BIRMINGHAM CITY
FOOTBALL CLUB THE OFFICIAL GUIDE 2006

Editorial
Peter Lewis
Paul Leedham

Sidan Press Team
Simon Rosen, Julian Hill-Wood, Marc Fiszman, Mark Peters, Karim Biria, Rob Cubbon,
Anette Lundebye, Marina Kravchenko, Gareth Peters, Janet Calcott, Trevor Scimes, John Fitzroy,
Jenny Middlemarch, Anders Rasmussen, Lim Wai-Lee, Emma Turner, Charles Grove, Tim Ryman

Photography
Action Images

Sidan Press, 63-64 Margaret St, London W1W 8SW
Tel: 020 7580 0200
Email: info@sidanpress.com

sidanpress.com

Club Directory

Chairman & Directors

Chairman Plc
David Sullivan

Chairman
David Gold

Managing Director
Karren Brady

Directors
Ralph Gold, Henri Brandman, Bradley Gold,
Michael Wiseman, Perry Deakin, Roger Bannister

Official Merchandise

Mail Order Hotline
0870 066 8286
shop@bcfc.com

Online Store
www.bcfc.com

Club Superstore
St. Andrew's, Cattell Road, Birmingham B9 4NH
0870 066 8239/240

City Centre Store
64 Dale End, Birmingham B4 7LS
0121 212 0873

Birthday Parties & Presentations
Stadium Tours
Junior Supporters Club
Helen Tims
0870 066 8245
helen.tims@bcfc.com

Customer Services
Matchday Announcements
Sarah Gould
0870 066 8265
sarah.gould@bcfc.com

Corporate Sales

Commercial Team
Matchday Hospitality
Advertising & Sponsorship
0871 226 1875
commercial@bcfc.com

Conference & Events

For your events at St. Andrew's
0871 226 1875
conferences@bcfc.com
events@bcfc.com

Community Department
0870 066 8210

Charity Requests
Please put in writing to the Club address

Website Enquiries
customerservices@premiumtv.co.uk

Contacts

Main Switchboard
0871 226 1875
Club Email
info@bcfc.com
Official Website
www.bcfc.com
Ticket Sales & Enquiries
0871 226 1875 Option 2
Online Ticket Sales
www.bcfc.com

Birmingham City Football Club
St. Andrew's, Birmingham B9 4NH

Contents

Birmingham City Official Partners

Principal Sponsor

LONDON

Kit Sponsor

Platinum Partners

Partners

Chairman's message
David Gold

Last season was obviously a bitterly disappointing experience for everyone connected with Birmingham City Football Club.

We are all feeling sorry for ourselves but we must believe that this is the beginning of the resurgence of the Blues.

We have done it before, back in 1995, after we were relegated to the Second Division and were all devastated. People may smile, laugh and giggle and call it a Mickey Mouse trophy, but we lifted the Auto Windscreens Shield that season too.

It was the beginning of a winning way, we returned as champions – and that's what we must do this time. We must pick ourselves up, dust ourselves down and come back next season as champions.

We believe that in Steve Bruce we have a manager with the right strengths to bring us back. The great thing about Steve is that people want to come and play for him. Steve is driven by a pride requirement to get this football club back into the Premier League.

It is important now to stay resolute and all pull together because we have a massive job ahead. That is where you, the fans, will have a vital part to play. Your support last season during a very difficult year for the club was incredible.

Please keep behind the team and the manager and hopefully this time next year we will be looking forward to another shot at Premier League football.

Manager's message

Steve Bruce

Our relegation from the Premiership last season was an awful experience for everybody but we are determined to bounce back at the first attempt.

Ultimately, as the manager, I took responsibility, but nobody took what happened harder than me.

When things like that occur you have to get through it, learn from your mistakes and make yourself better.

I still believe I have got the energy and enthusiasm to lead this club back into the top division where we undoubtedly belong.

At the time of penning these notes I am very pleased with the squad that has been assembled so far, which includes the additions of Cameron Jerome, Neil Danns and Stephen Kelly.

Cameron scored 20 goals in the Championship last season for Cardiff and Neil registered an impressive tally of 16 from midfield in the Colchester side that won promotion to this division.

Stephen is an international defender who played almost 50 games for Tottenham and more than held his own in the Premier League.

All three lads are under 24, they are young and hungry and have big futures ahead of them.

I thought that was the right direction to go down because we wanted to try and reduce the age of the squad and we have dramatically done that.

We've still got the nucleus of last season's team and with the addition of some exciting young players, we are confident that we can mount a serious challenge.

There is a young freshness about the place all of a sudden and I am really optimistic about the season ahead.

Having said all that, we are under no illusions as to how difficult this season is going to be because there are some big teams in this league.

Only 23 per cent of clubs that are relegated from the Premiership have gone straight back up at the first attempt.

But the bookies have us down as favourites and we've got to make sure that we live up to that billing.

Finally, can I thank all the fans for your tremendous support during some difficult times in the last 12 months.

Hopefully your loyalty will be rewarded with a season to remember this time around.

Premiership Wins 2002-2006

2-1

Birmingham City ○
Leeds United ○

Premiership

31.08.02

➡ Damien Johnson challenges Lee Bowyer

Event Line

12 ○ ▪	Viduka
27 ○ ▪	Devlin
32 ○ ⊕	Devlin / RF / C / OA
	Assist: Grainger
34 ○ ▪	Bakke
37 ○ ▪	Bowyer
44 ○ ▪	Johnson

Half time 1-0

50 ○ ⊕	Bowyer / LF / OP / IA
	Assist: Viduka
58 ○ ⊕	Johnson / RF / OP / OA
	Assist: John
60 ○ ⇄	Dacourt > Bakke
72 ○	Grainger
74 ○ ⇄	Horsfield > Morrison
84 ○ ⇄	Hughes > Devlin
89 ○ ⇄	Lazaridis > John

Full time 2-1

Two early contenders for goal of the season secured Blues' first ever Premiership victory in a thrilling St. Andrew's encounter.

After three games which saw plenty of effort and endeavour without much reward, Steve Bruce's new boys realised their potential with an awesome first half display against a shell-shocked Leeds side.

A sending-off in pre-season meant that this was Paul Devlin's first appearance of the season and he marked his top flight bow with a goal of supreme quality to open the scoring. Devlin could not have met Grainger's short corner any sweeter and his angled 30-yard shot nestled into the bottom right corner.

Blues went into the interval with their narrow lead still intact but five minutes after the break the scores were level. The home defence stopped expecting an offside flag which never came and Lee Bowyer kept his composure to beat Nico Vaesen.

But the stage was set for Damien Johnson to become the unlikely hero of Blues' first top flight win in 16 years – and in some style. The Northern Ireland international played a one-two with Stern John on the edge of the box before curling the ball expertly into the far corner.

Quote

🔴 **Steve Bruce**

All credit to the players for producing an unbelievable performance to beat a very good team.

Premiership Milestone

➡ **First Goal**

Paul Devlin marked his Premiership debut with a first goal in the competition.

Venue:	St Andrew's	Referee:	P.A.Durkin - 02/03	Birmingham City
Attendance:	27,164	Matches:	2	Leeds United
Capacity:	30,016	Yellow Cards:	8	
Occupancy:	90%	Red Cards:	0	

Form Coming into Fixture

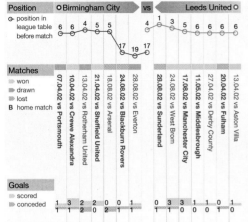

Position ○ Birmingham City vs Leeds United ○

○ position in league table before match

Birmingham City: 6 6 4 5 5 17 19 17
Leeds United: 4 3 5 6 6 6 6

Matches
- won
- drawn
- lost
- B home match

Birmingham City fixtures:
07.04.02 vs Portsmouth, 10.04.02 vs Crewe Alexandra, 13.04.02 vs Rotherham United, 21.04.02 vs Sheffield United, 18.08.02 vs Arsenal, 24.08.02 vs Blackburn Rovers, 28.08.02 vs Everton

Leeds United fixtures:
28.08.02 vs Sunderland, 24.08.02 vs West Brom, 17.08.02 vs Manchester City, 11.05.02 vs Middlesbrough, 27.04.02 vs Derby County, 20.04.02 vs Fulham, 13.04.02 vs Aston Villa

Goals
- scored
- conceded

| scored | 1 | 3 | 2 | 2 | 0 | 0 | 1 | 0 | 3 | 3 | 1 | 1 | 0 | 1 |
| conceded | 1 | 1 | 2 | 0 | 2 | 1 | 1 | 1 | 1 | 0 | 0 | 0 | 1 | 0 |

Goal Statistics

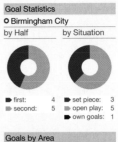

○ **Birmingham City**

by Half / by Situation
- first: 4
- second: 5
- set piece: 3
- open play: 5
- own goals: 1

○ **Leeds United**

by Half / by Situation
- first: 5
- second: 4
- set piece: 0
- open play: 9

Goals by Area

○ **Birmingham City**
Scored (Conceded)
- 3 (1)
- 4 (3)
- 2 (4)

○ **Leeds United**
Scored (Conceded)
- 2 (1)
- 6 (2)
- 1 (0)

Team Statistics

Starting Line-Ups

Grainger, Johnson, Bowyer, Mills D
Vaesen, Purse, Cisse, John Lazaridis, Viduka, Bakke Dacourt, Woodgate, Robinson
Cunningham, Savage, Morrison Horsfield, Smith, Barmby, Matteo
Kenna, Devlin Hughes, Kewell, Harte

▶ 4/4/2   ▶ 4/4/2

Unused Sub: Bennett, Johnson M

Unused Sub: Martyn, Kelly, Duberry, Wilcox

Premiership Totals	○ Birmingham	Leeds ○
Premiership Appearances	741	1,544
Team Appearances	33	1,075
Goals Scored	20	218
Assists	61	210
Clean Sheets (goalkeepers)	0	6
Yellow Cards	79	253
Red Cards	1	11

Age/Height

Birmingham City Age	Leeds United Age
▶ 28 yrs, 2 mo	▶ 25 yrs, 4 mo
Birmingham City Height	Leeds United Height
▶ 5'11"	▶ 6'

Match Statistics

League Table after Fixture

		Played	Won	Drawn	Lost	For	Against	Pts
●	4 Leeds	4	2	0	2	7	4	6
...		...	...	...	...	...	...	...
↑	14 Birmingham	4	1	1	2	3	5	4
↓	15 Newcastle	2	1	0	1	4	1	3
↓	16 Aston Villa	3	1	0	2	1	2	3
↑	17 West Brom	4	1	0	3	4	9	3
↓	18 Southampton	4	0	2	2	2	6	2
↓	19 West Ham	3	0	1	2	2	8	1
↓	20 Bolton	2	0	0	2	2	6	0

Statistics	○ Birmingham	Leeds ○
Goals	2	1
Shots on Target	4	3
Shots off Target	3	3
Hit Woodwork	0	2
Corners	2	3
Offsides	2	2
Fouls	10	16
Disciplinary Points	12	12

3-0

Birmingham City °
Aston Villa °

▶ A dejected Peter Enckelman leaves the field

Event Line

13 ○ ▪	Grainger	
27 ○ ▪	Alpay	
31 ○ ⊕	Morrison / RF / OP / IA	
	Assist: Savage	
34 ○ ▪	Purse	
Half time 1-0		
46 ○ ⇄	Dublin > Allback	
46 ○ ⇄	Vassell > Angel	
66 ○ ▪	Barry	
67 ○ ▪	Cisse	
69 ○ ⇄	Horsfield > Morrison	
77 ○ ⊕	Enckelman / LF / OG / 6Y	
78 ○ ▪	Staunton	
79 ○ ⇄	Powell > Devlin	
83 ○ ▪	Horsfield / RF / IFK / IA	
88 ○ ⇄	Hughes > Savage	
Full time 3-0		

Clinton Morrison's first half opener, a bizarre own goal and a late strike from super sub Geoff Horsfield clinched a first Premiership victory over local rivals Aston Villa at St. Andrew's.

Blues failed to emulate their wonderful display against Leeds in the previous home game with an often scrappy performance, but the majority of the fans amongst the sell-out crowd didn't care.

Blues rode their luck for long periods as Villa wasted numerous chances, particularly in the second half, and the first two goals had more than an element of luck involved in them.

Morrison kept his pre-match promise to the home fans and registered a first local derby goal just after the half hour mark.

Blues' lead was doubled as Peter Enckelman failed to control a throw-in from Olof Mellberg and the ball rolled under his foot and into the goal.

Horsfield scored a blistering third as he raced onto a through ball and fired the ball low into the bottom corner.

Quote

● **Steve Bruce**

It was an electric atmosphere and the fans have waited a long time for this. They will enjoy it tonight and they deserve to enjoy it.

Premiership Milestone

▶ **29,505**

The attendance of 29,505 was a Premiership record at St.Andrew's.

Venue:	St Andrew's	Referee:	D.R.Elleray - 02/03		Birmingham City
Attendance:	29,505	Matches:	2		Aston Villa
Capacity:	30,016	Yellow Cards:	7		
Occupancy:	98%	Red Cards:	0		

Form Coming into Fixture

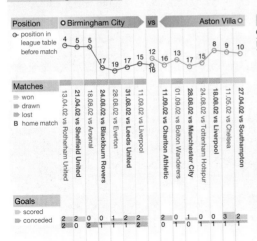

Position — o Birmingham City vs Aston Villa o

position in league table before match

4 5 5 17 19 17 15 12 16 16 13 17 15 8 9 10

Matches

- won
- drawn
- lost
- B home match

13.04.02 vs Rotherham United
21.04.02 vs Sheffield United
18.08.02 vs Arsenal
24.08.02 vs Blackburn Rovers
28.08.02 vs Everton
31.08.02 vs Leeds United
11.09.02 vs Liverpool
11.09.02 vs Charlton Athletic
01.09.02 vs Bolton Wanderers
28.08.02 vs Manchester City
24.08.02 vs Tottenham Hotspur
18.08.02 vs Liverpool
11.05.02 vs Chelsea
27.04.02 vs Southampton

Goals

- scored
- conceded

| scored | 2 | 2 | 0 | 0 | 1 | 2 | 2 | 2 | 0 | 1 | 0 | 0 | 3 | 2 |
| conceded | 2 | 0 | 0 | 2 | 1 | 1 | 2 | 2 | 1 | 0 | 1 | 1 | 1 | 1 |

Goal Statistics

o Birmingham City

by Half / **by Situation**

first:	2	set piece:	4
second:	7	open play:	4
		own goals:	1

o Aston Villa

by Half / **by Situation**

| first: | 3 | set piece: | 5 |
| second: | 5 | open play: | 3 |

Goals by Area

o Birmingham City — Scored (Conceded)

3 (1)
2 (3)
4 (5)

o Aston Villa — Scored (Conceded)

3 (1)
4 (3)
1 (1)

Team Statistics

Starting Line-Ups

Grainger Johnson De la Cruz

Johnsen

Purse Cisse Mellberg

Vaesen John Angel Vassall Enckelman

Kinsella Alpay

Cunningham Savage Hughes Morrison Horsfield Allback Dublin

Staunton

Barry

Kenna Devlin Powell Samuel

4/4/2 **5/3/2**

Unused Sub: Bennett, Lazaridis   Unused Sub: Postma, Hendrie, Moore

Premiership Totals	o Birmingham	Aston Villa o
Premiership Appearances	866	1,119
Team Appearances	56	732
Goals Scored	26	158
Assists	57	109
Clean Sheets (goalkeepers)	0	8
Yellow Cards	110	119
Red Cards	2	6

Age/Height

Birmingham City Age	Aston Villa Age
28 yrs, 4 mo	27 yrs, 8 mo
Birmingham City Height	Aston Villa Height
5'11"	6'

Match Statistics

League Table after Fixture

			Played	Won	Drawn	Lost	For	Against	Pts
●	7	West Brom	6	3	0	3	6	9	9
●	8	Middlesbrough	6	2	2	2	7	5	8
↑	9	Birmingham	6	2	2	2	8	7	8
↓	10	Man Utd	6	2	2	2	5	5	8
↓	11	Everton	6	2	2	2	7	8	8
↓	12	Man City	6	2	1	3	7	9	7
●	13	Blackburn	6	1	3	2	7	8	6
●	14	Bolton	5	2	0	3	6	9	6
↓	15	Aston Villa	6	2	0	4	3	6	6

Statistics	o Birmingham	Aston Villa o
Goals	3	0
Shots on Target	5	1
Shots off Target	6	6
Hit Woodwork	0	1
Corners	7	5
Offsides	4	4
Fouls	16	12
Disciplinary Points	12	12

1-2

West Ham United ○
Birmingham City ○

▶ Stern John is the hero in East London

Event Line

4 ○ ⊕	John / LF / OP / IA	
	Assist: Savage	
11 ○ ▦	Cisse	
17 ○ ⊕	Cole J / LF / OP / IA	
	Assist: Di Canio	
43 ○ ⊕	John / RF / OP / IA	
	Assist: Lazaridis	
Half time 1-2		
49 ○ ▦	Minto	
71 ○ ⇄	Camara > Cole J	
71 ○ ⇄	Pearce > Schemmel	
82 ○ ⇄	Horsfield > John	
83 ○ ⇄	Powell > Lazaridis	
90 ○ ▦	Carrick	
Full time 1-2		

Blues picked up a first away win of our debut Premiership campaign courtesy of an excellent victory in the Capital over West Ham.

A brace by Stern John either side of a Joe Cole equaliser gave Blues all three points against Glenn Roeder's star-studded Hammers.

Blues got off to a dream start at Upton Park by taking the lead after only three minutes. John shrugged off Scott Minto and raced into the six-yard box before firing a shot that went in off the helpless David James.

But the hosts were level shortly afterwards when Paulo Di Canio set up Cole, who nonchalantly chipped the ball over the advancing Nico Vaesen.

Chances began to be created at either end in an open and entertaining game and it was Blues that converted what turned out to be the decisive goal just two minutes before the break. John had hit a hat-trick in the League Cup win over Leyton Orient three days earlier and the former Nottingham Forest man was the match winner again. The Trinidad and Tobago international controlled well on his chest and then left Tomas Repka in his wake with a Cruyff-like turn before dispatching the ball confidently past James.

Quote

● Steve Bruce

I've got no doubt in my mind about Stern John's ability. We have all witnessed what he can do on the big stage.

Venue:	Upton Park	Referee:	P.Dowd - 02/03		West Ham United
Attendance:	35,010	Matches:	5		Birmingham City
Capacity:	35,647	Yellow Cards:	21		
Occupancy:	98%	Red Cards:	2		

Form Coming into Fixture

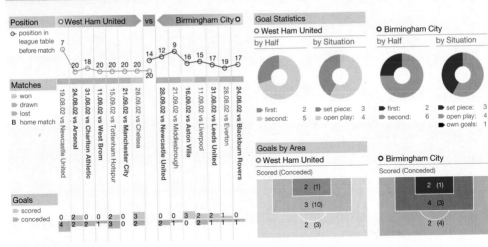

Team Statistics

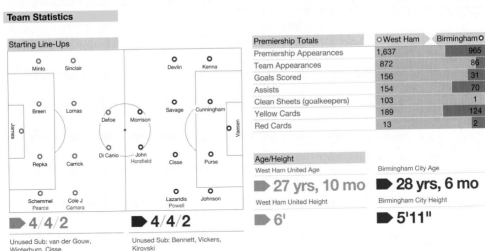

Starting Line-Ups

4/4/2

Unused Sub: van der Gouw, Winterburn, Cisse

4/4/2

Unused Sub: Bennett, Vickers, Kirovski

Premiership Totals	West Ham	Birmingham
Premiership Appearances	1,637	965
Team Appearances	872	86
Goals Scored	156	31
Assists	154	70
Clean Sheets (goalkeepers)	103	1
Yellow Cards	189	124
Red Cards	13	2

Age/Height

West Ham United Age: **27 yrs, 10 mo**
Birmingham City Age: **28 yrs, 6 mo**

West Ham United Height: **6'**
Birmingham City Height: **5'11"**

Match Statistics

League Table after Fixture

	Played	Won	Drawn	Lost	For	Against	Pts
↑ 12 Birmingham	9	3	2	4	10	11	11
↑ 13 Southampton	9	2	4	3	6	8	10
↓ 14 Aston Villa	8	3	0	5	6	9	9
↓ 15 West Brom	9	3	0	6	7	15	9
↓ 16 Man City	9	2	2	5	7	14	8
↓ 17 Sunderland	8	2	2	4	3	10	8
↓ 18 Bolton	8	2	1	5	8	14	7
● 19 Charlton	8	2	1	5	5	13	7
● 20 West Ham	8	1	2	5	8	16	5

Statistics	West Ham	Birmingham
Goals	1	2
Shots on Target	1	2
Shots off Target	10	9
Hit Woodwork	0	0
Corners	7	2
Offsides	3	6
Fouls	8	16
Disciplinary Points	8	4

3-1

Birmingham City ○
Bolton Wanderers ○

▶ Stern John fires in a shot at goal

Event Line

9 ○		Mendy
41 ○		Whitlow
45 ○		Morrison
Half time 0-0		
57 ○		Djorkaeff
60 ○	⇄	Horsfield > Lazaridis
61 ○	⊕	Purse / RF / C / IA
		Assist: Devlin
62 ○		Cisse
67 ○	◪	Gardner
		2nd Bookable Offence
70 ○	⇄	Holdsworth > Ricketts
72 ○	⊕	Okocha / RF / OP / IA
		Assist: Whitlow
72 ○	⊕	Savage / RF / OP / 6Y
		Assist: John
77 ○	⇄	Powell > John
78 ○	⇄	Charlton > Frandsen
78 ○	⇄	Nolan > Whitlow
83 ○	⊕	Horsfield / RF / OP / 6Y
		Assist: Morrison
84 ○	⇄	Hughes > Savage
Full time 3-1		

Second half goals from Darren Purse, Robbie Savage and Geoff Horsfield secured victory over ten man Bolton at a rain soaked St. Andrews.

It was never going to be a pretty game to watch on a slippery pitch with two teams desperate for a result.

It took just over an hour for the game's first goal to arrive but Purse's opener sparked an avalanche of net rippling. The visitors then had a man sent off after Ricardo Gardner received a second yellow card for a foul on Geoff Horsfield.

But despite their numerical disadvantage, Bolton drew level courtesy of a tremendous JayJay Okocha volley.

Inside a minute Blues were back in front though when Stern John's neat flick sent Savage clean though and he rounded Jussi Jaaskelainen before sliding home his first goal for the club.

Nico Vaesen had to be alert to save from Youri Djorkaeff before Horsfield made sure of victory. The sub was first to the rebound when Clinton Morrison's shot came back off a post to tap home into an empty net.

Quote
● **Steve Bruce**

We said it was going to be difficult in this division and we are realistic, but 15 points in the first 12 games is not a bad return for us.

Premiership Milestone
▶ **First Goal**

Robbie Savage netted his first Premiership goal for Birmingham.

Venue:	St Andrew's	Referee:	C.J.Foy - 02/03		Birmingham City
Attendance:	27,224	Matches:	5		Bolton Wanderers
Capacity:	30,016	Yellow Cards:	21		
Occupancy:	91%	Red Cards:	2		

Form Coming into Fixture

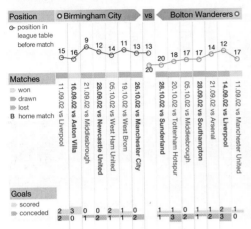

Goal Statistics

Birmingham City

by Half — first: 3, second: 5
by Situation — set piece: 1, open play: 5, own goals: 2

Bolton Wanderers

by Half — first: 0, second: 7
by Situation — set piece: 0, open play: 6, own goals: 1

Goals by Area

Birmingham City — Scored (Conceded): 3 (0), 5 (6), 0 (3)

Bolton Wanderers — Scored (Conceded): 4 (2), 2 (9), 1 (1)

Team Statistics

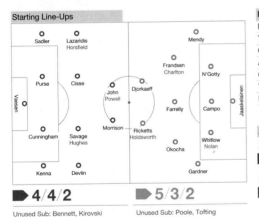

Starting Line-Ups

Unused Sub: Bennett, Kirovski   Unused Sub: Poole, Tofting

4/4/2   5/3/2

Premiership Totals	Birmingham	Bolton
Premiership Appearances	968	854
Team Appearances	118	492
Goals Scored	30	110
Assists	69	61
Clean Sheets (goalkeepers)	1	9
Yellow Cards	121	101
Red Cards	2	7

Age/Height

Birmingham City Age: 28 yrs
Bolton Wanderers Age: 28 yrs, 8 mo

Birmingham City Height: 5'11"
Bolton Wanderers Height: 6'

Match Statistics

League Table after Fixture

	Played	Won	Drawn	Lost	For	Against	Pts
↑ 12 Birmingham	12	4	3	5	14	15	15
↓ 13 Leeds	11	4	2	5	13	12	14
↑ 14 Man City	12	4	2	6	11	18	14
↓ 15 Aston Villa	11	3	2	6	7	11	11
↓ 16 West Ham	12	3	2	7	10	19	11
• 17 Charlton	11	3	1	7	9	16	10
• 18 West Brom	12	3	1	8	9	20	10
• 19 Sunderland	11	2	3	6	5	15	9
• 20 Bolton	11	2	2	7	11	21	8

Statistics	Birmingham	Bolton
Goals	3	1
Shots on Target	7	5
Shots off Target	4	5
Hit Woodwork	1	1
Corners	8	5
Offsides	3	2
Fouls	12	8
Disciplinary Points	8	22

17

0-1

Sunderland ○
Birmingham City ○

▶ Paul Devlin is brought down at the Stadium of Light

Event Line	
29 ○ ▢	Cisse
Half time 0-0	
56 ○ ⇄	Bellion > Proctor
59 ○ ▢	Savage
60 ○ ⇄	Powell > Savage
64 ○ ▢	Gray
75 ○ ▢	McCann
79 ○ ▢	Wright
83 ○ ▢	Tebily
84 ○ ⇄	Hughes > Devlin
85 ○ ⇄	Johnson > Powell
89 ○ ⊕	Morrison / RF / OP / IA
	Assist: Lazaridis
Full time 0-1	

Steve Bruce returned from his native north-east with a satisfying victory over the Black Cats at the Stadium of Light.

The win came in the most dramatic of circumstances with Clinton Morrison scoring in the very last minute.

Paul Devlin, Stan Lazaridis and Stern John all went close during an excellent first half performance from the visitors.

Lazaridis was in the thick of the action again with two chances in a minute. The first came when he intercepted Phil Babb's pass and raced forward before unleashing a shot which was deflected just wide by Gavin McCann. Then Devlin's pass inside found the Aussie who had another long range shot deflected inches past the post.

With just three minutes left on the clock, the hosts almost took the lead in comical fashion when Oliver Tebily's clearance cannoned off Damien Johnson and on to the bar.

But there was still time for Blues to grab victory as Morrison pounced to spark

Quote
● **Steve Bruce**

It's always cruel to lose in the last minute, but I think we were by far the better side. I thought we were a threat all day long.

Premiership Milestone
▶ **250**

Jeff Kenna made his 250th Premiership appearance.

Venue:	Stadium of Light	Referee:	R.Styles - 02/03		Sunderland
Attendance:	38,803	Matches:	9		Birmingham City
Capacity:	48,300	Yellow Cards:	36		
Occupancy:	80%	Red Cards:	3		

Form Coming into Fixture

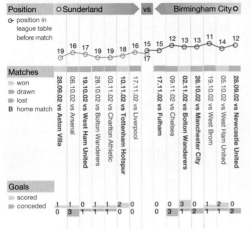

Position O Sunderland vs Birmingham City O
G- position in league table before match

Matches
- won
- drawn
- lost
- B home match

Goals
- scored
- conceded

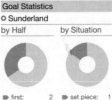

Goal Statistics

O Sunderland
by Half · by Situation

O Birmingham City
by Half · by Situation

▶ first: 2 ▶ set piece: 1
▶ second: 4 ▶ open play: 5

▶ first: 2 ▶ set piece: 1
▶ second: 4 ▶ open play: 4
▶ own goals: 1

Goals by Area

O Sunderland
Scored (Conceded)

| 1 (4) |
| 4 (2) |
| 1 (0) |

O Birmingham City
Scored (Conceded)

| 3 (0) |
| 3 (8) |
| 0 (2) |

Team Statistics

Starting Line-Ups

McCartney · Gray
Babb · Kilbane · Flo · Morrison
Macho
Craddock · McCann · Phillips · John
Wright · Proctor Bellion

Devlin · Tebily
Hughes
Savage Powell · Cunningham
Vaesen
Cisse · Purse
Lazaridis · Kenna

▶ 4/4/2   ▶ 4/4/2

Unused Sub: Poom, Bjorklund, Thirlwell, Stewart

Unused Sub: Bennett, Kirovski

Premiership Totals

	O Sunderland	Birmingham O
Premiership Appearances	958	1,037
Team Appearances	618	158
Goals Scored	119	34
Assists	68	76
Clean Sheets (goalkeepers)	3	2
Yellow Cards	112	134
Red Cards	4	3

Age/Height

Sunderland Age	Birmingham City Age
▶ 25 yrs, 9 mo	▶ 28 yrs, 4 mo
Sunderland Height	Birmingham City Height
▶ 6'	▶ 5'11"

Match Statistics

League Table after Fixture

		Played	Won	Drawn	Lost	For	Against	Pts
↑	9 Southampton	15	5	5	5	17	17	20
↓	10 Tottenham	14	6	2	6	17	21	20
↑	11 Aston Villa	15	5	4	6	14	13	19
↑	12 Fulham	15	5	4	6	20	20	19
↑	13 Birmingham	15	5	4	6	15	18	19
↓	14 Leeds	14	5	2	7	19	20	17
↓	15 Man City	15	5	2	8	15	23	17
●	16 Charlton	14	4	2	8	11	18	14
●	17 Sunderland	15	3	5	7	8	17	14

Statistics

	O Sunderland	Birmingham O
Goals	0	1
Shots on Target	2	4
Shots off Target	7	4
Hit Woodwork	1	0
Corners	5	7
Offsides	5	2
Fouls	17	19
Disciplinary Points	12	12

0-1

Fulham ○
Birmingham City ○

▶ Aliou Cisse puts the pressure on in midfield

Event Line

7 ○ ⊕	Kirovski / RF / OP / IA
	Assist: Morrison
23 ○ ▪	Johnson
25 ○ ▪	Horsfield
Half time 0-1	
46 ○ ⇄	Inamoto > Wome
52 ○ ⇄	Willock > Inamoto
54 ○ ▪	Malbranque
58 ○ ▪	Kirovski
66 ○ ⇄	Clark > Melville
68 ○ ▪	Clark
70 ○ ◢	Purse
	2nd Bookable Offence
73 ○ ⇄	Powell > Kirovski
75 ○ ⇄	Woodhouse > Johnson
78 ○ ▪	Powell
80 ○ ⇄	Hughes > Horsfield
82 ○ ▪	Tebily
89 ○ ▪	Brevett
90 ○ ▪	Cisse
Full time 0-1	

American international midfielder Jovan Kirovski capped his first Premiership start with the only goal of the game to secure victory for Blues at Fulham's temporary Loftus Road home.

Kirovski's spectacular early strike gave Steve Bruce the ideal present on the week of his first anniversary at the St. Andrew's helm.

Damien Johnson prevented his side from going a goal down early on when he was in the right place to head Sylvain Legwinski's goal-bound effort off the line. And Blues took full advantage soon afterwards when the lively Kirovski fired Blues into the lead with a superb curling strike into the far corner after collecting Clinton Morrison's lay off.

Referee Andy D'Urso had a busy afternoon taking the names of ten players – seven from Blues – and Bruce's men were forced to hang on after Purse received his second caution.

But hang on they did to give the delighted away fans an early Christmas treat of three welcome away points.

Quote

🔴 **Steve Bruce**

I can't hide my admiration for the way my players have gone about things. I've got an honest group of lads trying their hardest.

Premiership Milestone

▶ **First Goal**

Jovan Kirovski netted his first Premiership goal.

Venue:	Loftus Road	Referee:	A.P.D'Urso - 02/03
Attendance:	14,962	Matches:	11
Capacity:	18,500	Yellow Cards:	38
Occupancy:	81%	Red Cards:	1

Fulham
Birmingham City

Form Coming into Fixture

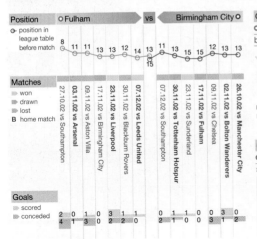

Position
- position in league table before match

Matches
- won
- drawn
- lost
- B home match

Goals
- scored
- conceded

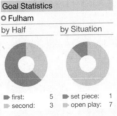

Goal Statistics

○ Fulham — by Half — by Situation

- first: 5
- second: 3
- set piece: 1
- open play: 7

○ Birmingham City — by Half — by Situation

- first: 0
- second: 5
- set piece: 1
- open play: 4

Goals by Area

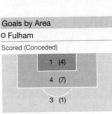

○ Fulham — Scored (Conceded)

- 1 (4)
- 4 (7)
- 3 (1)

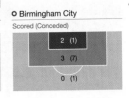

○ Birmingham City — Scored (Conceded)

- 2 (1)
- 3 (7)
- 0 (1)

Team Statistics

Starting Line-Ups

Brevett, Wome, Inamoto, Johnson, Woodhouse, Tebily, Melville, Clark, Davis, Boa Morte, Morrison, Savage, Cunningham, van der Sar, Vaesen, Goma, Djetou, Malbranque, Horsfield, Hughes, Cisse, Purse, Finnan, Legwinski, Kirovski, Powell, Kenna

▶ 4/4/1/1   ▶ 4/4/2

Unused Sub: Taylor Maik, Goldbaek   Unused Sub: Bennett, Fagan

Premiership Totals	○ Fulham	Birmingham ○
Premiership Appearances	741	983
Team Appearances	471	173
Goals Scored	36	31
Assists	49	57
Clean Sheets (goalkeepers)	20	3
Yellow Cards	93	130
Red Cards	5	3

Age/Height

Fulham Age	Birmingham City Age
▶ 27 yrs, 4 mo	▶ 27 yrs, 10 mo
Fulham Height	Birmingham City Height
▶ 5'11"	▶ 5'11"

Match Statistics

League Table after Fixture

		Played	Won	Drawn	Lost	For	Against	Pts
●	6 Newcastle	17	9	2	6	27	24	29
↑	7 Tottenham	18	8	4	6	24	24	28
↓	8 Southampton	18	7	6	5	21	18	27
●	9 Middlesbrough	18	7	5	6	22	16	26
●	10 Blackburn	18	6	6	6	24	22	24
●	11 Charlton	18	7	3	8	20	22	24
●	12 Man City	18	7	3	8	22	25	24
↑	13 Birmingham	18	6	5	7	17	21	23
↓	14 Fulham	18	6	4	8	22	23	22

Statistics	○ Fulham	Birmingham ○
Goals	0	1
Shots on Target	4	2
Shots off Target	6	1
Hit Woodwork	0	0
Corners	5	1
Offsides	6	2
Fouls	15	26
Disciplinary Points	12	34

2-1

Birmingham City ○
Liverpool ○

Premiership
23.02.03

▶ Matthew Upson keeps a close eye on Michael Owen

Event Line

34 ○ ⊕	Clemence / H / IFK / IA
	Assist: Savage
Half time 1-0	
54 ○ ▢	Dugarry
63 ○ ⇄	Owen > Carragher
63 ○ ▢	Upson
68 ○ ⊕	Morrison / RF / OP / 6Y
	Assist: Lazaridis
77 ○ ⊕	Owen / RF / OP / IA
	Assist: Murphy
79 ○ ⇄	Carter > Clemence
81 ○ ⇄	Horsfield > Dugarry
84 ○ ⇄	Mellor > Cheyrou
88 ○ ⇄	Devlin > Morrison
90 ○ ▢	Diao
Full time 2-1	

By the time Liverpool arrived at St. Andrew's in late February, Blues had gone ten games without a win and dropped perilously close to the Premiership drop zone.

But with Liverpool possibly having one eye on the return leg of their two-legged Champions League contest with Auxerre, Blues took full advantage to record a memorable victory.

And it was the son of an Anfield goalkeeping legend who put the home side on their way as midfielder Stephen Clemence scored a priceless first half goal. Clemence met Robbie Savage's inswinging free kick with a glancing header that bounced past Jerzy Dudek into the bottom left corner.

Clinton Morrison made it three goals in two Premiership games against Liverpool this season to double the lead in the second half.

The win restored Blues' six-point cushion above the relegation zone and put them in good heart for the second part of the eagerly-awaited Premiership derby with neighbours Aston Villa.

Quote

● **Stephen Clemence**

We have had a bad run of results and to go in front was a big confidence boost. We were disappointed to concede at the end, but the lads were brilliant today.

Premiership Milestone

▶ **50**

Damien Johnson made his 50th Premiership appearance.

Venue:	St Andrew's	Referee:	C.R.Wilkes - 02/03

Attendance: 29,449   Matches: 13
Capacity: 30,016   Yellow Cards: 37
Occupancy: 98%   Red Cards: 5

Birmingham City
Liverpool

Form Coming into Fixture

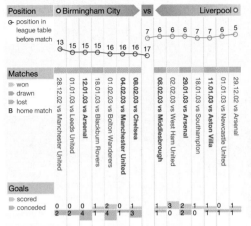

Position — O Birmingham City — vs — Liverpool O

position in league table before match

Matches
- won
- drawn
- lost
- B home match

Goals
- scored
- conceded

Goal Statistics

O Birmingham City

by Half   by Situation

- first: 1
- second: 3
- set piece: 2
- open play: 2

O Liverpool

by Half   by Situation

- first: 4
- second: 5
- set piece: 6
- open play: 3

Goals by Area

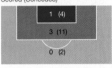

O Birmingham City
Scored (Conceded)

1 (4)
3 (11)
0 (2)

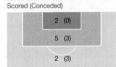

O Liverpool
Scored (Conceded)

2 (0)
5 (3)
2 (3)

Team Statistics

Starting Line-Ups

Clapham, Lazaridis, Diao, Carragher, Owen
Upson, Clemence, Carter, Dugarry/Horsfield, Baros, Murphy, Traore, Dudek
Vaesen, Morrison/Devlin, Heskey, Hamann, Hyypia
Cunningham, Savage
Kenna, Johnson, Cheyrou/Mellor, Riise

▶ 4/4/2   ▶ 4/4/2

Unused Sub: Bennett, John

Unused Sub: Arphexad, Babbel, Biscan

Premiership Totals	O Birmingham	Liverpool O
Premiership Appearances	1,128	1,180
Team Appearances	228	1,033
Goals Scored	39	214
Assists	90	127
Clean Sheets (goalkeepers)	4	26
Yellow Cards	119	116
Red Cards	1	8

Age/Height

Birmingham City Age   ▶ 27 yrs, 11 mo
Liverpool Age   ▶ 25 yrs, 1 mo
Birmingham City Height   ▶ 5'11"
Liverpool Height   ▶ 6'1"

Match Statistics

League Table after Fixture

		Played	Won	Drawn	Lost	For	Against	Pts
● 7	Liverpool	28	11	10	7	39	28	43
...		...	...	...	...	...	...	...
● 14	Leeds	28	10	4	14	34	37	34
● 15	Fulham	27	9	6	12	31	34	33
↑ 16	Birmingham	28	7	8	13	25	41	29
↓ 17	Bolton	28	5	11	12	31	45	26
↑ 18	West Ham	28	5	8	15	30	53	23
↓ 19	West Brom	28	5	6	17	21	43	21
● 20	Sunderland	28	4	7	17	19	45	19

Statistics	O Birmingham	Liverpool O
Goals	2	1
Shots on Target	2	9
Shots off Target	3	5
Hit Woodwork	0	0
Corners	2	6
Offsides	7	2
Fouls	14	11
Disciplinary Points	8	4

0-2

Aston Villa ○
Birmingham City ○

Premiership

03.03.03

▶ Stan Lazaridis celebrates his goal with Geoff Horsfield

Event Line

35 ○ ▪	Cunningham
Half time 0-0	
46 ○ ⇄	Hadji > Moore
51 ○ ▪	Dublin
	Violent Conduct
72 ○ ⇄	Horsfield > Morrison
74 ○ ⊕	Lazaridis / H / OP / 6Y
	Assist: Kenna
75 ○ ⇄	Devlin > Lazaridis
76 ○	Devlin
77 ○ ⊕	Horsfield / RF / OP / 6Y
81 ○ ◢	Gudjonsson
	2nd Bookable Offence
83 ○ ⇄	Carter > Savage
90 ○ ⇄	Crouch > Wright
Full time 0-2	

Blues secured a famous victory and a Premiership double over our big city rivals after an eventful second half at Villa Park.

The match came to life after the break with the dismissal of Villa striker Dion Dublin following an altercation with Robbie Savage.

The visitors did not immediately take advantage of their numerical advantage but the deadlock was eventually broken 16 minutes from time.

Jeff Kenna curled in an inviting cross that bounced through to Stan Lazaridis to head into an empty net.

Blues doubled their lead soon after with Geoff Horsfield yet again taking on the role of super sub.

Peter Enckelman failed to deal with JLloyd Samuel's weak header and Horsfield knocked the ball around the Villa keeper before rolling it into an empty net.

There was still time for the home side to be reduced to nine men as Joey Gudjonsson was sent off for a dreadful foul on Matthew Upson.

Quote
● **Steve Bruce**

I'm delighted with the discipline of my players. To come here and do the double over them is a great achievement.

Premiership Milestone
▶ **First Goal**

Stan Lazaridis netted his first Premiership goal for Birmingham.

Venue:	Villa Park		Referee:	M.R.Halsey - 02/03		Aston Villa
Attendance:	42,602		Matches:	23		Birmingham City
Capacity:	42,573		Yellow Cards:	54		
Occupancy:	100%		Red Cards:	1		

Form Coming into Fixture

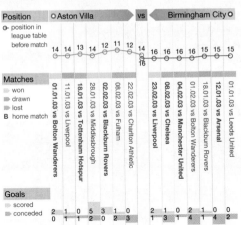

Goal Statistics

Aston Villa

by Half	by Situation

- first: 6
- second: 6
- set piece: 3
- open play: 9

Birmingham City

by Half	by Situation

- first: 2
- second: 4
- set piece: 3
- open play: 3

Goals by Area

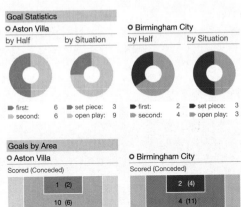

Aston Villa — Scored (Conceded)

1 (2)
10 (6)
1 (1)

Birmingham City — Scored (Conceded)

2 (4)
4 (11)
0 (1)

Team Statistics

Starting Line-Ups

Unused Sub: Postma, Edwards, Hitzlsperger

Unused Sub: Bennett, John

4 / 4 / 2

4 / 4 / 2

Premiership Totals

	Aston Villa	Birmingham
Premiership Appearances	1,396	1,142
Team Appearances	1,037	242
Goals Scored	185	41
Assists	131	92
Clean Sheets (goalkeepers)	12	4
Yellow Cards	138	121
Red Cards	9	1

Age/Height

Aston Villa Age	Birmingham City Age
26 yrs	27 yrs, 11 mo

Aston Villa Height	Birmingham City Height
5'11"	5'11"

Match Statistics

League Table after Fixture

	Played	Won	Drawn	Lost	For	Against	Pts
12 Fulham	29	10	7	12	33	35	37
13 Middlesbrough	28	9	8	11	34	32	35
14 Aston Villa	29	10	5	14	31	34	35
15 Leeds	28	10	4	14	34	37	34
16 Birmingham	29	8	8	13	27	41	32
17 Bolton	28	5	11	12	31	45	26
18 West Ham	29	6	8	15	32	53	26
19 West Brom	29	5	6	18	21	44	21
20 Sunderland	29	4	7	18	19	46	19

Statistics

	Aston Villa	Birmingham
Goals	0	2
Shots on Target	4	3
Shots off Target	7	2
Hit Woodwork	0	0
Corners	4	3
Offsides	0	4
Fouls	20	17
Disciplinary Points	22	8

1-0

Birmingham City ○
West Bromwich Albion ○

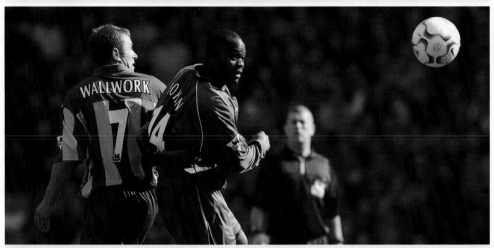

▶ Stern John spins away from Ronnie Wallwork

Event Line
Half time 0-0
56 ○ ⇄ Horsfield > Morrison
68 ○ ⇄ Carter > Kenna
79 ○ ⇄ John > Clemence
86 ○ ⇄ Hughes > Koumas
90 ○ ⊕ Horsfield / H / OP / IA
Assist: John
Full time 1-0

Geoff Horsfield was once again the derby day hero with a last minute injury time goal to beat the Baggies.

The goal was rough justice on an Albion side that had battled hard all afternoon but this result realistically ended their hopes of Premiership survival.

A capacity crowd were forced to endure a largely lacklustre performance until Horsfield grabbed the winner after Stern John's effort was blocked.

Clinton Morrison should have opened the scoring on 36 minutes when Christophe Dugarry's sideways ball found the striker inside the six-yard box but the Republic of Ireland international miscued his shot and it went narrowly wide.

Albion came out for the second half with more purpose and it almost paid dividends when Ian Bennett was forced to scramble away Jason Koumas's low shot. And from the resultant corner, Blues had a lucky escape as Jason Roberts' powerful header rebounded back off the bar.

With less than 60 seconds left on the clock, Horsfield was in the right place at the right time to head home and seal the points.

Quote

● **Steve Bruce**

They say that fortune favours the brave and we deserved the win for our bravery.

Premiership Milestone

▶ **200**

Robbie Savage made his 200th Premiership appearance.

Venue:	St Andrew's	Referee:	P.A.Durkin - 02/03	**Birmingham City**
Attendance:	29,449	Matches:	21	**West Bromwich Albion**
Capacity:	30,016	Yellow Cards:	53	
Occupancy:	98%	Red Cards:	2	

Form Coming into Fixture

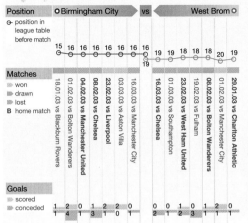

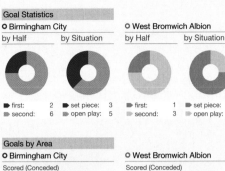

Team Statistics

Starting Line-Ups

4/4/2

5/3/2

Unused Sub: Marriott, Johnson M

Unused Sub: Murphy J, Lyttle, Chambers, Dobie

Premiership Totals

	O Birmingham / West Brom O
Premiership Appearances	1,073 / 418
Team Appearances	242 / 267
Goals Scored	43 / 28
Assists	78 / 17
Clean Sheets (goalkeepers)	0 / 20
Yellow Cards	117 / 48
Red Cards	1 / 5

Age/Height

Birmingham City Age	West Bromwich Albion Age
27 yrs, 6 mo	**27 yrs, 7 mo**
Birmingham City Height	West Bromwich Albion Height
6'	**6'**

Match Statistics

League Table after Fixture

	Played	Won	Drawn	Lost	For	Against	Pts
● 11 Middlesbrough	31	11	9	11	39	35	42
● 12 Man City	31	12	5	14	40	49	41
● 13 Fulham	31	10	8	13	35	40	38
● 14 Aston Villa	31	10	6	15	33	37	36
↑ 15 Birmingham	31	9	8	14	28	42	35
↓ 16 Leeds	30	10	4	16	37	42	34
↑ 17 West Ham	31	7	9	15	34	53	30
↓ 18 Bolton	30	6	11	13	33	47	29
● 19 West Brom	31	5	6	20	21	47	21

Statistics

	O Birmingham / West Brom O
Goals	1 / 0
Shots on Target	2 / 4
Shots off Target	6 / 7
Hit Woodwork	0 / 1
Corners	7 / 3
Offsides	1 / 1
Fouls	10 / 18
Disciplinary Points	0 / 0

2-0

Birmingham City ○
Sunderland ○

➡ Geoff Horsfield volleys the ball goalwards

Event Line

22 ○ ⇄	McCartney > Bjorklund
43 ○ ⊕	Hughes / LF / OP / OA
Half time 1-0	
55 ○ ⇄	Wright > El Karkouri
59 ○ ▨	McCartney
60 ○ ⊕	Dugarry / H / IFK / IA
	Assist: Kenna
64 ○ ⇄	John > Dugarry
81 ○ ⇄	Carter > Devlin
84 ○ ⇄	Kirovski > Hughes
86 ○ ▨	Stewart
	Foul
Full time 2-0	

Blues took another step closer to Premiership survival with victory over Sunderland – a result that condemned our opponents to Division One football.

Bryan Hughes gave Blues a first half lead just two minutes from the break with an audacious lob to register his first Premiership goal. Stan Lazaridis whipped in a cross towards Christophe Dugarry but the striker was beaten to the ball by Black Cats keeper Mart Poom who punched clear. But the ball feel to the feet of Hughes who kept his composure to hit an inch perfect chip over the reach of Poom and into the net.

It was a day of firsts as the imperial Frenchman notched his first goal since joining the club on loan from Bordeaux. Lazaridis's free kick was punched clear by Poom and successive headers by Hughes and Jeff Kenna set up Dugarry who stooped to nod the ball inside the far post. New fans' favourite Dugarry turned away to take the plaudits of the Tilton Road faithful.

A thoroughly depressing day for the visitors was complete as Marcus Stewart received his marching orders after a wild challenge on Stern John with five minutes remaining.

Quote

🔵 **Steve Bruce**

I was pleased that Christophe Dugarry scored his first goal for us. That was probably his least effective game since coming here, but I was delighted that he got on the scoresheet.

Premiership Milestone

➡ **First Goal**

Both Bryan Hughes and Christophe Dugarry netted their first Premiership goals.

Venue:	St Andrew's	Referee:	P.Dowd - 02/03	Birmingham City
Attendance:	29,132	Matches:	25	Sunderland
Capacity:	30,016	Yellow Cards:	86	
Occupancy:	97%	Red Cards:	5	

Form Coming into Fixture

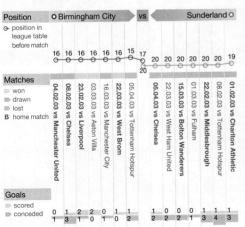

Position ○ Birmingham City vs Sunderland ○
○- position in league table before match

Position: 16 16 16 16 16 16 15 17 20 20 20 20 20 20 20 20 19

Matches (Birmingham City): 04.02.03 vs Manchester United | 08.02.03 vs Chelsea | 23.02.03 vs Liverpool | 03.03.03 vs Aston Villa | 16.03.03 vs Manchester City | 22.03.03 vs West Brom | 05.04.03 vs Tottenham Hotspur

Matches (Sunderland): 05.04.03 vs Chelsea | 22.03.03 vs West Ham United | 15.03.03 vs Bolton Wanderers | 01.03.03 vs Fulham | 22.02.03 vs Middlesbrough | 08.02.03 vs Tottenham Hotspur | 01.02.03 vs Charlton Athletic

■ won
■ drawn
■ lost
B home match

Goals
■ scored
■ conceded

Birmingham City Goals scored: 0 1 2 2 0 1 1
Birmingham City Goals conceded: 1 3 1 0 1 0 2

Sunderland Goals scored: 1 0 0 0 1 1 1
Sunderland Goals conceded: 2 2 2 1 3 4 3

Goal Statistics

○ Birmingham City
by Half | by Situation

■ first: 1 | ■ set piece: 3
■ second: 6 | ■ open play: 4

○ Sunderland
by Half | by Situation

■ first: 2 | ■ set piece: 2
■ second: 2 | ■ open play: 2

Goals by Area

○ Birmingham City
Scored (Conceded)

3 (0)
4 (8)
0 (0)

○ Sunderland
Scored (Conceded)

1 (4)
1 (12)
2 (1)

Team Statistics

Starting Line-Ups

Clapham, Lazaridis, Stewart, Williams D, Thornton, Upson, Clemence, Dugarry John, Bjorklund McCartney, Bennett, Phillips, McCann, Poom, Cunningham, Hughes Kirovski, Horsfield, El Karkouri Wright, Kilbane, Kenna, Devlin Carter, Kyle, Gray

■ 4/4/2   ■ 4/3/3

Unused Sub: Marriott, Purse
Unused Sub: Turns, Arca, Proctor

Premiership Totals

	○ Birmingham	Sunderland ○
Premiership Appearances	941	963
Team Appearances	243	743
Goals Scored	30	110
Assists	75	70
Clean Sheets (goalkeepers)	1	41
Yellow Cards	71	125
Red Cards	1	4

Age/Height

Birmingham City Age
■ **28 yrs, 2 mo**
Birmingham City Height
■ **6'**

Sunderland Age
■ **26 yrs, 5 mo**
Sunderland Height
■ **5'11"**

Match Statistics

League Table after Fixture

	Played	Won	Drawn	Lost	For	Against	Pts
● 12 Man City	33	12	6	15	40	51	42
↑ 13 Leeds	33	11	5	17	46	48	38
↑ 14 Aston Villa	33	10	8	15	36	40	38
↓ 15 Fulham	33	10	8	15	35	46	38
↑ 16 Birmingham	33	10	8	15	31	44	38
↓ 17 Bolton	33	8	11	14	36	48	35
● 18 West Ham	33	7	11	15	37	56	32
● 19 West Brom	33	5	6	22	22	52	21
● 20 Sunderland	33	4	7	22	20	54	19

Statistics

	○ Birmingham	Sunderland ○
Goals	2	0
Shots on Target	3	1
Shots off Target	4	2
Hit Woodwork	0	0
Corners	6	6
Offsides	7	6
Fouls	22	19
Disciplinary Points	0	16

0-2

Charlton Athletic ○
Birmingham City ○

▶ Jeff Kenna makes progress down the right flank

Event Line

20 ○ ⊕	Dugarry / RF / OP / 6Y	
	Assist: Horsfield	
31 ○ ▪	Parker	
33 ○ ▪	Svensson	
Half time 0-1		
46 ○ ⇄	Robinson > Kishishev	
46 ○ ⇄	Lisbie > Svensson	
55 ○ ⊕	Savage / RF / P / IA	
	Assist: Savage	
68 ○	Clemence	
68 ○ ⇄	John > Dugarry	
82 ○ ⇄	Konchesky > El Khalej	
87 ○ ⇄	Devlin > Horsfield	
90 ○ ⇄	Purse > Johnson	
Full time 0-2		

Blues started the crucial Easter period with a deserved victory over Charlton at the Valley.

A convincing win arrived courtesy of a goal in each half from Christophe Dugarry and Robbie Savage – the latter coming from the penalty spot.

Blues squandered two chances early on as Dugarry broke clear and raced into the box before hitting a poor pass behind the unmarked Geoff Horsfield. Then Horsfield got clear but fired his shot across goal and out for a throw-in.

Blues' dominance paid off midway through the first half as Dugarry bagged his second goal for the club in real style. The French star sublimely back heeled Horsfield's cross past Dean Kiely to open the scoring.

Blues went two goals up ten minutes after the break when Savage was tripped in the box by Chris Powell. Despite prolonged protests from the Charlton players, the referee had no hesitation in pointing to the spot. Savage dusted himself down and took the kick himself sending the keeper the wrong way to double his side's lead.

Horsfield almost capped his man-of-the-match display with a goal when he turned his marker but saw his shot kept out by Kiely.

Quote

 Steve Bruce

Considering the enormity of the game and the pressure of the relegation fight, it's a bit special when we play like that. We were very, very worthy winners.

Venue:	The Valley	Referee:	N.S.Barry - 02/03	Charlton Athletic
Attendance:	25,732	Matches:	23	Birmingham City
Capacity:	27,111	Yellow Cards:	82	
Occupancy:	95%	Red Cards:	5	

Form Coming into Fixture

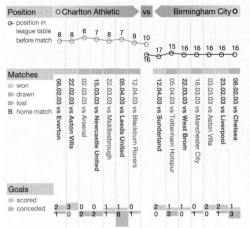

Position — ○ Charlton Athletic vs Birmingham City ○

○ position in league table before match

8 8 6 7 8 7 9 10
16 17 15 16 16 16 16 16

Matches
- won
- drawn
- lost
- B home match

08.02.03 vs Everton
22.02.03 vs Aston Villa
02.03.03 vs Arsenal
15.03.03 vs Newcastle United
22.03.03 vs Middlesbrough
05.04.03 vs Leeds United
12.04.03 vs Blackburn Rovers
12.04.03 vs Sunderland
05.04.03 vs Tottenham Hotspur
22.03.03 vs West Brom
16.03.03 vs Manchester City
03.03.03 vs Aston Villa
23.02.03 vs Liverpool
08.02.03 vs Chelsea

Goals
- scored
- conceded

| 2 | 3 | 0 | 0 | 1 | 1 | 0 | 2 | 1 | 1 | 0 | 2 | 2 | 1 |
| 1 | 0 | 2 | 2 | 1 | 6 | 1 | 0 | 2 | 0 | 1 | 0 | 1 | 3 |

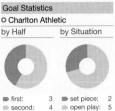

Goal Statistics

○ Charlton Athletic

by Half / by Situation

- first: 3
- second: 4
- set piece: 2
- open play: 5

○ Birmingham City

by Half / by Situation

- first: 2
- second: 7
- set piece: 4
- open play: 5

Goals by Area

○ Charlton Athletic
Scored (Conceded)

3 (4)
4 (8)
0 (1)

○ Birmingham City
Scored (Conceded)

3 (0)
5 (7)
1 (0)

Team Statistics

Starting Line-Ups

Powell   Jensen C   Johnson   Kenna
                                      Purse

Fortune   Euell   Savage   Cunningham
          Johansson Horsfield
                     Devlin
Kiely   Bennett

          Svensson — Dugarry
El Khalej   Lisbie John   Clemence   Upson
Konchesky Parker

Young   Kishishev   Hughes   Clapham
          Robinson

▶ 4/4/2   ▶ 4/4/2

Unused Sub: Roberts, Blomqvist   Unused Sub: Marriott, Lazaridis

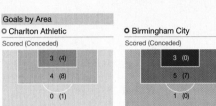

Premiership Totals	○ Charlton	Birmingham ○
Premiership Appearances	1,311	1,102
Team Appearances	1,020	272
Goals Scored	109	41
Assists	104	78
Clean Sheets (goalkeepers)	29	2
Yellow Cards	145	119
Red Cards	4	2

Age/Height

	Charlton Athletic Age	Birmingham City Age
	▶ 27 yrs, 6 mo	▶ 28 yrs, 4 mo
	Charlton Athletic Height	Birmingham City Height
	▶ 5'11"	▶ 5'11"

Match Statistics

League Table after Fixture

	Played	Won	Drawn	Lost	For	Against	Pts
↓ 11 Charlton	34	13	7	14	41	48	46
• 12 Man City	34	13	6	15	42	51	45
↑ 13 Aston Villa	34	11	8	15	38	41	41
↑ 14 Fulham	34	11	8	15	37	47	41
↑ 15 Birmingham	34	11	8	15	33	44	41
↓ 16 Leeds	34	11	5	18	48	51	38
• 17 Bolton	34	9	11	14	37	48	38
• 18 West Ham	34	7	11	16	37	57	32
• 19 West Brom	34	6	6	22	24	53	24

Statistics	○ Charlton	Birmingham ○
Goals	0	2
Shots on Target	5	8
Shots off Target	2	6
Hit Woodwork	0	0
Corners	8	5
Offsides	4	6
Fouls	16	12
Disciplinary Points	8	4

31

3-2

Birmingham City ○
Southampton ○

► Christophe Dugarry levels the scores with a sublime free-kick

Event Line

26 ○ ⊕ Svensson / RF / OP / IA	
Assist: Beattie	
43 ○ ▪ Bridge	
Half time 0-1	
46 ○ ⇄ Ormerod > Delap	
54 ○ ⇄ Lazaridis > Clemence	
64 ○ ⇄ Devlin > Kenna	
71 ○ ▪ Telfer	
75 ○ ⊕ Dugarry / RF / DFK / OA	
Assist: Cunningham	
76 ○ ⇄ Higginbotham > Fernandes	
77 ○ ⊕ Ormerod / RF / OP / IA	
Assist: Svensson	
79 ○ ⊕ Hughes / LF / OP / IA	
Assist: Horsfield	
79 ○ ⇄ John > Johnson	
82 ○ ⊕ Dugarry / H / OP / 6Y	
Assist: John	
85 ○ ⇄ Tessem > Telfer	
Full time 3-2	

Christophe Dugarry continued his rich vein of form with two goals as a sell-out home crowd were treated to a superb Bank Holiday feast.

Bryan Hughes scored his side's other goal in an eventful encounter against FA Cup finalists Southampton.

Anders Svensson opened the scoring completely against the run of play with the Saints' first real effort on goal.

Steve Bruce's side had to wait until 15 minutes from time to eventually draw level. Dugarry's twice-taken free-kick curled around the wall and Paul Jones's left hand could not stop the ball from nestling into the bottom corner.

The lead lasted less than two minutes as Brett Ormerod latched on to Michael Svensson's flick and powered an unstoppable shot into the top left corner. But the home side equalised within 90 seconds, Hughes collecting from Geoff Horsfield before side-footing the ball past Jones.

An incredible match took a final twist one minute later when substitute Stern John produced a superb cross and Dugarry headed home his fourth goal in three games.

Quote

● **Steve Bruce**

I've got a bunch of honest and committed players here, superb characters who deserve to stay in the Premiership.

Venue:	St Andrew's	Referee:	S.G.Bennett - 02/03		Birmingham City
Attendance:	29,115	Matches:	25		Southampton
Capacity:	30,016	Yellow Cards:	97		
Occupancy:	97%	Red Cards:	5		

Form Coming into Fixture

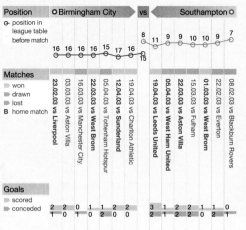

Goal Statistics

Birmingham City
by Half / by Situation

- first: 3
- second: 7
- set piece: 4
- open play: 6

Southampton
by Half / by Situation

- first: 6
- second: 4
- set piece: 4
- open play: 6

Goals by Area

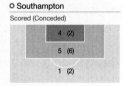

Birmingham City — Scored (Conceded)

- 4 (0)
- 5 (4)
- 1 (0)

Southampton — Scored (Conceded)

- 4 (2)
- 5 (6)
- 1 (2)

Team Statistics

Starting Line-Ups

Birmingham City 4/4/2

Clapham, Hughes
Upson, Clemence, Lazaridis
Dugarry, Svensson
Cunningham, Savage
Bennett
Horsfield, Beattie
Kenna, Johnson
Devlin, John

Unused Sub: Marriott, Purse

Southampton 4/4/1/1

Fernandes, Telfer
Higginbotham, Tessem
Delap, Lundekvam
Ormerod
Oakley, Svensson
Jones P
Prutton, Bridge

Unused Sub: Blayney, Williams

Premiership Totals

	Birmingham	Southampton
Premiership Appearances	1,193	1,677
Team Appearances	294	1,312
Goals Scored	46	110
Assists	99	116
Clean Sheets (goalkeepers)	3	49
Yellow Cards	122	138
Red Cards		8

Age/Height

	Birmingham City	Southampton
Age	28 yrs, 8 mo	27 yrs, 1 mo
Height	5'11"	6'

Match Statistics

League Table after Fixture

		Played	Won	Drawn	Lost	For	Against	Pts
↓ 9	Southampton	34	12	12	10	40	38	48
↑ 10	Man City	35	14	6	15	45	51	48
↓ 11	Middlesbrough	35	12	10	13	42	38	46
↓ 12	Charlton	35	13	7	15	42	50	46
↑ 13	Birmingham	35	12	8	15	36	46	44
↓ 14	Aston Villa	35	11	9	15	39	42	42
↓ 15	Fulham	34	11	8	15	37	47	41
↑ 16	Bolton	35	9	12	14	37	48	39
↓ 17	Leeds	34	11	5	18	48	51	38

Statistics

	Birmingham	Southampton
Goals	3	2
Shots on Target	9	7
Shots off Target	6	5
Hit Woodwork	0	0
Corners	5	3
Offsides	10	1
Fouls	10	19
Disciplinary Points	0	8

3-0

Birmingham City ○
Middlesbrough ○

▸ Geoff Horsfield is a picture of concentration

Event Line

18 ○ ⊕	Dugarry / RF / OP / IA
	Assist: Clemence
40 ○ ⊕	Clemence / LF / DFK / O/
	Assist: Dugarry

Half time 2-0

46 ○ ⇄	Doriva > Cooper
63 ○ ▢	Boateng
63 ○ ▢	Hughes
67 ○ ⇄	Nemeth > Ricketts
70 ○ ⇄	Lazaridis > Hughes
75 ○ ⇄	Devlin > Horsfield
78 ○ ⇄	Maccarone > Job
80 ○ ⊕	Lazaridis / H / OP / 6Y
	Assist: Savage
81 ○ ⇄	John > Dugarry
89 ○ ▢	Maccarone

Full time 3-0

Blues stormed to their fourth successive victory with a convincing performance over a lacklustre Middlesbrough side.

Steve Bruce elected to stick with the same 16 players that did so well against Southampton.

Christophe Dugarry opened the scoring on 18 minutes when he cleverly beat the Boro offside trap before collecting Damien Johnson's chipped ball, swivelling and firing the ball home on the volley to the delight of the Blues faithful.

Blues continued to press and with five minutes of the first half to go Dugarry was brought down on the edge of the box. While the visiting defence were still organising their wall, Stephen Clemence took a quick free kick and sent a low left-footed shot into the bottom corner.

Despite being two goals down, Boro seemed incapable of bringing any urgency to the game and Blues strolled to a comfortable win capped off with a third goal. Paul Devlin laid the ball back for Robbie Savage and he drilled in a first time cross which was met at the far post by a Stan Lazaridis header to complete the scoring.

Quote

● **Steve Bruce**

It's been the toughest season of my career, but also the most satisfying. We will now be able to enjoy the last two fixtures.

Venue:	St Andrew's	Referee:	M.L.Dean - 02/03	**Birmingham City**
Attendance:	28,821	Matches:	25	**Middlesbrough**
Capacity:	30,016	Yellow Cards:	109	
Occupancy:	96%	Red Cards:	9	

Form Coming into Fixture

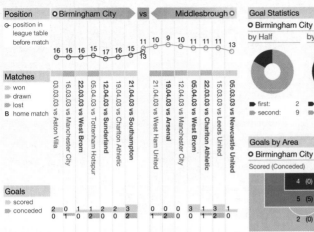

Position ○ Birmingham City vs Middlesbrough ○

Position in league table before match

16 16 16 15 17 16 15 13 11 10 9 10 11 11 11 13

Matches
- won
- drawn
- lost
- B home match

03.03.03 vs Aston Villa
16.03.03 vs Manchester City
22.03.03 vs West Brom
05.04.03 vs Tottenham Hotspur
12.04.03 vs Sunderland
19.04.03 vs Charlton Athletic
21.04.03 vs Southampton
21.04.03 vs West Ham United
19.04.03 vs Arsenal
12.04.03 vs Manchester City
05.04.03 vs West Brom
22.03.03 vs Charlton Athletic
15.03.03 vs Leeds United
05.03.03 vs Newcastle United

Goals
- scored
- conceded

2	0	1	1	2	2	3		0	0	0	3	1	3	1	
0	1	0	2	0	0	2		1	2	0	0	1	2	0	

Goal Statistics

○ Birmingham City

by Half | by Situation

- first: 2
- second: 9
- set piece: 4
- open play: 7

○ Middlesbrough

by Half | by Situation

- first: 3
- second: 5
- set piece: 1
- open play: 7

Goals by Area

○ Birmingham City — Scored (Conceded)

4 (0)
5 (5)
2 (0)

○ Middlesbrough — Scored (Conceded)

1 (2)
5 (3)
2 (1)

Team Statistics

Starting Line-Ups

Clapham, Hughes, Lazaridis, Parnaby, Greening, Southgate, Upson, Clemence, Dugarry, John, Ricketts, Nemeth, Boateng, Ehiogu, Schwarzer, Bennett, Cunningham, Savage, Horsfield, Devlin, Christie, Cooper, Doriva, Kenna, Johnson, Job, Maccarone, Queudrue

4/4/2

5/3/2

Unused Sub: Marriott, Purse

Unused Sub: Jones, Stockdale

Premiership Totals

	○ Birmingham	Boro ○
Premiership Appearances	1,207	1,666
Team Appearances	308	748
Goals Scored	49	129
Assists	102	83
Clean Sheets (goalkeepers)	3	47
Yellow Cards	122	193
Red Cards	1	10

Age/Height

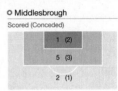

Birmingham City Age	Middlesbrough Age
28 yrs, 8 mo	**27 yrs, 3 mo**
Birmingham City Height	Middlesbrough Height
5'11"	**6'**

Match Statistics

League Table after Fixture

			Played	Won	Drawn	Lost	For	Against	Pts
●	5	Liverpool	36	18	10	8	59	37	64
●	6	Everton	36	17	8	11	47	45	59
●	7	Blackburn	36	15	11	10	47	42	56
●	8	Tottenham	35	14	8	13	50	51	50
↑	9	Charlton	36	14	7	15	44	51	49
↓	10	Southampton	35	12	12	11	41	40	48
↓	11	Man City	35	14	6	15	45	51	48
↑	12	Birmingham	36	13	8	15	39	46	47
↓	13	Middlesbrough	36	12	10	14	42	41	46

Statistics

	○ Birmingham	Boro ○
Goals	3	0
Shots on Target	6	4
Shots off Target	1	2
Hit Woodwork	0	0
Corners	3	3
Offsides	3	9
Fouls	17	18
Disciplinary Points	4	8

1-0

Birmingham City ○
Tottenham Hotspur ○

▶ Jeff Kenna slides in on Mauricio Taricco

Event Line

25 ○ ■	Savage	
31 ○ ■	Clemence	
35 ○ ■	Gardner	
36 ○ ⊕	Dunn / RF / P / IA	
	Assist: Savage	
38 ○ ■	Carr	
38 ○ ■	Dunn	

Half time 1-0

47 ○ ■	Davies	
57 ○ ⇄	Zamora > Postiga	
69 ○ ⇄	John > Horsfield	
70 ○ ⇄	Marney > Taricco	
72 ○ ⇄	Devlin > Dugarry	
89 ○ ■	Ricketts	
90 ○ ■	Marney	
90 ○ ⇄	Tebily > Savage	

Full time 1-0

A first-half penalty from debutant David Dunn was enough to give Blues victory on the opening day of the season at St Andrew's.

Blues went desperately close to opening the scoring when Dunn's 30-yard free-kick evaded the visitors' wall before skewing off the post.

But Spurs had certainly come for a battle and began to exert pressure of their own and Maik Taylor was forced into action when he tipped away Simon Davies's dangerous cross.

Steve Bruce's side finally got their just reward when Robbie Savage was brought down in the area by Anthony Gardner. Dunn coolly stepped up and hit the ball hard to Kasey Keller's left to send the home crowd into raptures.

Christophe Dugarry very nearly made it 2-0 when Geoff Horsfield lofted the ball over the top of the Spurs defence but the Frenchman's half-volley bounced narrowly wide.

Blues defended well in the second half to keep hold of their lead and ensure an opening day victory.

Quote

● **Steve Bruce**

David Dunn proved he has some real quality. He's got something about him and is a special player.

Premiership Milestone

▶ **Debut**

Both Maik Taylor and David Dunn made their first Premiership appearances in the colours of Birmingham.

Venue:	St Andrew's	Referee:	R.Styles - 03/04	Birmingham City
Attendance:	29,358	Matches:	0	Tottenham Hotspur
Capacity:	30,016	Yellow Cards:	0	
Occupancy:	98%	Red Cards:	0	

Form Coming into Fixture

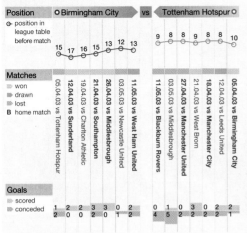

Position o Birmingham City vs Tottenham Hotspur o

G- position in league table before match

Matches
- won
- drawn
- lost
- B home match

Goals
- scored
- conceded

Goal Statistics

o Birmingham City — by Half | by Situation

- first: 4
- second: 9
- set piece: 5
- open play: 8

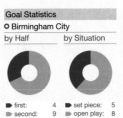

o Tottenham Hotspur — by Half | by Situation

- first: 4
- second: 4
- set piece: 3
- open play: 5

Goals by Area

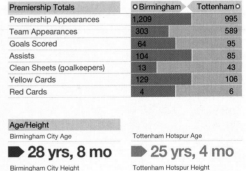

o Birmingham City — Scored (Conceded)

4 (2) / 6 (4) / 3 (1)

o Tottenham Hotspur — Scored (Conceded)

2 (3) / 5 (12) / 1 (3)

Team Statistics

Starting Line-Ups

Clapham, Dunn, Carr, Davies, Doherty, Purse, Clemence, Dugarry (Devlin), Keane, Redknapp, Bunjevcevic, Keller, Cunningham, Savage (Tebily), Horsfield (John), Postiga (Zamora), Gardner, Ricketts, Kenna, Johnson, Taricco (Marney), Taylor, Maik

4/4/2

Unused Sub: Bennett, Lazaridis

5/3/2

Unused Sub: Sullivan, Kelly, Acimovic

Premiership Totals

	o Birmingham	Tottenham o
Premiership Appearances	1,209	995
Team Appearances	303	589
Goals Scored	64	95
Assists	104	85
Clean Sheets (goalkeepers)	13	43
Yellow Cards	129	106
Red Cards	4	6

Age/Height

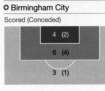 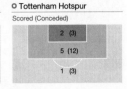

Birmingham City Age: **28 yrs, 8 mo**

Tottenham Hotspur Age: **25 yrs, 4 mo**

Birmingham City Height: **6'**

Tottenham Hotspur Height: **6'**

Match Statistics

League Table after Fixture

		Played	Won	Drawn	Lost	For	Against	Pts
1	Blackburn	1	1	0	0	5	1	3
2	Man Utd	1	1	0	0	4	0	3
3	Fulham	1	1	0	0	3	2	3
4	Arsenal	1	1	0	0	2	1	3
5	Portsmouth	1	1	0	0	2	1	3
6	Birmingham	1	1	0	0	1	0	3
7	Leicester	1	0	1	0	2	2	1
...		...	...	...	...	...	...	...
18	Tottenham	1	0	0	1	0	1	0

Statistics

	o Birmingham	Tottenham o
Goals	1	0
Shots on Target	3	3
Shots off Target	6	8
Hit Woodwork	1	1
Possession %	43	57
Corners	1	4
Offsides	3	1
Fouls	22	27
Disciplinary Points	12	20

0-1

Newcastle United ○
Birmingham City ○

▶ David Dunn threads the ball through the Newcastle defence

Event Line

34 ○ ▪	Jenas
Half time 0-0	
59 ○ ▪	Speed
61 ○ ⊕	Dunn / LF / P / 6Y
	Assist: Johnson
66 ○ ⇄	Chopra > Ameobi
66 ○ ⇄	Bowyer > Solano
66 ○ ⇄	Robert > Viana
71 ○ ⇄	Horsfield > John
79 ○ ⇄	Cisse > Lazaridis
84 ○ ▪	Kenna
88 ○ ⇄	Tebily > Dunn
Full time 0-1	

Blues continued an unbeaten start to the 2003/04 season with a memorable victory at St. James' Park when David Dunn was once again the match winner.

The game burst into life in the 19th minute when Blues created the first chance as Dunn hit a dipping shot which Newcastle keeper Shay Given spectacularly tipped over for a corner.

Nolberto Solano went closest for Newcastle in the first half when his injury time free kick was caught easily under the bar by Taylor.

After the interval Dunn proved to be the Blues hero at both ends of the pitch. First he was in the right place to clear Shola Ameobi's header off the line and soon afterwards came the moment that clinched victory.

Dunn sent Damien Johnson clear in the box and he was caught by a mistimed tackle by Gary Speed to earn Blues a penalty.

Although Given saved Dunn's weakly-struck spot kick, Blues' record signing from Blackburn followed up to slot the ball under the Newcastle keeper.

Quote	Premiership Milestone
● **Steve Bruce**	▶ **50**
We're absolutely delighted. We seem to have come a long way in 12 months.	Matthew Upson made his 50th Premiership appearance.

Venue:	St James' Park	Referee:	M.D.Messias - 03/04
Attendance:	52,006	Matches:	1
Capacity:	52,327	Yellow Cards:	5
Occupancy:	99%	Red Cards:	0

Newcastle United
Birmingham City

Form Coming into Fixture

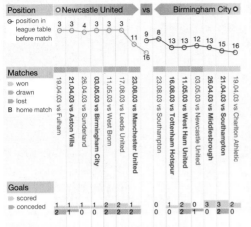

Position

	O Newcastle United	vs	Birmingham City O

position in league table before match

3 3 4 3 3 3 11 9 8 13 13 12 13 15 16
16

Matches
- won
- drawn
- lost
- B home match

19.04.03 vs Fulham
21.04.03 vs Aston Villa
26.04.03 vs Sunderland
03.05.03 vs Birmingham City
11.05.03 vs West Brom
17.08.03 vs Leeds United
23.08.03 vs Manchester United
23.08.03 vs Southampton
16.08.03 vs Tottenham Hotspur
11.05.03 vs West Ham United
03.05.03 vs Newcastle United
26.04.03 vs Middlesbrough
21.04.03 vs Southampton
19.04.03 vs Charlton Athletic

Goals
- scored
- conceded

| 1 | 1 | 1 | 1 | 2 | 2 | 1 | 0 | 1 | 2 | 0 | 3 | 3 | 2 |
| 2 | 1 | 0 | 0 | 2 | 2 | 2 | 0 | 0 | 2 | 1 | 0 | 2 | 0 |

Goal Statistics

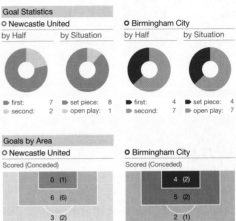

O Newcastle United

by Half		by Situation	
first:	7	set piece:	8
second:	2	open play:	1

O Birmingham City

by Half		by Situation	
first:	4	set piece:	4
second:	7	open play:	7

Goals by Area

O Newcastle United
Scored (Conceded)

0	(1)
6	(6)
3	(2)

O Birmingham City
Scored (Conceded)

4	(2)
5	(2)
2	(1)

Team Statistics

Starting Line-Ups

Speed Viana Robert Johnson Kenna

Bramble Jenas Shearer Dunn Tebily Savage Cunningham

Given Taylor Maik

O'Brien Dyer Ameobi Chopra John Horsfield Clemence Upson

Griffin Solano Bowyer Lazaridis Cisse Clapham

4/4/2
Unused Sub: Harper, Hughes

4/4/1/1
Unused Sub: Bennett, Morrison

Premiership Totals	O Newcastle	Birmingham O
Premiership Appearances	1,854	1,332
Team Appearances	1,202	323
Goals Scored	403	61
Assists	269	122
Clean Sheets (goalkeepers)	51	15
Yellow Cards	212	142
Red Cards	9	5

Age/Height

Newcastle United Age	Birmingham City Age
25 yrs, 5 mo	**28 yrs, 2 mo**

Newcastle United Height	Birmingham City Height
5'10"	**5'11"**

Match Statistics

League Table after Fixture

		Played	Won	Drawn	Lost	For	Against	Pts
●	1 Arsenal	3	3	0	0	8	1	9
●	2 Man Utd	3	3	0	0	7	1	9
●	3 Portsmouth	4	2	2	0	7	2	8
●	4 Man City	3	2	1	0	7	3	7
●	5 Chelsea	3	2	1	0	6	4	7
↑	6 Birmingham	3	2	1	0	2	0	7
↑	7 Fulham	3	2	0	1	7	5	6
...	...	...	...	...	...	...	...	...
↓	18 Newcastle	3	0	1	2	3	5	1

Statistics	O Newcastle	Birmingham O
Goals	0	1
Shots on Target	4	5
Shots off Target	8	4
Hit Woodwork	0	0
Possession %	57	43
Corners	9	6
Offsides	4	1
Fouls	15	15
Disciplinary Points	8	4

0-2

Leeds United o
Birmingham City o

▶ Matthew Upson prepares to send the ball forward

Event Line		
13 O ■	Olembe	
45 O ■	Savage	
Half time 0-0		
61 O ■	Sakho	
70 O ■	Dugarry	
77 O ◼	Roque Junior	
	2nd Bookable Offence	
79 O ⊕	Savage / RF / P / IA	
	Assist: Forssell	
81 O ⇄	Lennon > Sakho	
83 O ■	Camara	
84 O ⊕	Forssell / RF / OP / IA	
	Assist: Dunn	
85 O ⇄	Cisse > Dugarry	
88 O ⇄	Tebily > Forssell	
90 O ⇄	Morrison > Dunn	
Full time 0-2		

It was the late, late show as Blues got out of jail to collect all three points over Leeds and extend the unbeaten start to the league season to five games.

After an uneventful first half, Maik Taylor in the Blues goal had to be alert to punch away Ian Harte's inswinging free-kick.

Another Harte free-kick set up Leeds' next chance as Mark Viduka flicked on to Alan Smith who turned Kenny Cunningham before hitting a fierce shot that Taylor smothered at the second attempt.

Blues seemed to be content in soaking up the pressure as Leeds continued to dominate. But it was the visitors that took the lead after conjuring up a goal out of nothing. Christophe Dugarry's back-heel sent Mikael Forssell through on goal and he was eventually brought down by Roque Junior to earn Blues a penalty that was converted by Robbie Savage.

The victory was sealed six minutes from time after a neat move involving Damien Johnson, Dugarry and David Dunn was finished neatly by Forssell.

Quote

● Steve Bruce

Mikael Forssell has got us the penalty and then the second goal with the best bit of quality in the whole game.

Venue:	Elland Road	Referee:	D.J.Gallagher - 03/04	Leeds United
Attendance:	34,305	Matches:	3	Birmingham City
Capacity:	40,204	Yellow Cards:	13	
Occupancy:	85%	Red Cards:	0	

Form Coming into Fixture

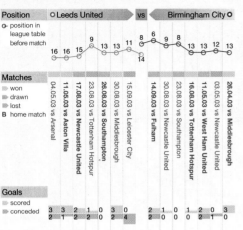

Position

○ Leeds United vs Birmingham City ○

○ position in league table before match

Matches
- won
- drawn
- lost
- B home match

Goals
- scored
- conceded

scored	3	3	2	1	0	3	0		2	1	0	1	2	0	3
conceded	2	1	2	2	0	2	4		2	0	0	2	1	0

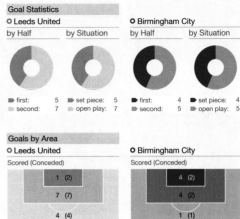

Goal Statistics

○ Leeds United

by Half
- first: 5
- second: 7

by Situation
- set piece: 5
- open play: 7

○ Birmingham City

by Half
- first: 4
- second: 5

by Situation
- set piece: 4
- open play: 5

Goals by Area

○ Leeds United — Scored (Conceded)

1 (2)
7 (7)
4 (4)

○ Birmingham City — Scored (Conceded)

4 (2)
4 (2)
1 (1)

Team Statistics

Starting Line-Ups

Leeds United (left): Robinson; Harte, Sakho, Lennon, Roque Junior, Olembe, Viduka (Tebily), Camara, Morris, Smith, Dugarry (Cisse), Kelly, Pennant

▶ 4/4/2

Unused Sub: Carson, Radebe, Batty, Chapuis

Birmingham City (right): Dunn, Johnson, Morrison, Forssell, Savage, Cunningham, Taylor Maik, Clemence, Upson, Lazaridis, Clapham

▶ 4/4/2

Unused Sub: Bennett, John

Premiership Totals

	○ Leeds	Birmingham ○
Premiership Appearances	949	1,093
Team Appearances	820	287
Goals Scored	120	65
Assists	119	109
Clean Sheets (goalkeepers)	16	16
Yellow Cards	126	137
Red Cards	8	4

Age/Height

Leeds United Age

▶ **24 yrs, 4 mo**

Birmingham City Age

▶ **27 yrs, 5 mo**

Leeds United Height

▶ **5'10"**

Birmingham City Height

▶ **5'11"**

Match Statistics

League Table after Fixture

		Played	Won	Drawn	Lost	For	Against	Pts
↑ 1	Chelsea	5	4	1	0	15	6	13
↓ 2	Arsenal	5	4	1	0	11	3	13
↓ 3	Man Utd	5	4	0	1	9	2	12
↑ 4	Southampton	6	3	3	0	8	3	12
↓ 5	Man City	6	3	2	1	14	8	11
↑ 6	Liverpool	6	3	2	1	9	4	11
↑ 7	Birmingham	5	3	2	0	6	2	11
...	...	...	...	...	...	...	...	...
↓ 16	Leeds	6	1	2	3	6	12	5

Statistics

	○ Leeds	Birmingham ○
Goals	0	2
Shots on Target	6	3
Shots off Target	4	4
Hit Woodwork	0	0
Possession %	56	44
Corners	6	1
Offsides	5	3
Fouls	15	14
Disciplinary Points	22	8

41

2-0

Birmingham City ○
Portsmouth ○

➡ Jamie Clapham climbs above Teddy Sheringham

Event Line

21 ○ ⊕	Clemence / LF / IFK / 6Y	
	Assist: Lazaridis	
33 ○ ▪	Faye	
Half time 1-0		
50 ○ ⊕	Lazaridis / LF / OP / IA	
	Assist: Clemence	
55 ○ ⇄	Roberts > Taylor	
65 ○ ⇄	Sherwood > Faye	
71 ○ ⇄	Cisse > Dugarry	
74 ○ ▪	Cisse	
79 ○ ▪	Sheringham	
83 ○ ▪	Sherwood	
84 ○ ⇄	Tebily > Lazaridis	
87 ○ ⇄	Figueroa > Forssell	
Full time 2-0		

Stephen Clemence went from Carling Cup villain to Premiership hero as he scored one goal and set up another in this win over Portsmouth at St. Andrew's.

Clemence had blasted a penalty high over the bar in a humiliating defeat to Blackpool just four days earlier. But that howler was soon forgotten as the former Spurs man put Blues ahead on 21 minutes.

Lazaridis swung in a free kick towards the far post and the ball came through a forest of legs to Clemence who poked it past Shaka Hislop with his left foot.

The roles were reversed early in the second half when Clemence set up Lazaridis for the clinching second goal and the Australian winger coolly slotted the ball past Hislop into the bottom right corner.

The South Coast visitors did look dangerous in parts during the first half and enjoyed plenty of possession after the break but Blues always looked like holding on to the victory. It wasn't the best performance but there were few complaints from the home fans as their side's unbeaten league start continued.

Quote

● Steve Bruce

Obviously the more games you win early on, the easier it becomes. We've got our feet on the ground at the moment though.

Premiership Milestone

➡ Debut

Luciano Figueroa made his Premiership debut.

Venue:	St Andrew's	Referee:	S.G.Bennett - 03/04		Birmingham City
Attendance:	29,057	Matches:	4		Portsmouth
Capacity:	30,016	Yellow Cards:	18		
Occupancy:	97%	Red Cards:	2		

Form Coming into Fixture

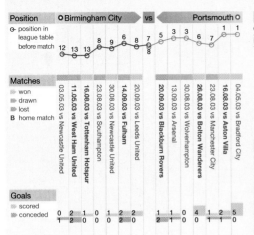

Position

- position in league table before match

Matches

- won
- drawn
- lost
- B home match

Goals

- scored
- conceded

0	2	1	0	1	2	2	1	1	0	4	1	2	5	
1	2	0	0	0	2	0	2	1	0	0	1	1	0	

Matches (vs):
03.05.03 vs Newcastle United, 11.05.03 vs West Ham United, 16.08.03 vs Tottenham Hotspur, 23.08.03 vs Southampton, 30.08.03 vs Newcastle United, 14.09.03 vs Fulham, 20.09.03 vs Leeds United, 20.09.03 vs Blackburn Rovers, 13.09.03 vs Arsenal, 30.08.03 vs Wolverhampton, 26.08.03 vs Bolton Wanderers, 23.08.03 vs Manchester City, 16.08.03 vs Aston Villa, 04.05.03 vs Bradford City

Goal Statistics

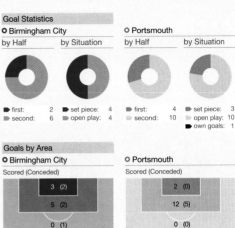

Birmingham City

by Half		by Situation	
first:	2	set piece:	4
second:	6	open play:	4

Portsmouth

by Half		by Situation	
first:	4	set piece:	3
second:	10	open play:	10
		own goals:	1

Goals by Area

Birmingham City

Scored (Conceded)

| 3 (2) |
| 5 (2) |
| 0 (1) |

Portsmouth

Scored (Conceded)

| 2 (0) |
| 12 (5) |
| 0 (0) |

Team Statistics

Starting Line-Ups

Birmingham City:
Clapham, Lazaridis / Tebily, Stone, Schemmel, Upson, Clemence, Faye / Sherwood, De Zeeuw, Dugarry / Cisse, Sheringham, Hislop, Cunningham, Savage, Forssell / Figueroa, Yakubu, Smertin, Stefanovic, Johnson, Dunn, Taylor / Roberts, Zivkovic

4/4/2 — **4/4/2**

Unused Sub: Bennett, Morrison

Unused Sub: Wapenaar, Primus, Foxe

Premiership Totals

	Birmingham	Portsmouth
Premiership Appearances	1,075	1,282
Team Appearances	270	60
Goals Scored	60	203
Assists	108	163
Clean Sheets (goalkeepers)	17	47
Yellow Cards	133	153
Red Cards	4	11

Age/Height

Birmingham City Age	Portsmouth Age
27 yrs, 4 mo	**29 yrs, 3 mo**
Birmingham City Height	Portsmouth Height
5'11"	**6'**

Match Statistics

League Table after Fixture

		Played	Won	Drawn	Lost	For	Against	Pts
●	1 Arsenal	7	5	2	0	14	5	17
●	2 Chelsea	6	5	1	0	16	6	16
●	3 Man Utd	7	5	1	1	13	3	16
↑	4 Birmingham	6	4	2	0	8	2	14
↓	5 Southampton	7	3	3	1	8	4	12
↓	6 Man City	6	3	2	1	14	8	11
↓	7 Liverpool	6	3	2	1	9	4	11
●	8 Portsmouth	7	2	3	2	9	7	9
●	9 Blackburn	6	2	2	2	14	12	8

Statistics

	Birmingham	Portsmouth
Goals	2	0
Shots on Target	6	3
Shots off Target	5	8
Hit Woodwork	0	1
Possession %	38	62
Corners	4	4
Offsides	0	6
Fouls	13	16
Disciplinary Points	4	12

0-1 Bolton Wanderers ○
Birmingham City ○

► Matthew Upson tries to hold off Kevin Davies

Event Line	
31 ○ ⊕ Forssell / LF / OP / IA	
34 ○ ▢ Dunn	
44 ○ ▢ Tebily	
Half time 0-1	
54 ○ ▢ Giannakopoulos	
58 ○ ⇄ Kenna > Tebily	
65 ○ ⇄ Jardel > Campo	
77 ○ ⇄ Hughes > Lazaridis	
81 ○ ⇄ Pedersen > Giannakopoulos	
84 ○ ⇄ Little > Nolan	
88 ○ ⇄ Morrison > Dugarry	
Full time 0-1	

After suffering a first Premiership defeat of the season at Manchester United followed by successive home goalless draws with Chelsea and Aston Villa, Blues returned to winning ways at the Reebok Stadium.

The decisive goal came just after the hour mark. Mikael Forssell sent David Dunn clear and he raced 50 yards into the Bolton half before knocking the ball wide to Christophe Dugarry. The Frenchman cut inside and the ball squirmed past former Blues defender Simon Charlton, who slipped allowing Forssell to slot the ball beyond Jussi Jaaskelainen to give Blues the lead.

Forssell almost doubled his tally soon afterwards but his fierce shot from Dunn's through ball was kept out by Jaaskelainen.

At the other end Blues had Taylor to thank for maintaining the lead with a spectacular one-handed save to tip over Kevin Davies's goal-bound volley.

But Blues held on despite concerted pressure from the home side in the second half and Forssell's goal had finally broken a 38-year hoodoo away to the Trotters.

Quote

● Steve Bruce

Maik Taylor has produced a hell of a save during that game. He's got a big presence, big safe hands and is a cracking professional.

Premiership Milestone

► 50

Mikael Forssell's goal was the 50th scored by Birmingham in the Premiership.

44

Venue:	Reebok Staduim	Referee:	C.J.Foy - 03/04	**Bolton Wanderers**
Attendance:	25,023	Matches:	7	**Birmingham City**
Capacity:	28,723	Yellow Cards:	24	
Occupancy:	87%	Red Cards:	3	

Form Coming into Fixture

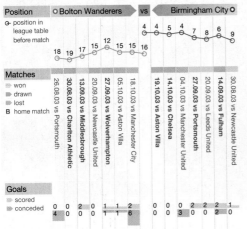

Position	○ Bolton Wanderers	vs	Birmingham City ○

G- position in league table before match

Matches
- won
- drawn
- lost

B home match

Goals
- scored
- conceded

scored	0	0	2	0	1	1	2		0	0	0	2	2	2	1
conceded	4	0	0	0	1	1	6		0	0	3	0	0	2	0

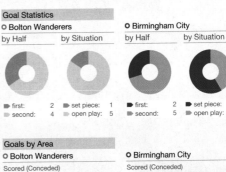

Goal Statistics

○ Bolton Wanderers

by Half | by Situation

- first: 2
- second: 4
- set piece: 1
- open play: 5

○ Birmingham City

by Half | by Situation

- first: 2
- second: 5
- set piece: 4
- open play: 3

Goals by Area

○ Bolton Wanderers
Scored (Conceded)

2 (2)
3 (8)
1 (2)

○ Birmingham City
Scored (Conceded)

3 (0)
4 (4)
0 (1)

Team Statistics

Starting Line-Ups

Gardner, Giannakopoulos, Pedersen, Okocha, Charlton, Jaaskelainen, Campo, Jardel, Davies, Thome, Frandsen, N'Gotty, Nolan, Little

Dunn, Tebily, Kenna, Cisse, Cunningham, Forssell, Dugarry, Morrison, Clemence, Upson, Lazaridis, Hughes, Clapham, Taylor Maik

4/3/3

4/4/2

Unused Sub: Poole, Barness

Unused Sub: Bennett, Figueroa

Premiership Totals	○ Bolton	Birmingham ○
Premiership Appearances	995	1,176
Team Appearances	628	335
Goals Scored	71	61
Assists	69	105
Clean Sheets (goalkeepers)	20	19
Yellow Cards	135	107
Red Cards	7	5

Age/Height

Bolton Wanderers Age	Birmingham City Age
29 yrs, 1 mo	**28 yrs**
Bolton Wanderers Height	Birmingham City Height
6'	**5'11"**

Match Statistics

League Table after Fixture

		Played	Won	Drawn	Lost	For	Against	Pts
↑	1 Chelsea	10	7	2	1	20	9	23
↓	2 Arsenal	9	7	2	0	18	7	23
↓	3 Man Utd	10	7	1	2	18	6	22
●	4 Birmingham	10	5	4	1	9	5	19
↑	5 Fulham	10	5	3	2	20	13	18
↑	6 Southampton	10	4	4	2	10	5	16
↓	7 Man City	10	4	3	3	20	12	15
...	...	...	...	...	...	...	...	...
↓	17 Bolton	10	1	5	4	8	19	8

Statistics	○ Bolton	Birmingham ○
Goals	0	1
Shots on Target	2	9
Shots off Target	3	3
Hit Woodwork	0	0
Possession %	51	49
Corners	3	17
Offsides	6	1
Fouls	16	5
Disciplinary Points	4	8

45

0-2

Leicester City ⚬
Birmingham City ⚬

▶ Clinton Morrison spares a thought for Ian Walker

Event Line	
31 ⚬ ■	Scowcroft
32 ⚬ ■	Johnson
38 ⚬ ■	Elliott
	Violent Conduct
42 ⚬ ⊕	Morrison / RF / OP / IA
	Assist: Clapham
44 ⚬ ■	Clemence
Half time 0-1	
46 ⚬ ⇄	Curtis > Ferdinand
58 ⚬ ■	Dickov
61 ⚬ ■	Walker
	Handball
62 ⚬ ⇄	Coyne > Dickov
66 ⚬ ⊕	Forssell / H / C / IA
	Assist: Savage
66 ⚬ ⇄	Lazaridis > Clemence
72 ⚬ ⇄	Bent M > Thatcher
72 ⚬ ⇄	Cisse > Savage
83 ⚬ ⇄	John > Forssell
Full time 0-2	

After a run of four defeats and one draw had seen Steve Bruce's men fall from the heady heights of fourth to eighth, we headed for a noon showdown at the Walkers Stadium looking to get the season back on track.

A goal in each half from Clinton Morrison and Mikael Forssell deservedly gave Blues all three points in an ill-tempered contest that saw the hosts finish the game with only nine men.

Matt Elliott was sent off in the first half after aiming an elbow into the face of David Dunn and it took Blues just four minutes to take full advantage. Dunn sent Jamie Clapham clear and he put in a great for Morrison to side foot home his first goal of the season.

The home side's numbers were further reduced just after the hour mark when goalkeeper Ian Walker was dismissed after handling outside the area.

And Forssell made sure of victory as he headed home a cross from former Leicester man Robbie Savage.

Quote

● **Steve Bruce**

Clinton Morrison has had a tough time because of injury. He wasn't fit for pre-season, but he has got his reward for working hard.

Premiership Milestone

▶ **100**

Jamie Clapham made his 100th Premiership appearance.

46

Venue:	Walkers Stadium	Referee:	M.A.Riley - 03/04
Attendance:	30,639	Matches:	15
Capacity:	32,500	Yellow Cards:	46
Occupancy:	94%	Red Cards:	2

Leicester City
Birmingham City

Form Coming into Fixture

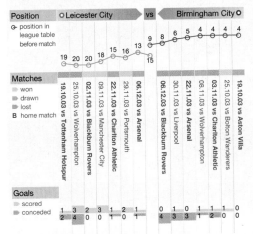

Goal Statistics

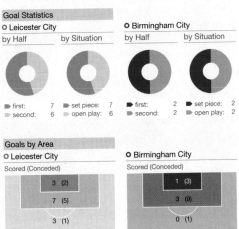

O Leicester City

by Half | by Situation

- first: 7
- second: 6
- set piece: 7
- open play: 6

O Birmingham City

by Half | by Situation

- first: 2
- second: 2
- set piece: 2
- open play: 2

Goals by Area

O Leicester City
Scored (Conceded)

3 (2)
7 (5)
3 (1)

O Birmingham City
Scored (Conceded)

1 (3)
3 (9)
0 (1)

Team Statistics

Starting Line-Ups

Thatcher, Stewart, Bent M, Scimeca, Izzet, Dickov, Coyne, Forssell, John, Walker, Ferdinand, Curtis, Morrison, Elliott, Davidson, Impey, Scowcroft

Johnson, Kenna, Savage, Cisse, Cunningham, Clemence, Lazaridis, Upson, Taylor Maik, Dunn, Clapham

▶ 4/4/2

Unused Sub: Gillespie, Hignett

▶ 4/4/2

Unused Sub: Bennett, Purse

Premiership Totals	O Leicester	Birmingham O
Premiership Appearances	1,874	1,494
Team Appearances	771	452
Goals Scored	259	78
Assists	160	137
Clean Sheets (goalkeepers)	73	20
Yellow Cards	190	155
Red Cards	11	4

Age/Height

Leicester City Age
▶ 29 yrs, 5 mo

Birmingham City Age
▶ 27 yrs, 9 mo

Leicester City Height
▶ 5'11"

Birmingham City Height
▶ 5'11"

Match Statistics

League Table after Fixture

		Played	Won	Drawn	Lost	For	Against	Pts
↑ 8	Birmingham	16	6	5	5	14	18	23
↓ 9	Liverpool	16	6	4	6	23	18	22
↑ 10	Bolton	16	5	6	5	16	22	21
● 11	Middlesbrough	16	5	6	5	12	15	20
↓ 12	Man City	16	5	4	7	23	22	19
↓ 13	Tottenham	16	5	3	8	18	24	18
● 14	Blackburn	15	5	2	8	23	24	17
↑ 15	Everton	16	4	5	7	17	20	17
↓ 16	Leicester	16	4	4	8	23	25	16

Statistics	O Leicester	Birmingham O
Goals	0	2
Shots on Target	3	3
Shots off Target	2	5
Hit Woodwork	0	0
Possession %	42	58
Corners	6	7
Offsides	4	2
Fouls	19	16
Disciplinary Points	32	8

47

2-1

Birmingham City °
Manchester City °

► Maik Taylor pounces on a loose ball

Event Line

11 ○ ▪	Savage
14 ○ ⊕	Fowler / H / OP / IA
	Assist: Wright-Phillips
Half time 0-1	
61 ○ ⇄	Kirovski > Dunn
61 ○ ⇄	John > Morrison
68 ○	Upson
69 ○ ⇄	Sibierski > Fowler
69 ○ ⇄	Sinclair > McManaman
78 ○	Jihai
81 ○ ⊕	Kenna / H / IFK / IA
	Assist: Savage
87 ○ ⊕	Forssell / LF / IFK / IA
89 ○ ⇄	Cisse > Clemence
Full time 2-1	

There was Boxing Day delight for a sell-out St. Andrew's crowd as Blues recorded back-to-back Premiership wins with a last gasp comeback victory over Man City.

Robbie Fowler gave the visitors an early lead when he dived full length to head in from Shaun Wright-Phillips's right wing cross.

Mikael Forssell went close to an equaliser soon after the break with a back-heel which skimmed the outside of the post.

Blues continued to dominate but were almost caught on the break when Maik Taylor had to make an excellent double save, first from Nicolas Anelka and then to block Trevor Sinclair's rebound effort.

Blues finally got a deserved equaliser as Robbie Savage's curling free-kick thumped off the post and came back out to the unlikely figure of Jeff Kenna to register only his second goal for the club.

Blues completed an amazing turn-around just three minutes from time as Forssell blocked an attempted clearance and the ball flew past a helpless David Seaman.

Quote

● **Steve Bruce**

Kevin Keegan probably thought his side had weathered the storm, but my lads are a great bunch and they showed huge commitment to get that victory.

Venue:	St Andrew's	Referee:	U.D.Rennie - 03/04
Attendance:	29,520	Matches:	10
Capacity:	30,016	Yellow Cards:	36
Occupancy:	98%	Red Cards:	1

Birmingham City
Manchester City

Form Coming into Fixture

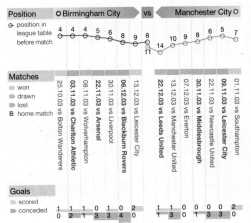

Position
O- position in league table before match

Matches
- won
- drawn
- lost
- B home match

Goals
- scored
- conceded

Goal Statistics

O Birmingham City
by Half | by Situation

O Manchester City
by Half | by Situation

Birmingham City:
- first: 3
- second: 3
- set piece: 3
- open play: 3

Manchester City:
- first: 1
- second: 3
- set piece: 0
- open play: 4

Goals by Area

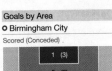

O Birmingham City — Scored (Conceded)
- 1 (3)
- 5 (9)
- 0 (1)

O Manchester City — Scored (Conceded)
- 0 (3)
- 3 (7)
- 1 (1)

Team Statistics

Starting Line-Ups

Lazaridis, Dunn/Kirovski, Upson, Clemence/Cisse, Morrison/John, Cunningham, Savage, Forssell, Fowler/Sibierski, Kenna, Johnson — Taylor/Maik

Wright-Phillips, Jihai, Reyna, Dunne, Anelka, Barton, Sommeil, McManaman/Sinclair, Distin — Seaman

4/4/2   **4/4/2**

Unused Sub: Bennett, Purse
Unused Sub: Stuhr-Ellegaard, Tarnat, Macken

Premiership Totals

	O Birmingham	Man City O
Premiership Appearances	1,426	1,719
Team Appearances	452	408
Goals Scored	78	291
Assists	131	210
Clean Sheets (goalkeepers)	21	141
Yellow Cards	155	137
Red Cards	4	13

Age/Height

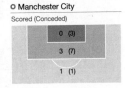

Birmingham City Age: **27 yrs, 9 mo**
Manchester City Age: **28 yrs, 3 mo**
Birmingham City Height: **5'11"**
Manchester City Height: **5'11"**

Match Statistics

League Table after Fixture

		Played	Won	Drawn	Lost	For	Against	Pts
↑ 5	Charlton	18	7	6	5	26	22	27
● 6	Newcastle	18	6	8	4	26	21	26
↓ 7	Southampton	18	7	5	6	18	14	26
● 8	Birmingham	17	7	5	5	16	19	26
● 9	Liverpool	17	7	4	6	26	19	25
● 10	Bolton	18	5	7	6	18	26	22
↑ 11	Middlesbrough	17	5	6	6	14	17	21
↑ 12	Aston Villa	18	5	6	7	16	23	21
↓ 13	Man City	18	5	5	8	25	25	20

Statistics

	O Birmingham	Man City O
Goals	2	1
Shots on Target	4	5
Shots off Target	7	3
Hit Woodwork	1	0
Possession %	52	48
Corners	9	3
Offsides	2	0
Fouls	19	14
Disciplinary Points	8	4

2-1

Birmingham City o
Southampton o

➡ Damien Johnson goes in bravely

Event Line

6 O ⊕	Ormerod / RF / C / 6Y	
	Assist: Delap	
16 O ⊕	Clemence / H / C / IA	
	Assist: Hughes	
18 O	Delap	
Half time 1-1		
67 O ⊕	Kenna / RF / OP / IA	
	Assist: Morrison	
69 O ■	Prutton	
	Violent Conduct	
71 O ⇄	McCann > Fernandes	
72 O ⇄	Phillips > Ormerod	
85 O ⇄	Pahars > Delap	
90 O ⇄	Carter > Dunn	
90 O ⇄	Kirovski > Morrison	
Full time 2-1		

Jeff Kenna was on the scoresheet again as his goal was enough to give Blues an excellent victory against his former club at St. Andrew's.

It was the Saints who started brightest and it took them just three minutes to create the first chance of the game. Anders Svensson's fine ball from the left wing found striker James Beattie free in the box but the visitors' number nine headed over Maik Taylor's bar from just eight yards out.

But it didn't take long for the South Coast outfit to make amends and take an early lead. Maik Taylor brilliantly pushed away Rory Delap's shot but Brett Ormerod was on hand to shoot through a crowded penalty area.

Stung by the opener Blues hit back as Stephen Clemence's powerful header from Bryan Hughes's corner was deflected into his own net by Saints defender Fitz Hall. And midway through the second half a superb move started and finished by former Saints player Jeff Kenna saw Blues come from behind to claim victory for the second successive Premiership home game.

Kenna found Clinton Morrison on the left of the box and continued his run to meet the striker's cross and secure the win.

Quote

● **Steve Bruce**

I just wish Jeff Kenna was at the start of his career. He is a tremendous professional and has been playing at the top for a decade.

Premiership Milestone

➡ **50**

Kenny Cunningham made his 50th Premiership appearance in the colours of Birmingham.

Venue:	St Andrew's	Referee:	S.G.Bennett - 03/04		**Birmingham City**
Attendance:	29,071	Matches:	16		**Southampton**
Capacity:	30,016	Yellow Cards:	52		
Occupancy:	97%	Red Cards:	6		

Form Coming into Fixture

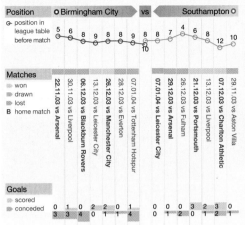

Position: position in league table before match

Matches: won / drawn / lost / B home match

Goals: scored / conceded

	22.11.03 vs Arsenal	30.11.03 vs Liverpool	06.12.03 vs Blackburn Rovers	13.12.03 vs Leicester City	26.12.03 vs Manchester City	28.12.03 vs Everton	07.01.04 vs Tottenham Hotspur	07.01.04 vs Leicester City	29.12.03 vs Arsenal	26.12.03 vs Fulham	21.12.03 vs Portsmouth	13.12.03 vs Liverpool	07.12.03 vs Charlton Athletic	29.11.03 vs Aston Villa
scored	0	1	0	2	2	0	1	0	0	0	3	2	3	0
conceded	3	3	4	0	1	1	4	0	1	2	0	1	2	1

Goal Statistics

Birmingham City

by Half / by Situation

Southampton

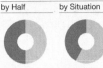

by Half / by Situation

- first: 2
- second: 4
- set piece: 5
- open play: 1

- first: 4
- second: 4
- set piece: 3
- open play: 4
- own goals: 1

Goals by Area

Birmingham City

Scored (Conceded)

1 (2)
5 (12)
0 (2)

Southampton

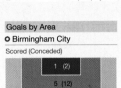

Scored (Conceded)

4 (1)
3 (4)
1 (2)

Team Statistics

Starting Line-Ups

Kenna, Dunn, Carter, Purse, Clemence, Morrison, Kirovski, Ormerod, Phillips, Cunningham, Hughes, Forssell, Beattie, Tebily, Johnson, Taylor Maik

Prutton, Dodd, Svensson, Hall F, Delap, Pahars, Svensson, Fernandes, McCann, Higginbotham, Niemi

4/4/2   **4/4/2**

Unused Sub: Bennett, Cisse, John   Unused Sub: Blayney, Kenton

Premiership Totals

	Birmingham	Southampton
Premiership Appearances	1,079	1,356
Team Appearances	380	1,043
Goals Scored	59	208
Assists	81	134
Clean Sheets (goalkeepers)	21	14
Yellow Cards	97	139
Red Cards	5	9

Age/Height

Birmingham City Age

27 yrs

Southampton Age

27 yrs, 4 mo

Birmingham City Height

6'

Southampton Height

5'11"

Match Statistics

League Table after Fixture

		Played	Won	Drawn	Lost	For	Against	Pts
↑	1 Arsenal	21	14	7	0	40	14	49
↓	2 Man Utd	20	16	1	3	40	14	49
●	3 Chelsea	20	13	3	4	36	17	42
●	4 Charlton	21	9	7	5	30	23	34
●	5 Liverpool	20	9	5	6	30	21	32
↑	6 Fulham	21	9	4	8	33	29	31
↓	7 Newcastle	20	7	8	5	27	22	29
↑	8 Birmingham	20	8	5	7	19	25	29
↓	9 Southampton	21	7	6	8	19	17	27

Statistics

	Birmingham	Southampton
Goals	2	1
Shots on Target	7	4
Shots off Target	9	4
Hit Woodwork	1	0
Possession %	51	49
Corners	7	10
Offsides	1	2
Fouls	14	25
Disciplinary Points	0	16

3-0

Birmingham City ○
Everton ○

▶ Mikael Forssell celebrates his goal with Robbie Savage

Event Line	
8 ○ ⊕	Johnson / RF / C / OA
39 ○ ⊕	Lazaridis / LF / OP / IA
Half time 2-0	
46 ○ ⇄	Campbell > Ferguson
46 ○ ⇄	Pistone > Unsworth
49 ○ ⊕	Forssell / LF / OP / OA
	Assist: Savage
60 ○ ⇄	McFadden > Radzinski
63 ○ ▢	Tebily
63 ○ ⇄	Dugarry > Savage
76 ○ ⇄	John > Lazaridis
80 ○ ⇄	Taylor Martin > Forssell
Full time 3-0	

Goals from Damien Johnson, Stan Lazaridis and Mikael Forssell saw Blues run riot to record an impressive victory over Everton.

The win could easily have been more comprehensive as Steve Bruce's team also hit the woodwork twice and came close on other occasions to increasing their lead as time and again they cut open the visiting defence with ease.

Blues opened the scoring when Johnson's cross-cum-shot nestled into the corner of the net.

Any nerves were well and truly settled six minutes before the interval. Robbie Savage released Lazaridis who set off on another trademark run but his finish into the top corner belied a player who had recorded just seven goals in just short of 170 appearances up to that night. It was a quality strike that earned the winger the coveted 'Goal of the Season' accolade.

And the big Blues crowd were celebrating again within four minutes of the restart courtesy of Forssell's excellent turn and shot that fairly flew into the bottom corner.

Quote
● Steve Bruce

I thought we played some excellent football tonight and were worthy winners. We've got on an unbeaten run and who knows what we can achieve.

Premiership Milestone
▶ Debut

Martin Taylor made his first Premiership appearance in the colours of Birmingham.

Venue:	St Andrew's	Referee:	M.R.Halsey - 03/04		**Birmingham City**
Attendance:	29,004	Matches:	19		**Everton**
Capacity:	30,016	Yellow Cards:	42		
Occupancy:	97%	Red Cards:	3		

Form Coming into Fixture

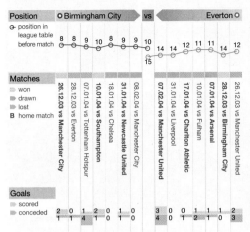

Position	o Birmingham City	vs	Everton o

position in league table before match: 8 8 9 10 8 9 9 10 14 14 12 11 11 14 12 / 15

Matches
- won
- drawn
- lost
- B home match

26.12.03 vs Manchester City
07.01.04 vs Tottenham Hotspur
10.01.04 vs Southampton
18.01.04 vs Chelsea
31.01.04 vs Newcastle United
08.02.04 vs Manchester United
07.02.04 vs Manchester United
31.01.04 vs Liverpool
10.01.04 vs Fulham
07.01.04 vs Arsenal
28.12.03 vs Birmingham City
26.12.03 vs Manchester United

Goals
- scored
- conceded

| 2 | 0 | 1 | 2 | 0 | 1 | 0 | 3 | 0 | 0 | 1 | 1 | 1 | 2 |
| 1 | 1 | 4 | 1 | 0 | 1 | 0 | 4 | 0 | 1 | 2 | 1 | 0 | 3 |

Goal Statistics

o Birmingham City		o Everton	
by Half	by Situation	by Half	by Situation

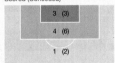

Birmingham City:
- first: 1
- second: 5
- set piece: 5
- open play: 1

Everton:
- first: 1
- second: 7
- set piece: 3
- open play: 3
- own goals: 2

Goals by Area

o Birmingham City	o Everton
Scored (Conceded)	Scored (Conceded)

Birmingham City: 1 (3) / 5 (3) / 0 (2)

Everton: 3 (3) / 4 (6) / 1 (2)

Team Statistics

Starting Line-Ups

Birmingham City: Upson, Lazaridis, John, Purse, Hughes, Morrison, Ferguson, Campbell, Cunningham, Savage, Dugarry, Forssell, Taylor Martin, Tebily, Johnson, Taylor Maik

Everton: Rooney, Hibbert, Gravesen, Unsworth, Pistone, Radzinski, McFadden, Carsley, Stubbs, Kilbane, Naysmith, Menru

▶ 4/4/2   **▶ 4/4/2**

Unused Sub: Bennett, Kenna   Unused Sub: Simonsen, Linderoth

Premiership Totals	o Birmingham	Everton o
Premiership Appearances	1,122	2,000
Team Appearances	480	1,229
Goals Scored	61	240
Assists	89	176
Clean Sheets (goalkeepers)	23	114
Yellow Cards	128	237
Red Cards	7	17

Age/Height

Birmingham City Age	Everton Age
▶ 27 yrs, 10 mo	**▶ 28 yrs, 5 mo**
Birmingham City Height	Everton Height
▶ 6'	**▶ 6'**

Match Statistics

League Table after Fixture

		Played	Won	Drawn	Lost	For	Against	Pts
↑	7 Aston Villa	25	10	6	9	30	28	36
↓	8 Fulham	25	10	5	10	37	35	35
↑	9 Birmingham	24	9	8	7	23	26	35
↓	10 Bolton	25	8	10	7	31	37	34
↑	11 Tottenham	25	10	3	12	35	38	33
↓	12 Southampton	25	8	7	10	23	23	31
●	13 Middlesbrough	24	8	7	9	26	29	31
●	14 Blackburn	25	7	6	12	36	40	27
●	15 Everton	25	6	7	12	28	36	25

Statistics	o Birmingham	Everton o
Goals	3	0
Shots on Target	7	2
Shots off Target	7	4
Hit Woodwork	0	0
Possession %	45	55
Corners	8	11
Offsides	1	4
Fouls	13	13
Disciplinary Points	4	0

3-1

Birmingham City ○
Middlesbrough ○

▶ Stephen Clemence congratulates goalscorer Martin Taylor

Event Line

19 ○ ▨	Mills D
19 ○ ▨	Savage
23 ○ ⊕	Taylor Martin / H / IFK / 6Y
	Assist: Forssell

Half time 1-0

46 ○ ⇄	Doriva > Downing
46 ○ ⇄	Maccarone > Job
50 ○ ▨	Ricketts
56 ○ ▨	Boateng
57 ○ ⊕	Savage / RF / DFK / OA
	Assist: Clemence
63 ○ ⇄	Nemeth > Greening
70 ○ ▨	Ehiogu
75 ○ ⊕	Nemeth / RF / OP / OA
79 ○ ⊕	Forssell / RF / OP / 6Y
	Assist: Johnson
80 ○	Forssell
83 ○ ⇄	John > Forssell
86 ○	Morrison
87 ○ ▨	Zenden
	2nd Bookable Offence
88 ○ ⇄	Carter > Morrison
90 ○ ⇄	Kenna > Savage

Full time 3-1

After a bitterly disappointment FA Cup exit at the hands of First Division side Sunderland, Blues recorded a morale-boosting victory over Carling Cup winners Middlesbrough at St. Andrew's.

Martin Taylor was handed his first start following his January transfer window signing from Blackburn and marked his full debut with a rather fortunate opening goal. Bryan Hughes raced down the left and pulled the ball back for Mikael Forssell and his shot took a wicked deflection off Taylor to beat Mark Schwarzer.

Blues almost doubled their lead just two minutes later when Clinton Morrison broke clear and crossed for Hughes who hit a cracking first time shot which Schwarzer did well to stop.

The second goal did arrive after the interval courtesy of a fierce free-kick from Robbie Savage that gave the keeper no chance.

Szilard Nemeth halved Blues' advantage with 15 minutes remaining but the win was guaranteed when Forssell notched his 13th goal of the season. Johnson's cross eluded Morrison but was met by Forssell's volley which looped up into the top corner.

Quote

● **Steve Bruce**

We were first to every ball and the players got the victory they deserved.

Premiership Milestone

▶ **First Goal**

Martin Taylor netted his first Premiership goal for Birmingham.

Venue:	St Andrew's	Referee:	R.Styles - 03/04	Birmingham City
Attendance:	29,369	Matches:	17	Middlesbrough
Capacity:	30,016	Yellow Cards:	58	
Occupancy:	98%	Red Cards:	8	

Form Coming into Fixture

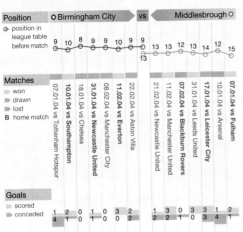

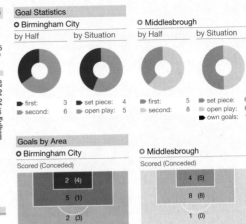

Position

o- position in league table before match

Birmingham City: 9 10 8 9 9 10 9 9 / 13
Middlesbrough: 13 13 12 13 14 12 15

Matches
- won
- drawn
- lost
- B home match

Birmingham City:
- 07.01.04 vs Tottenham Hotspur
- 10.01.04 vs Southampton
- 18.01.04 vs Chelsea
- 31.01.04 vs Newcastle United
- 08.02.04 vs Manchester City
- 11.02.04 vs Everton
- 22.02.04 vs Aston Villa

Middlesbrough:
- 21.02.04 vs Newcastle United
- 11.02.04 vs Manchester United
- 07.02.04 vs Blackburn Rovers
- 31.01.04 vs Leeds United
- 17.01.04 vs Leicester City
- 10.01.04 vs Arsenal
- 07.01.04 vs Fulham

Goals
- scored
- conceded

Birmingham City scored: 1 2 0 1 0 3 2
Birmingham City conceded: 4 1 0 1 0 0 2

Middlesbrough scored: 1 3 0 3 3 1 2
Middlesbrough conceded: 2 2 1 0 3 4 1

Goal Statistics

Birmingham City

by Half
- first: 3
- second: 6

by Situation
- set piece: 4
- open play: 5

Middlesbrough

by Half
- first: 5
- second: 8

by Situation
- set piece: 6
- open play: 6
- own goals: 1

Goals by Area

Birmingham City Scored (Conceded)
- 2 (4)
- 5 (1)
- 2 (3)

Middlesbrough Scored (Conceded)
- 4 (5)
- 8 (8)
- 1 (0)

Team Statistics

Starting Line-Ups

Birmingham City:
Upson, Hughes, Taylor Martin, Clemence, Taylor Maik, Morrison Carter, Job Maccarone, Cunningham, Savage Kenna, Forssell John, Ricketts, Tebily, Johnson

Middlesbrough:
Greening Nemeth, Mills D, Boateng, Ehiogu, Schwarzer, Zenden, Southgate, Downing Doriva, Queudrue

Birmingham City: ▶ 4/4/2
Unused Sub: Bennett, Purse

Middlesbrough: ▶ 4/4/2
Unused Sub: Jones, Riggott

Premiership Totals	o Birmingham	Boro o
Premiership Appearances	1,399	1,758
Team Appearances	500	860
Goals Scored	66	119
Assists	99	105
Clean Sheets (goalkeepers)	24	57
Yellow Cards	140	218
Red Cards	4	13

Age/Height

Birmingham City Age: ▶ 27 yrs, 1 mo
Middlesbrough Age: ▶ 27 yrs, 5 mo

Birmingham City Height: ▶ 6'
Middlesbrough Height: ▶ 5'11"

Match Statistics

League Table after Fixture

		Played	Won	Drawn	Lost	For	Against	Pts
●	5 Charlton	27	11	7	9	38	34	40
●	6 Liverpool	26	10	9	7	38	29	39
↑	7 Birmingham	26	10	9	7	28	29	39
↓	8 Aston Villa	27	10	7	10	32	32	37
↓	9 Fulham	27	10	6	11	39	38	36
●	10 Tottenham	26	10	4	12	39	42	34
●	11 Bolton	26	8	10	8	32	40	34
●	12 Southampton	27	8	9	10	27	27	33
●	13 Middlesbrough	26	8	7	11	28	34	31

Statistics	o Birmingham	Boro o
Goals	3	1
Shots on Target	5	6
Shots off Target	4	2
Hit Woodwork	0	0
Possession %	52	48
Corners	4	2
Offsides	2	2
Fouls	13	20
Disciplinary Points	12	26

2-0

Birmingham City ○
Bolton Wanderers ○

➧ Olivier Tebily does well to block a dangerous Kevin Nolan drive

Event Line
24 ○ ⊕ Forssell / LF / OP / IA
Assist: Morrison
Half time 1-0
48 ○ ⇄ Pedersen > Djorkaeff
63 ○ ⇄ Ba > Okocha
69 ○ ⊕ Hughes / H / OP / 6Y
Assist: Johnson
76 ○ ⇄ Cisse > Clemence
79 ○ ⇄ Giannakopoulos > Frandsen
84 ○ ▢ Savage
86 ○ ▢ Hunt
86 ○ ⇄ John > Forssell
88 ○ ⇄ Kenna > Johnson
Full time 2-0

Blues soared up to fifth place in the Premiership table with an excellent win over Bolton at St Andrew's.

Steve Bruce's men looked bright throughout and thoroughly deserved their victory courtesy of a first half strike from Mikael Forssell and a second half header from Bryan Hughes.

The Blues boss kept faith with the same side that beat Boro and they deservedly took the lead midway through the first half. The goal came about following Robbie Savage's hopeful ball over the top towards Clinton Morrison. The Republic of Ireland international headed the ball back into the path of his strike partner Forssell who controlled it well before scrambling the ball home.

Blues doubled their lead with a superbly worked second half goal. Morrison released Damien Johnson on the right and he beat his marker with pace before lofting a wonderful ball to the far post. Bryan Hughes did well to leap above Nicky Hunt to nod home a simple header.

It should have been 3-0 soon after when Johnson dispossessed Anthony Barness before breaking through on goal but the midfielder screwed his shot just wide.

Quote	Premiership Milestone
● **Steve Bruce**	➧ **50**
We are on an adventure and we are enjoying it. The longer you stay in this division, the easier it becomes.	Clinton Morrison made his 50th Premiership appearance.

Venue:	St Andrew's	Referee:	A.P.D'Urso - 03/04	Birmingham City
Attendance:	28,003	Matches:	18	Bolton Wanderers
Capacity:	30,016	Yellow Cards:	58	
Occupancy:	93%	Red Cards:	6	

Form Coming into Fixture

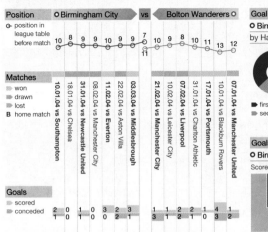

Position

O Birmingham City vs Bolton Wanderers O

position in league table before match

10 8 9 9 10 9 9 7 11 10 9 8 10 11 13 12

Matches
- won
- drawn
- lost
- B home match

10.01.04 vs Southampton
18.01.04 vs Chelsea
31.01.04 vs Newcastle United
08.02.04 vs Manchester City
11.02.04 vs Everton
22.02.04 vs Aston Villa
03.03.04 vs Middlesbrough
21.02.04 vs Manchester City
10.02.04 vs Leicester City
07.02.04 vs Liverpool
31.01.04 vs Charlton Athletic
17.01.04 vs Portsmouth
10.01.04 vs Blackburn Rovers
07.01.04 vs Manchester United

Goals
- scored
- conceded

| 2 | 0 | 1 | 0 | 3 | 2 | 3 | | 1 | 1 | 2 | 2 | 1 | 4 | 1 |
| 1 | 0 | 1 | 0 | 0 | 2 | 1 | | 3 | 1 | 2 | 1 | 0 | 3 | 2 |

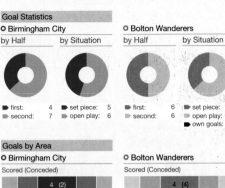

Goal Statistics

O Birmingham City

by Half		by Situation	
first:	4	set piece:	5
second:	7	open play:	6

O Bolton Wanderers

by Half		by Situation	
first:	6	set piece:	4
second:	6	open play:	7
		own goals:	1

Goals by Area

O Birmingham City

Scored (Conceded)

| 4 (2) |
| 4 (0) |
| 3 (3) |

O Bolton Wanderers

Scored (Conceded)

| 4 (4) |
| 8 (7) |
| 0 (1) |

Team Statistics

Starting Line-Ups

Upson   Hughes   Nolan   Hunt

Frandsen Giannakopoulos

Taylor Martin   Clemence Cisse   Morrison   N'Gotty

Taylor Malik   Davies   Campo   Jaaskelainen

Cunningham   Savage   Forssell John   Charlton

Okocha Ba

Tebily   Johnson Kenna   Djorkaeff Pedersen   Barness

4/4/2   4/3/3

Unused Sub: Bennett, Purse

Unused Sub: Poole, Howey

Premiership Totals

	O Birmingham	Bolton O
Premiership Appearances	1,430	1,104
Team Appearances	531	846
Goals Scored	69	97
Assists	103	86
Clean Sheets (goalkeepers)	24	25
Yellow Cards	157	134
Red Cards	5	5

Age/Height

Birmingham City Age	Bolton Wanderers Age
▶ **27 yrs, 8 mo**	▶ **29 yrs, 7 mo**
Birmingham City Height	Bolton Wanderers Height
▶ **6'**	▶ **5'11"**

Match Statistics

League Table after Fixture

		Played	Won	Drawn	Lost	For	Against	Pts
●	3 Man Utd	27	18	4	5	51	25	58
●	4 Newcastle	27	10	12	5	38	28	42
↑	5 Birmingham	27	11	9	7	30	29	42
●	6 Charlton	27	11	7	9	38	34	40
↓	7 Liverpool	26	10	9	7	38	29	39
●	8 Aston Villa	27	10	7	10	32	32	37
●	9 Fulham	27	10	6	11	39	38	36
●	10 Tottenham	26	10	4	12	39	42	34
●	11 Bolton	27	8	10	9	32	42	34

Statistics

	O Birmingham	Bolton O
Goals	2	0
Shots on Target	6	2
Shots off Target	4	8
Hit Woodwork	0	0
Possession %	55	45
Corners	3	5
Offsides	2	1
Fouls	10	15
Disciplinary Points	4	4

4-1

Birmingham City ○
Leeds United ○

▶ Bryan Hughes wheels away after finding the back of the net

Event Line

3 ○ ⊕ Viduka / LF / OP / IA
　　Assist: Pennant
12 ○ ⊕ Hughes / RF / OP / IA
　　Assist: Lazaridis
37 ○ ▪ Domi
Half time 1-1
67 ○ ⊕ Hughes / RF / OP / IA
　　Assist: Lazaridis
69 ○ ⊕ Forssell / RF / OP / IA
　　Assist: Cunningham
78 ○ ⇄ Johnson S > Milner
82 ○ ⊕ Forssell / RF / P / IA
　　Assist: Morrison
83 ○ ⇄ John > Forssell
84 ○ ⇄ Tebily > Morrison
Full time 4-1

Blues boosted their hopes of UEFA Cup qualification with a fine victory over a relegation-haunted Leeds side.

A brace apiece from Bryan Hughes and Mikael Forssell secured a deserved win despite going a goal down early on to a Mark Viduka strike.

Blues drew level when Hughes met Clinton Morrison's cross with an angled first time shot low into the far corner.

Hughes scored his second goal of the game midway through the second half to put his side in front in an entertaining contest. Kenny Cunningham set up Stan Lazaridis and he rolled the ball across for Hughes to smash home.

Cunningham was involved again in the third goal when his clearance fell into the path of Forssell who raced into the box before driving the ball past Paul Robinson.

Blues made it 4-1 when Dominic Matteo gave away a penalty after flattening Morrison inside the area. Hughes grabbed the ball in the hope of scoring his first Premiership hat-trick but Forssell had other ideas, taking charge and smashing the spot kick past Robinson.

Quote

● **Steve Bruce**

Leeds will be really disappointed with the goals that they conceded and the defensive performances of the two sides was the difference in the second half.

58

Venue:	St Andrew's	Referee:	M.R.Halsey - 03/04		**Birmingham City**
Attendance:	29,069	Matches:	24		**Leeds United**
Capacity:	30,016	Yellow Cards:	53		
Occupancy:	97%	Red Cards:	3		

Form Coming into Fixture

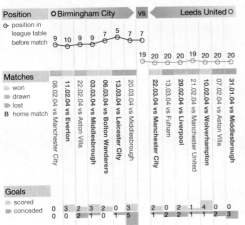

Position
- ⊙ position in league table before match
- B home match

Matches
- won
- drawn
- lost

Goals
- scored
- conceded

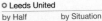

Goal Statistics

○ Birmingham City

by Half / by Situation

first:	6	set piece:	4
second:	7	open play:	9

○ Leeds United

by Half / by Situation

first:	5	set piece:	4
second:	4	open play:	5

Goals by Area

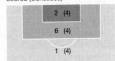

○ Birmingham City
Scored (Conceded)

| 5 (5) |
| 5 (2) |
| 3 (2) |

○ Leeds United
Scored (Conceded)

| 2 (4) |
| 6 (4) |
| 1 (4) |

Team Statistics

Starting Line-Ups

Birmingham City
- Grainger
- Lazaridis
- Upson
- Clemence
- Morrison / Tebily
- Cunningham
- Hughes
- Forssell / John
- Taylor Martin
- Johnson
- Taylor Malik

Leeds United
- Pennant
- Kelly
- McPhail
- Caldwell
- Smith
- Viduka
- Johnson S
- Matteo
- Milner / Johnson S
- Domi
- Robinson

▶ 4/4/2   **▶ 4/4/2**

Unused Sub: Bennett, Cisse, Carter   Unused Sub: Carson, Harte, Radebe, Keegan

Premiership Totals

	○ Birmingham	Leeds ○
Premiership Appearances	1,044	1,286
Team Appearances	484	1,002
Goals Scored	58	117
Assists	86	129
Clean Sheets (goalkeepers)	25	18
Yellow Cards	92	171
Red Cards	4	12

Age/Height

Birmingham City Age	Leeds United Age
▶ **27 yrs, 9 mo**	▶ **24 yrs, 7 mo**
Birmingham City Height	Leeds United Height
▶ **6'**	▶ **5'10"**

Match Statistics

League Table after Fixture

		Played	Won	Drawn	Lost	For	Against	Pts
●	1 Arsenal	29	22	7	0	57	19	73
●	2 Chelsea	30	21	4	5	57	24	67
●	3 Man Utd	29	19	4	6	55	29	61
●	4 Liverpool	29	12	9	8	42	31	45
●	5 Newcastle	29	11	12	6	41	30	45
↑	6 Birmingham	30	12	9	9	37	36	45
↑	7 Aston Villa	30	12	7	11	38	35	43
...	...	...	...	...	...	...	...	...
●	19 Leeds	30	6	7	17	29	60	25

Statistics

	○ Birmingham	Leeds ○
Goals	4	1
Shots on Target	8	7
Shots off Target	10	5
Hit Woodwork	1	0
Possession %	52	48
Corners	7	7
Offsides	3	1
Fouls	11	19
Disciplinary Points	0	4

1-0

Birmingham City ○
Manchester City ○

▶ Stan Lazaridis takes on Robbie Fowler

Event Line

8 ○ ⊕ Heskey / H / OP / IA	
Assist: Lazaridis	
31 ○ ■ Mills D	
Half time 1-0	
54 ○ ⇄ John > Heskey	
57 ○ ⇄ Sinclair > Sibierski	
59 ○ ⇄ Clemence > Lazaridis	
69 ○ ■ Izzet	
79 ○ ⇄ Barton > Bosvelt	
79 ○ ⇄ Macken > Fowler	
79 ○ ⇄ Tebily > Forssell	
Full time 1-0	

The St. Andrew's faithful breathed a collective sigh of relief as their team secure a first victory in 11 Premiership games courtesy of a first half goal from Emile Heskey.

The crucial goal came after just eight minutes as Heskey notched his first for the club. A typically mazy run from Stan Lazaridis ended with a pinpoint cross and the England international scored with a powerful header into the top corner.

City almost responded immediately as Wright-Phillips stung Taylor's hands with a shot from the edge of the box.

Robbie Fowler produced a glaring miss when Sun Jihai found him totally unmarked at the far post with a deep cross but his header sailed back towards the corner flag.

Forssell went close with an early second half header and substitute Stern John missed a one-on-one that could have sealed victory.

Fortunately it didn't prove costly and Blues hung on for their first victory of the 2004/05 campaign.

Quote

● **Steve Bruce**

Emile Heskey has been awesome since the start of the season. How many other players could have scored that kind of header?

Premiership Milestone

▶ **First Goal**

Emile Heskey netted his first Premiership goal for Birmingham.

60

Venue:	St Andrew's	Referee:	P.Dowd - 04/05	**Birmingham City**
Attendance:	28,551	Matches:	2	**Manchester City**
Capacity:	30,016	Yellow Cards:	4	
Occupancy:	95%	Red Cards:	0	

Form Coming into Fixture

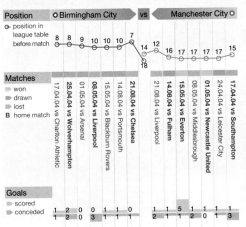

Position	O Birmingham City	vs	Manchester City O
position in league table before match			

Matches
- won
- drawn
- lost
- B home match

Goals
- scored
- conceded

Goal Statistics

O Birmingham City			O Manchester City		
by Half	by Situation		by Half	by Situation	

Birmingham City:
- first: 3
- second: 2
- set piece: 3
- open play: 2

Manchester City:
- first: 7
- second: 4
- set piece: 1
- open play: 10

Goals by Area

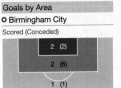
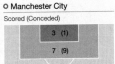

O Birmingham City — Scored (Conceded)
- 2 (2)
- 2 (6)
- 1 (1)

O Manchester City — Scored (Conceded)
- 3 (1)
- 7 (9)
- 1 (0)

Team Statistics

Starting Line-Ups

Lazaridis, Gray, Wright-Phillips, Jihai
Clemence
Upson, Johnson, Reyna, Mills D
Taylor Malik
Heskey John, Anelka
James
Cunningham, Izzet, Forssell Tebily, Fowler Macken, Bosvelt Barton, Distin
Melchiot, Gronkjaer, Sibierski Sinclair, Thatcher

4/4/2
Unused Sub: Bennett, Taylor Martin

4/4/2
Unused Sub: Stuhr-Ellegaard, Bischoff

Premiership Totals	O Birmingham	Man City O
Premiership Appearances	1,678	1,880
Team Appearances	470	533
Goals Scored	164	280
Assists	186	175
Clean Sheets (goalkeepers)	26	114
Yellow Cards	183	196
Red Cards	8	16

Age/Height

Birmingham City Age	Manchester City Age
28 yrs	**28 yrs, 6 mo**
Birmingham City Height	Manchester City Height
6'	**5'11"**

Match Statistics

League Table after Fixture

		Played	Won	Drawn	Lost	For	Against	Pts
↑	1 Chelsea	3	3	0	0	4	0	9
↓	2 Arsenal	2	2	0	0	9	4	6
●	3 Aston Villa	2	1	1	0	3	1	4
●	4 Fulham	2	1	1	0	3	1	4
●	5 Liverpool	2	1	1	0	3	2	4
●	6 Tottenham	2	1	1	0	2	1	4
↑	7 Birmingham	3	1	1	1	2	2	4
...	...	...	...	...	...	...	...	...
↓	19 Man City	3	0	1	2	2	4	1

Statistics	O Birmingham	Man City O
Goals	1	0
Shots on Target	2	1
Shots off Target	4	3
Hit Woodwork	0	0
Possession %	55	45
Corners	2	5
Offsides	0	4
Fouls	20	14
Disciplinary Points	4	4

0-1

Liverpool ○
Birmingham City ○

Premiership

06.11.04

▶ Muzzy Izzet gives Luis Garcia little room in which to work

Event Line

44 ○ ▢	Josemi
Half time 0-0	
61 ○ ▢	Garcia
63 ○ ⇄	Anderton > Clemence
63 ○ ⇄	Lazaridis > Gronkjaer
65 ○ ⇄	Finnan > Sinama-Pongolle
72 ○ ▢	Hamann
73 ○ ⇄	Mellor > Riise
74 ○ ▢	Johnson
77 ○ ⊕	Anderton / RF / C / 6Y
	Assist: Upson
85 ○ ⇄	Biscan > Hamann
88 ○ ⇄	Clapham > Izzet
Full time 0-1	

After a run of eight Premiership games without a win, hopes were not high as Blues headed for Anfield – a ground where we had not won since 1978.

Steve Bruce's side had also failed to win on their travels throughout 2004 but both sequences were spectacularly brought to an end by substitute Darren Anderton's late strike.

Steve Bruce's team had Maik Taylor to thank for a string of fine saves throughout the game.

Blues' best chance of the first half was created by a clever dummy from Heskey on his return to Anfield which let in Muzzy Izzet, but with only the keeper to beat he misjudged the flight of the ball and the opportunity was gone.

But the former Leicester man made up for it with a double goal line clearance after the interval.

And Blues took full advantage with just 13 minutes remaining as Anderton tapped home from close range to score his side's first goal in 470 minutes.

Quote

● **Steve Bruce**

This away win has been a long time coming, but we've earned the little bit of luck that we enjoyed today.

Premiership Milestone

▶ **100**

Jesper Gronkjaer made his 100th Premiership appearance.

Venue:	Anfield	Referee:	U.D.Rennie - 04/05		Liverpool
Attendance:	42,669	Matches:	7		Birmingham City
Capacity:	45,362	Yellow Cards:	11		
Occupancy:	94%	Red Cards:	1		

Form Coming into Fixture

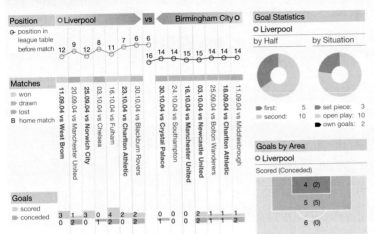

Position
○ Liverpool vs Birmingham City ○

position in league table before match

Liverpool: 12, 9, 12, 8, 11, 7, 6, 6
Birmingham City: 16, 14, 14, 15, 15, 14, 14, 14

Matches
- won
- drawn
- lost
- B home match

Liverpool matches:
- 11.09.04 vs West Brom
- 20.09.04 vs Manchester United
- 25.09.04 vs Norwich City
- 03.10.04 vs Chelsea
- 16.10.04 vs Fulham
- 23.10.04 vs Charlton Athletic
- 30.10.04 vs Blackburn Rovers

Birmingham City matches:
- 30.10.04 vs Crystal Palace
- 24.10.04 vs Southampton
- 16.10.04 vs Manchester United
- 03.10.04 vs Newcastle United
- 25.09.04 vs Bolton Wanderers
- 18.09.04 vs Charlton Athletic
- 11.09.04 vs Middlesbrough

Goals
- scored
- conceded

Liverpool: scored 3, 1, 3, 0, 4, 2, 2 ; conceded 0, 2, 0, 1, 2, 0, 2
Birmingham City: scored 0, 0, 0, 2, 1, 1, 1 ; conceded 1, 0, 0, 2, 1, 1, 2

Goal Statistics

○ Liverpool

by Half		by Situation	
▶ first:	5	▶ set piece:	3
second:	10	open play:	10
		▶ own goals:	2

○ Birmingham City

by Half		by Situation	
▶ first:	2	▶ set piece:	3
second:	3	open play:	2

Goals by Area

○ Liverpool
Scored (Conceded)
- 4 (2)
- 5 (5)
- 6 (0)

○ Birmingham City
Scored (Conceded)
- 1 (2)
- 4 (5)
- 0 (0)

Team Statistics

Starting Line-Ups

Liverpool: Kirkland, Traore, Hyypia, Carragher, Josemi, Riise/Mellor, Alonso, Hamann/Biscan, Garcia, Sinama-Pongolle/Finnan, Heskey, Kewell

4/4/1/1

Unused Sub: Dudek, Diao

Birmingham City: Taylor Maik, Johnson, Meichiot, Savage, Cunningham, Izzet/Clapham, Upson, Gronkjaer/Lazaridis, Clemence/Anderton, Gray

4/5/1

Unused Sub: Bennett, Yorke

Premiership Totals

Premiership Totals	○ Liverpool	Birmingham ○
Premiership Appearances	1,228	2,259
Team Appearances	931	544
Goals Scored	105	191
Assists	106	296
Clean Sheets (goalkeepers)	8	29
Yellow Cards	129	269
Red Cards	9	9

Age/Height

Liverpool Age	Birmingham City Age
▶ 25 yrs, 8 mo	▶ 29 yrs
Liverpool Height	Birmingham City Height
▶ 6'1"	▶ 6'

Match Statistics

League Table after Fixture

		Played	Won	Drawn	Lost	For	Against	Pts
↓ 7	Liverpool	11	5	2	4	18	11	17
↓ 8	Man Utd	11	4	5	2	11	9	17
↓ 9	Newcastle	11	4	4	3	22	19	16
↓ 10	Portsmouth	11	4	3	4	15	15	15
↑ 11	Charlton	12	4	3	5	13	21	15
↓ 12	Tottenham	12	3	4	5	8	11	13
↓ 13	Man City	12	3	3	5	13	12	12
↑ 14	Birmingham	12	2	6	4	8	10	12
↓ 15	Crystal Palace	12	3	3	6	13	16	12

Statistics

Statistics	○ Liverpool	Birmingham ○
Goals	0	1
Shots on Target	8	1
Shots off Target	9	5
Hit Woodwork	1	0
Possession %	54	46
Corners	4	5
Offsides	2	3
Fouls	24	17
Disciplinary Points	12	4

1-2

Aston Villa ○
Birmingham City ○

➡ David Dunn accelerates away from Gavin McCann

Event Line

9 ○ ⊕	Morrison / RF / OP / IA	
	Assist: Heskey	
18 ○ ⊕	Dunn / RF / OP / IA	
	Assist: Johnson	
37 ○ ◼	Mellberg	
37 ○	Johnson	
45 ○ ◼	Dunn	
Half time 0-2		
59 ○ ⇄	Gray > Dunn	
66 ○ ◼	Barry	
66 ○ ◼	Tebily	
77 ○ ◼	Carter	
82 ○ ⇄	Anderton > Morrison	
90 ○ ⊕	Barry / LF / OP / IA	
	Assist: Mellberg	
90 ○ ⇄	Clapham > Lazaridis	
Full time 1-2		

Blues' voodoo sign over local rivals Aston Villa continued with goals from Clinton Morrison and David Dunn securing a magnificent away victory.

Villa went into the game undefeated on their own soil and must have fancied their chances of registering a first Premiership victory over their Second City neighbours. But Steve Bruce's side showed a steely determination combined with no little skill and raced into a two-goal lead within the first 18 minutes.

Emile Heskey flicked on for Clinton Morrison and the former Crystal Palace striker hit a volley that bobbled up deceiving Thomas Sorensen and bounced over the keeper to gift Blues a lead. Morrison then turned provider to release Damien Johnson down the right and the diminutive midfielder skipped past JLloyd Samuel before pulling the ball back for Dunn to smash home from eight yards.

The visitors had to weather a storm after the break but fantastic performances in the centre of defence from Matthew Upson and Kenny Cunningham ensured there was no way through for Villa until two minutes into injury time.

Gareth Barry's strike made it a nervy final two minutes of added-on time but Blues held out to earn the Birmingham bragging rights yet again.

Quote

🔴 **Robbie Savage**

This win is even sweeter after Olof Mellberg's comments. We'd like to dedicate the win to him.

Premiership Milestone

➡ **250**

Robbie Savage made his 250th Premiership appearance.

Venue:	Villa Park	Referee:	S.W.Dunn - 04/05	Aston Villa
Attendance:	41,329	Matches:	14	Birmingham City
Capacity:	42,573	Yellow Cards:	23	
Occupancy:	97%	Red Cards:	2	

Form Coming into Fixture

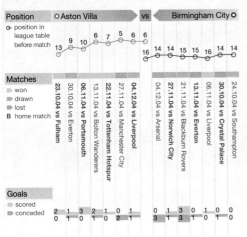

Position
O Aston Villa vs Birmingham City O
position in league table before match

Matches
- won
- drawn
- lost
- B home match

Matches (Aston Villa): 23.10.04 vs Fulham, 30.10.04 vs Everton, 06.11.04 vs Portsmouth, 13.11.04 vs Bolton Wanderers, 22.11.04 vs Tottenham Hotspur, 27.11.04 vs Manchester City, 04.12.04 vs Liverpool

Matches (Birmingham City): 04.12.04 vs Arsenal, 27.11.04 vs Norwich City, 21.11.04 vs Blackburn Rovers, 13.11.04 vs Liverpool, 06.11.04 vs Everton, 30.10.04 vs Crystal Palace, 24.10.04 vs Southampton

Goals
- scored
- conceded

scored	2	1	3	2	1	0	1		0	1	3	0	1	0	0
conceded	0	1	0	1	0	2	1		3	1	3	1	0	1	0

Goal Statistics

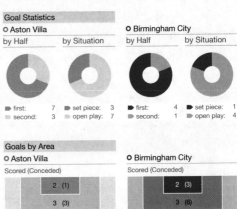

O Aston Villa

by Half | by Situation
- first: 7
- second: 3
- set piece: 3
- open play: 7

O Birmingham City

by Half | by Situation
- first: 4
- second: 1
- set piece: 1
- open play: 4

Goals by Area

O Aston Villa
Scored (Conceded)

| 2 (1) |
| 3 (3) |
| 5 (1) |

O Birmingham City
Scored (Conceded)

| 2 (3) |
| 3 (6) |
| 0 (0) |

Team Statistics

Starting Line-Ups

Aston Villa:
Samuel, Barry
Mellberg, McCann, Cole C
Sorensen
Angel
Delaney, Davis
De la Cruz, Solano

Birmingham City:
Johnson, Tebily
Savage, Cunningham, Heskey
Taylor Walk
Morrison Anderton, Carter, Upson
Dunn, Lazaridis Gray Clapham

▶ 4/4/2   ▶ 4/4/2

Unused Sub: Ridgewell, Postma, Berson, Whittingham, Moore

Unused Sub: Vaesen, Yorke

Premiership Totals	O Aston Villa	Birmingham O
Premiership Appearances	1,333	1,915
Team Appearances	882	657
Goals Scored	104	174
Assists	128	258
Clean Sheets (goalkeepers)	54	30
Yellow Cards	145	209
Red Cards	5	9

Age/Height

Aston Villa Age	Birmingham City Age
▶ 26 yrs, 4 mo	▶ 28 yrs, 3 mo
Aston Villa Height	Birmingham City Height
▶ 6'	▶ 6'

Match Statistics

League Table after Fixture

		Played	Won	Drawn	Lost	For	Against	Pts
●	6 Aston Villa	17	6	7	4	22	19	25
●	7 Liverpool	16	7	3	6	24	18	24
●	8 Charlton	17	7	3	7	19	27	24
●	9 Bolton	17	6	5	6	26	25	23
●	10 Portsmouth	16	6	4	6	22	23	22
●	11 Tottenham	17	6	4	7	16	17	22
●	12 Newcastle	17	5	6	6	28	32	21
●	13 Man City	17	5	5	7	21	18	20
↑	14 Birmingham	17	3	8	6	14	19	17

Statistics	O Aston Villa	Birmingham O
Goals	1	2
Shots on Target	2	4
Shots off Target	7	5
Hit Woodwork	0	1
Possession %	68	32
Corners	6	0
Offsides	1	3
Fouls	9	28
Disciplinary Points	8	16

65

4-0

Birmingham City ○
West Bromwich Albion ○

➡ Clinton Morrison makes it 2-0

Event Line

4 ○ ⊕ Savage / RF / P / IA	
Assist: Morrison	
20 ○ ▨ Koumas	
23 ○ ⊕ Morrison / LF / IFK / IA	
Assist: Carter	
30 ○ ⊕ Heskey / RF / OP / IA	
Assist: Dunn	
32 ○ ▨ Haas	
44 ○ ▨ Greening	
Half time 3-0	
46 ○ ⇄ Earnshaw > Gera	
60 ○ ▨ Gaardsoe	
75 ○ ⇄ Wallwork > Haas	
78 ○ ⇄ Anderton > Johnson	
80 ○ ⊕ Anderton / RF / DFK / OA	
Assist: Heskey	
83 ○ ⇄ Gray > Heskey	
87 ○ ⇄ Clapham > Savage	
Full time 4-0	

Blues cemented their King of the Midlands' title with an impressive demolition of a disappointing West Brom side at St. Andrew's.

Blues raced into a three-goal lead within the first half an hour.

Robbie Savage opened the scoring after just three minutes when he converted from the penalty spot after former Blues defender Darren Purse was adjudged to have fouled Clinton Morrison.

Blues did have one scare in the 13th minute when Zoltan Gera's shot struck the woodwork and Jonathan Greening's follow-up volley was saved by Maik Taylor.

Blues doubled their lead with Clinton Morrison's third goal in as many games after pouncing on Darren Carter's cross. Emile Heskey then blasted a third goal past Russell Hoult.

Substitute Darren Anderton completed the rout by scoring the fourth goal with his first touch of the game. Anderton hit a powerful free-kick that took a deflection off the wall and gave Hoult no chance as the ball bounced past him into the net.

Quote	Premiership Milestone
● **Steve Bruce**	➡ **100**
We started really well and that gave us the springboard to go on and get the win.	Clinton Morrison's goal was the 100th scored by Birmingham in the Premiership.

Venue:	St Andrew's	Referee:	M.A.Riley - 04/05	**Birmingham City**
Attendance:	28,880	Matches:	16	**West Bromwich Albion**
Capacity:	30,016	Yellow Cards:	55	
Occupancy:	96%	Red Cards:	6	

Form Coming into Fixture

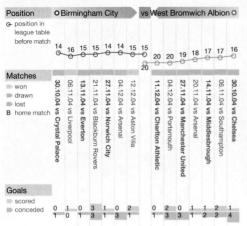

Position ○ Birmingham City vs West Bromwich Albion ○

○ position in league table before match

14 16 15 15 14 14 15 15 20 20 19 18 17 17 16
20

Matches
- won
- drawn
- lost
- B home match

30.10.04 vs Crystal Palace
06.11.04 vs Liverpool
13.11.04 vs Everton
21.11.04 vs Blackburn Rovers
27.11.04 vs Norwich City
04.12.04 vs Arsenal
12.12.04 vs Aston Villa
11.12.04 vs Charlton Athletic
04.12.04 vs Portsmouth
27.11.04 vs Manchester United
20.11.04 vs Arsenal
14.11.04 vs Middlesbrough
06.11.04 vs Southampton
30.10.04 vs Chelsea

Goals
- scored
- conceded

| scored | 0 | 1 | 0 | 3 | 1 | 0 | 2 | | 0 | 2 | 0 | 1 | 1 | 2 | 1 |
| conceded | 1 | 0 | 1 | 3 | 1 | 3 | 1 | | 1 | 3 | 3 | 1 | 2 | 2 | 4 |

Goal Statistics

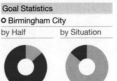

○ Birmingham City

by Half | by Situation

▶ first: 6 ▶ set piece: 1
second: 1 ▶ open play: 6

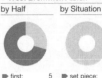

○ West Bromwich Albion

by Half | by Situation

▶ first: 5 ▶ set piece: 0
second: 2 ▶ open play: 6
▶ own goals: 1

Goals by Area

○ Birmingham City
Scored (Conceded)

| 2 (3) |
| 5 (7) |
| 0 (0) |

○ West Bromwich Albion
Scored (Conceded)

| 2 (6) |
| 4 (7) |
| 1 (3) |

Team Statistics

Starting Line-Ups

Lazaridis, Dunn, Gera, Haas, Earnshaw, Wallwork, Koumas, Upson, Carter, Purse, Morrison, Taylor, Malik, Kanu, Gaardsoe, Hoult, Cunningham, Savage, Clapham, Heskey Gray, Scimeca, Tebily, Johnson Anderton, Greening, Clement, Johnson

▶ 4/4/2   ▶ 4/5/1

Unused Sub: Vaesen, Clemence | Unused Sub: Kuszczak, Dyer, Horsfield

Premiership Totals

	○ Birmingham	West Brom ○
Premiership Appearances	1,929	849
Team Appearances	671	331
Goals Scored	176	60
Assists	260	65
Clean Sheets (goalkeepers)	30	21
Yellow Cards	213	79
Red Cards	9	9

Age/Height

Birmingham City Age	West Bromwich Albion Age
▶ **28 yrs, 3 mo**	▶ **27 yrs, 3 mo**
Birmingham City Height	West Bromwich Albion Height
▶ **6'**	▶ **6'1"**

Match Statistics

League Table after Fixture

	Played	Won	Drawn	Lost	For	Against	Pts
↓ 12 Portsmouth	17	6	5	6	23	24	23
↓ 13 Newcastle	17	5	6	6	28	32	21
↑ 14 Birmingham	18	4	8	6	18	19	20
↓ 15 Fulham	17	5	3	9	19	28	18
↑ 16 Blackburn	18	2	9	7	16	30	15
↓ 17 Norwich	18	2	9	7	17	32	15
↓ 18 Crystal Palace	18	3	5	10	19	29	14
● 19 Southampton	18	2	7	9	18	31	13
● 20 West Brom	18	1	7	10	15	36	10

Statistics

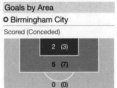

	○ Birmingham	West Brom ○
Goals	4	0
Shots on Target	5	6
Shots off Target	3	3
Hit Woodwork	0	1
Possession %	54	46
Corners	2	2
Offsides	4	1
Fouls	14	20
Disciplinary Points	0	16

2-0

Birmingham City °
Middlesbrough °

▶ Darren Carter brings the ball under control

Event Line

10	⊕ Morrison / RF / IFK / IA	
	Assist: Heskey	
23	⇄ Job > Viduka	
42	▢ Dunn	
45	⊕ Heskey / H / C / IA	
	Assist: Savage	
Half time 2-0		
50	⇄ Gray > Heskey	
54	⇄ Clapham > Dunn	
61	⇄ Nemeth > Doriva	
80	⇄ Melchiot > Morrison	
81	⇄ Morrison > Cooper	
Full time 2-0		

Blues made it three wins on the bounce with a fairly comfortable Boxing Day win over high-flying Middlesbrough.

Clinton Morrison set the home side on their way with the first goal after just ten minutes. Maik Taylor's long kick was flicked on by Emile Heskey and Morrison finished clinically with a superb low shot past Mark Schwarzer.

Blues continued to press and got the vital second goal in first half injury time.

The move began when Damien Johnson skipped past Franck Queudrue and raced into the box before pulling the ball back for Carter whose goal-bound shot was deflected inches wide of the post by Southgate.

Johnson reacted quickest and played a short corner to Savage and he swung the ball in for Heskey who made no mistake with a firm header from six yards.

The two goals were enough to secure victory in a fixture that was a repeat of the first ever game played at St. Andrew's exactly 98 years earlier.

Quote

● **Steve Bruce**

Despite picking up a couple of injuries, it was still a very good win against a Middlesbrough side that has been playing well this season.

Venue:	St Andrew's	Referee:	S.G.Bennett - 04/05

Venue: St Andrew's
Attendance: 29,082
Capacity: 30,016
Occupancy: 97%

Referee: S.G.Bennett - 04/05
Matches: 15
Yellow Cards: 44
Red Cards: 2

Birmingham City
Middlesbrough

Form Coming into Fixture

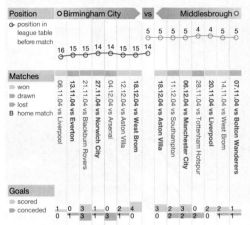

Position ○ Birmingham City **vs** Middlesbrough ○
- position in league table before match

Goal Statistics

○ Birmingham City
by Half	by Situation
first: 9	set piece: 4
second: 2	open play: 7

○ Middlesbrough
by Half	by Situation
first: 4	set piece: 1
second: 9	open play: 10
	own goals: 2

Goals by Area

○ Birmingham City
Scored (Conceded)

| 2 (3) |
| 8 (6) |
| 1 (0) |

○ Middlesbrough
Scored (Conceded)

| 4 (1) |
| 7 (7) |
| 2 (0) |

Team Statistics

Starting Line-Ups

Lazaridis, Dunn, Clapham, Parlour, Reiziger, Upson, Carter, Morrison, Melchiot, Hasselbaink, Doriva, Nemeth, Cooper, Morrison, Taylor Maik, Schwarzer, Cunningham, Savage, Heskey, Gray, Viduka, Job, Zenden, Southgate, Tebily, Johnson, Downing, Queudrue

▶ 4/4/2   ▶ 4/4/2

Unused Sub: Vaesen, Anderton   Unused Sub: Nash, McMahon

Premiership Totals	○ Birmingham	Boro ○
Premiership Appearances	1,780	2,029
Team Appearances	691	944
Goals Scored	147	280
Assists	182	205
Clean Sheets (goalkeepers)	31	64
Yellow Cards	194	219
Red Cards	8	14

Age/Height

Birmingham City Age
▶ **27 yrs, 11 mo**

Middlesbrough Age
▶ **29 yrs, 4 mo**

Birmingham City Height
▶ **6'**

Middlesbrough Height
▶ **5'11"**

Match Statistics

League Table after Fixture

		Played	Won	Drawn	Lost	For	Against	Pts
● 5	Middlesbrough	19	9	5	5	32	24	32
● 6	Liverpool	19	9	4	6	33	20	31
↑ 7	Tottenham	19	8	4	7	23	18	28
↓ 8	Charlton	19	8	4	7	21	28	28
↑ 9	Portsmouth	19	7	5	7	24	25	26
↓ 10	Aston Villa	19	6	7	6	22	23	25
↓ 11	Man City	19	6	5	8	23	20	23
↑ 12	Birmingham	19	5	8	6	20	19	23
↓ 13	Bolton	19	6	5	8	26	28	23

Statistics	○ Birmingham	Boro ○
Goals	2	0
Shots on Target	7	3
Shots off Target	1	3
Hit Woodwork	0	0
Possession %	49	51
Corners	5	3
Offsides	6	6
Fouls	17	9
Disciplinary Points	4	0

2-3

Fulham ○
Birmingham City ○

▶ Emile Heskey opens the scoring in fine style

Event Line

25 ○ ⊕ Heskey / LF / OP / IA
    Assist: Morrison
34 ○ ⊕ Legwinski / RF / OP / IA
    Assist: Radzinski
41 ○ ⊕ Carter / RF / OP / IA
    Assist: Heskey

Half time 1-2

46 ○ ⇄ Rehman > Pearce
53 ○ ⊕ Savage / LF / OP / IA
56 ○ ⇄ Malbranque > McBride
57 ○ ⇄ Hammond > John
67 ○   Rehman
75 ○ ⇄ Gray > Heskey
82 ○ ⇄ Clemence > Morrison
86 ○ ⇄ Anderton > Savage
90 ○ ⊕ Radzinski / LF / C / 6Y
    Assist: Volz

Full time 2-3

It continued to be a happy Christmas for Blues as we recorded a fourth straight league victory for the first time in the Premiership.

Emile Heskey fired the visitors in front on 25 minutes when he played a one-two with Clinton Morrison before firing an unstoppable shot past Edwin Van Der Sar.

Fulham were briefly in the game when Sylvain Legwinski drew level for the Cottagers but the parity was short-lived.

Blues were back in front when Robbie Savage swung the ball into the box and Heskey bravely headed the ball down for Darren Carter. The midfielder finished clinically from a narrow angle to record his first Premiership goal for the club.

And it was 3-1 soon after the break courtesy of a wonder goal by Savage. The Welsh international hit a fantastic looping shot over the grasp of Van Der Sar.

Tomasz Radzinski grabbed a late goal deep into injury time to give Fulham a lifeline but it was too little, too late and the visitors held on for a deserved victory.

Quote

● **Steve Bruce**

It was as excellent result for us and a good performance. Four wins in a row have certainly made my job easier.

Premiership Milestone

▶ **150**

Stephen Clemence made his 150th Premiership appearance.

Venue:	Craven Cottage	Referee:	M.Clattenburg - 04/05	**Fulham**
Attendance:	18,706	Matches:	12	**Birmingham City**
Capacity:	22,646	Yellow Cards:	22	
Occupancy:	83%	Red Cards:	2	

Form Coming into Fixture

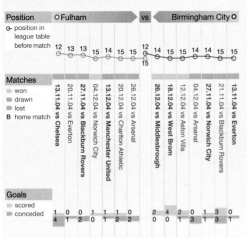

Goal Statistics

○ Fulham

by Half		by Situation	
▶ first:	1	▶ set piece:	1
▶ second:	3	▶ open play:	3

○ Birmingham City

by Half		by Situation	
▶ first:	11	▶ set piece:	5
▶ second:	1	▶ open play:	7

Goals by Area

○ Fulham
Scored (Conceded)

| 1 (4) |
| 1 (7) |
| 2 (1) |

○ Birmingham City
Scored (Conceded)

| 1 (3) |
| 10 (6) |
| 1 (0) |

Team Statistics

Starting Line-Ups

▶ 4/4/2   ▶ 4/4/2

Unused Sub: Crossley, Pembridge   Unused Sub: Vaesen, Taylor Martin

Premiership Totals

	○ Fulham	Birmingham ○
Premiership Appearances	1,265	2,010
Team Appearances	650	673
Goals Scored	254	165
Assists	154	238
Clean Sheets (goalkeepers)	38	32
Yellow Cards	114	223
Red Cards	13	9

Age/Height

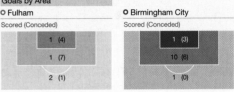

Fulham Age	Birmingham City Age
▶ 27 yrs, 3 mo	▶ 28 yrs, 1 mo
Fulham Height	Birmingham City Height
▶ 6'	▶ 6'

Match Statistics

League Table after Fixture

		Played	Won	Drawn	Lost	For	Against	Pts
↓	8 Tottenham	20	8	5	7	24	19	29
↑	9 Birmingham	20	6	8	6	23	21	26
↓	10 Portsmouth	20	7	5	8	24	27	26
↓	11 Aston Villa	20	6	7	7	22	24	25
↓	12 Man City	20	6	6	8	24	21	24
●	13 Bolton	20	6	5	9	26	29	23
↓	14 Newcastle	19	5	7	7	31	37	22
↑	15 Blackburn	20	3	10	7	19	32	19
↓	16 Fulham	20	5	3	12	22	35	18

Statistics

	○ Fulham	Birmingham ○
Goals	2	3
Shots on Target	5	5
Shots off Target	3	1
Hit Woodwork	0	0
Possession %	47	53
Corners	5	3
Offsides	5	4
Fouls	9	13
Disciplinary Points	4	0

2-1

Birmingham City ○
Southampton ○

Premiership
02.02.05

▶ Damien Johnson brushes aside Jamie Redknapp

Event Line

12 ○ ⊕ Pandiani / H / OP / 6Y
    Assist: Pennant
41 ○ ⊕ Blake / RF / P / IA
    Assist: Melchiot
43 ○ ▦ Prutton

Half time 2-0

46 ○ ⇄ Camara > Jones
48 ○ ▦ Bernard
52 ○ ⊕ Camara / LF / OP / IA
    Assist: Crouch
69 ○ ⇄ Svensson > Van Damme
77 ○ ⇄ Carter > Pennant
80 ○ ⇄ Tebily > Pandiani
90 ○ ⇄ Morrison > Blake

Full time 2-1

New boy Walter Pandiani and Robbie Blake grabbed their first goals for the club as Blues scraped past Southampton in a nervy encounter at St. Andrew's.

Steve Bruce handed full debuts to Pandiani and Jermaine Pennant with the third deadline day loanee Mehdi Nafti taking his place amongst the substitutes.

The debutant pairing combined to scintillating effect to open the scoring on 12 minutes, Pennant racing down the right and finding Pandiani, who made no mistake with a guided header back across goal and past the helpless Antti Niemi.

It was all one-way traffic and Robbie Blake put Blues in cruise control with a second from the penalty spot just before the break after Mario Melchiot was caught by Jamie Redknapp's trailing leg.

Henri Camara's early second half goal for Saints ensured that the home fans were on the edge of their seat for the remainder of the contest.

But Blues survived some hairy moments to collect their first league victory of 2005.

Quote

● **Steve Bruce**

Walter Pandiani didn't meet the lads until 5pm, but he indicated that he wanted to play and showed what he can bring to our team.

Premiership Milestone

▶ **Debut**

Jermaine Pennant made his first Premiership appearance in the colours of Birmingham.

Venue:	St Andrew's	Referee:	P.Walton - 04/05		Birmingham City
Attendance:	28,797	Matches:	20		Southampton
Capacity:	30,016	Yellow Cards:	52		
Occupancy:	96%	Red Cards:	2		

Form Coming into Fixture

Goal Statistics

O Birmingham City

by Half | by Situation

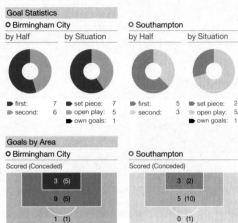

	first:	7	set piece:	7
	second:	6	open play:	5
			own goals:	1

O Southampton

by Half | by Situation

	first:	5	set piece:	2
	second:	3	open play:	5
			own goals:	1

Goals by Area

O Birmingham City
Scored (Conceded)

| 3 (5) |
| 9 (5) |
| 1 (1) |

O Southampton
Scored (Conceded)

| 3 (2) |
| 5 (10) |
| 0 (1) |

Team Statistics

Starting Line-Ups

Birmingham City: Clapham, Gray, Jones, Telfer, Camara, Prutton, Upson, Clemence, Blake, Morrison, Lundekvam, Crouch, Redknapp, Cunningham, Johnson, Pandiani, Tebily, Davenport, Delap, Melchiot, Pennant, Carter, Van Damme, Svensson, Bernard

Taylor/Malk

▶ 4/4/2   **▶ 4/5/1**

Unused Sub: Vaesen, Nafti

Unused Sub: Smith, Higginbotham, Jakobsson

Premiership Totals

	O Birmingham	Southampton O
Premiership Appearances	1,303	1,512
Team Appearances	615	769
Goals Scored	48	93
Assists	87	127
Clean Sheets (goalkeepers)	32	22
Yellow Cards	111	180
Red Cards	7	8

Age/Height

Birmingham City Age	Southampton Age
▶ 27 yrs, 5 mo	**▶ 27 yrs**
Birmingham City Height	Southampton Height
▶ 6'	**▶ 6'**

Match Statistics

League Table after Fixture

	Played	Won	Drawn	Lost	For	Against	Pts
● 10 Man City	25	8	8	9	31	27	32
● 11 Aston Villa	25	8	8	9	28	30	32
↑ 12 Newcastle	25	7	9	9	36	42	30
↓ 13 Portsmouth	25	8	6	11	28	35	30
↑ 14 Birmingham	25	7	8	10	29	31	29
↓ 15 Fulham	25	8	5	12	32	41	29
● 16 Blackburn	25	5	10	10	21	35	25
● 17 Crystal Palace	25	5	7	13	29	39	22
● 18 Southampton	25	3	9	13	26	41	18

Statistics

	O Birmingham	Southampton O
Goals	2	1
Shots on Target	5	3
Shots off Target	7	3
Hit Woodwork	0	0
Possession %	56	44
Corners	8	1
Offsides	1	4
Fouls	11	18
Disciplinary Points	0	8

2-0

Birmingham City ○
Liverpool ○

▶ Jermaine Pennant forces a save from Jerzy Dudek

Event Line

18 ○ ⇄	Tebily > Melchiot
38 ○ ⊕	Pandiani / RF / P / IA
	Assist: Heskey
45 ○ ⊕	Gray / LF / OP / 6Y
	Assist: Pennant

Half time 2-0

46 ○ ⇄	Smicer > Biscan
50 ○	Tebily
63 ○ ⇄	Nunez > Riise
71 ○	Heskey
79 ○ ⇄	Pellegrino > Finnan
84 ○ ⇄	Nafti > Pennant
89 ○ ⇄	Blake > Pandiani

Full time 2-0

Blues recorded their first double over the Reds in 69 years with an impressive victory at St. Andrew's.

The home side came flying out of the blocks and put Liverpool under pressure from the start without creating any clear cut chances.

After a few scares at the other end, Steve Bruce's side were handed a golden opportunity to take the lead seven minutes from half-time. Former Liverpool striker Emile Heskey won a penalty after being pulled down by Sami Hyypia. Walter Pandiani grabbed the ball and made no mistake with his spot kick, blasting it past Jerzy Dudek for his second goal in three games.

Then on the stroke of half time Julian Gray scored his first goal for the club to send them on their way to a well-earned and vital victory. Jamie Clapham started the move with a deep cross that found Jermaine Pennant. The former Arsenal man tricked his way past John Arne Riise before crossing to Gray whose volley gave Dudek no chance.

Damien Johnson ensured Blues kept a clean sheet when he hooked Jamie Carragher's late header off the line.

Quote

🔵 Steve Bruce

Considering the opposition, it was as well as we have played since coming into the Premiership. I was very pleased with the entire team performance.

Premiership Milestone

▶ First Goal

Julian Gray netted his first Premiership goal.

Venue:	St Andrew's	Referee:	H.M.Webb - 04/05		Birmingham City
Attendance:	29,318	Matches:	21		Liverpool
Capacity:	30,016	Yellow Cards:	62		
Occupancy:	98%	Red Cards:	0		

Form Coming into Fixture

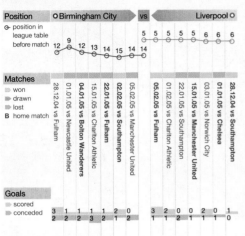

Position
O Birmingham City vs Liverpool O

- position in league table before match

5 5 5 5 5 6 6 6
12 9 12 13 14 15 14 14

Matches
- won
- drawn
- lost
- B home match

28.12.04 vs Fulham
01.01.05 vs Newcastle United
04.01.05 vs Bolton Wanderers
15.01.05 vs Charlton Athletic
22.01.05 vs Fulham
02.02.05 vs Southampton
05.02.05 vs Manchester United

05.02.05 vs Fulham
01.01.05 vs Charlton Athletic
22.01.05 vs Southampton
15.01.05 vs Manchester United
03.01.05 vs Norwich City
01.01.05 vs Chelsea
28.12.04 vs Southampton

Goals
- scored
- conceded

| scored | 3 | 1 | 1 | 1 | 2 | 0 | | 3 | 2 | 0 | 0 | 2 | 0 | 1 |
| conceded | 2 | 2 | 2 | 3 | 2 | 1 | 2 | 1 | 1 | 2 | 1 | 1 | 1 | 0 |

Goal Statistics

O Birmingham City

by Half | by Situation

- first: 4
- second: 5

- set piece: 3
- open play: 5
- own goals: 1

O Liverpool

by Half | by Situation

- first: 2
- second: 6

- set piece: 1
- open play: 7

Goals by Area

O Birmingham City

Scored (Conceded)

4 (5)
5 (8)
0 (1)

O Liverpool

Scored (Conceded)

1 (2)
6 (2)
1 (3)

Team Statistics

Starting Line-Ups

Clapham, Gray, Baros, Finnan / Pellegrino

Upson, Clemence, Pandiani / Blake, Gerrard, Hamann, Carragher

Taylor Maik, Dudek

Cunningham, Johnson, Heskey, Morientes, Biscan / Smicer, Hyypia

Melchiot / Tebily, Pennant / Nafti, Riise / Nunez, Traore

▶ 4/4/2

▶ 4/4/1/1

Unused Sub: Bennett, Anderton

Unused Sub: Carson, Warnock

Premiership Totals	O Birmingham	Liverpool O
Premiership Appearances	1,523	1,497
Team Appearances	562	1,404
Goals Scored	112	107
Assists	130	136
Clean Sheets (goalkeepers)	32	46
Yellow Cards	142	138
Red Cards	8	10

Age/Height

Birmingham City Age	Liverpool Age
▶ 27 yrs, 11 mo	▶ 28 yrs, 2 mo
Birmingham City Height	Liverpool Height
▶ 6'	▶ 6'1"

Match Statistics

League Table after Fixture

			Played	Won	Drawn	Lost	For	Against	Pts
●	5	Liverpool	27	13	4	10	41	29	43
●	6	Middlesbrough	27	11	8	8	41	35	41
●	7	Bolton	27	11	7	9	35	32	40
●	8	Charlton	26	11	5	10	30	36	38
●	9	Tottenham	26	10	6	10	33	30	36
↑	10	Aston Villa	27	9	8	10	31	34	35
↓	11	Man City	26	8	9	9	31	27	33
↑	12	Birmingham	27	8	8	11	31	33	32
↓	13	Newcastle	26	7	10	9	37	43	31

Statistics	O Birmingham	Liverpool O
Goals	2	0
Shots on Target	4	2
Shots off Target	2	4
Hit Woodwork	0	0
Possession %	51	49
Corners	10	4
Offsides	7	2
Fouls	16	10
Disciplinary Points	8	0

75

2-0

Birmingham City ○
Aston Villa ○

▶ Julian Gray does well to maintain possession

Event Line		
30 ○ ▨	Melchiot	
40 ○ ▨	Upson	
41 ○ ▨	Johnson	
Half time 0-0		
52 ○ ⊕	Heskey / RF / OP / IA	
	Assist: Pandiani	
54 ○ ▨	Berson	
57 ○ ▨	Laursen	
60 ○ ⇄	Vassell > Berson	
60 ○ ⇄	Cole C > Moore	
71 ○ ⇄	Hitzlsperger > Solano	
76 ○ ⇄	Nafti > Clemence	
80 ○ ⇄	Gray > Lazaridis	
88 ○ ⇄	Morrison > Pandiani	
89 ○ ⊕	Gray / RF / OP / IA	
90 ○ ▨	Hendrie	
Full time 2-0		

Blues completed a memorable double over local rivals Aston Villa at St. Andrew's.

After two woeful away performances at Crystal Palace and West Bromwich Albion, Steve Bruce demanded a big improvement. And that is exactly what he got as Blues took the game to their arch rivals and were rarely troubled in the defensive third.

Blues took the Second City derby honours as defensive bloopers by Thomas Sorensen and Martin Laursen helped gift the home side a deserved victory.

Bruce's boys took the lead in the 52nd minute courtesy of another Sorensen howler. Emile Heskey powered his way past two defenders before hitting a low angled shot that squeezed through the keeper's grasp and bobbled into the net.

Victory was secured in the final minute when Gray struck Blues' second and killer goal.

A mix-up in the visiting defence saw Olof Mellberg kick the ball off Martin Laursen and it rolled kindly into the path of Gray who had the simple task of running on and placing the ball home in front of the ecstatic fans in the Tilton Road stand.

Quote	Premiership Milestone
● **Steve Bruce**	▶ **300**
We were back to our best again today and Emile Heskey was outstanding. He is England's best centre-forward of his type.	Emile Heskey made his 300th Premiership appearance.

Venue:	St Andrew's	Referee:	M.A.Riley - 04/05	Birmingham City
Attendance:	29,382	Matches:	28	Aston Villa
Capacity:	30,016	Yellow Cards:	79	
Occupancy:	98%	Red Cards:	9	

Form Coming into Fixture

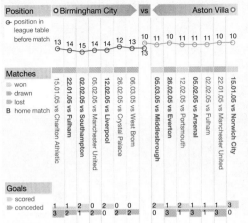

Position

○ Birmingham City vs Aston Villa ○

○- position in league table before match

Matches
- won
- drawn
- lost
- B home match

15.01.05 vs Charlton Athletic
22.01.05 vs Fulham
02.02.05 vs Southampton
05.02.05 vs Manchester United
12.02.05 vs Liverpool
26.02.05 vs Crystal Palace
06.03.05 vs West Brom

05.03.05 vs Middlesbrough
26.02.05 vs Everton
12.02.05 vs Portsmouth
05.02.05 vs Arsenal
02.02.05 vs Fulham
22.01.05 vs Manchester United
15.01.05 vs Norwich City

Goals
- scored
- conceded

| scored | 1 | 1 | 2 | 0 | 2 | 0 | 0 | 2 | 1 | 2 | 1 | 1 | 1 | 3 |
| conceded | 3 | 2 | 1 | 2 | 0 | 2 | 2 | 0 | 3 | 1 | 3 | 1 | 3 | 0 |

Goal Statistics

○ **Birmingham City**

by Half | by Situation

- first: 4
- second: 2
- set piece: 3
- open play: 2
- own goals: 1

○ **Aston Villa**

by Half | by Situation

- first: 3
- second: 8
- set piece: 3
- open play: 6
- own goals: 2

Goals by Area

○ **Birmingham City**

Scored (Conceded)

4 (3)
2 (8)
0 (1)

○ **Aston Villa**

Scored (Conceded)

6 (3)
3 (7)
2 (1)

Team Statistics

Starting Line-Ups

Clapham, Lazaridis / Gray, Upson, Carter, Pandiani / Morrison, Taylor Maik, Cunningham, Clemence / Nafti, Heskey, Melchiot, Johnson

Solano / Hitzlsperger, De la Cruz, Davis, Laursen, Moore / Cole C, Hendrie, Sorensen, Mellberg, Berson / Vassell, Barry, Samuel

▶ 4/4/2 | ▶ 4/5/1

Unused Sub: Vaesen, Blake | Unused Sub: Postma, Ridgewell

Premiership Totals

	○ Birmingham	Aston Villa ○
Premiership Appearances	1,645	1,541
Team Appearances	710	1,206
Goals Scored	125	136
Assists	155	170
Clean Sheets (goalkeepers)	33	57
Yellow Cards	146	159
Red Cards	7	8

Age/Height

Birmingham City Age	Aston Villa Age
▶ **28 yrs**	▶ **25 yrs, 4 mo**
Birmingham City Height	Aston Villa Height
▶ **6'**	▶ **5'11"**

Match Statistics

League Table after Fixture

		Played	Won	Drawn	Lost	For	Against	Pts
↓	11 Aston Villa	30	10	8	12	34	39	38
●	12 Man City	30	9	9	12	35	34	36
●	13 Birmingham	30	9	8	13	33	37	35
●	14 Blackburn	30	7	11	12	25	37	32
●	15 Portsmouth	30	8	7	15	32	46	31
●	16 Fulham	29	8	6	15	33	47	30
↑	17 Southampton	30	5	12	13	33	45	27
↓	18 Crystal Palace	30	6	8	16	33	49	26
●	19 West Brom	30	4	12	14	29	51	24

Statistics

	○ Birmingham	Aston Villa ○
Goals	2	0
Shots on Target	4	3
Shots off Target	8	2
Hit Woodwork	0	1
Possession %	52	48
Corners	2	3
Offsides	1	1
Fouls	12	20
Disciplinary Points	12	12

2-1

Birmingham City ○
Blackburn Rovers ○

Premiership
30.04.05

➤ Emile Heskey is mobbed after scoring the winning goal

Event Line

13 ○ ⊕	Stead / H / OP / IA
	Assist: Emerton
22 ○ ⇄	Clemence > Anderton
44 ○ ■	Mokoena
Half time 0-1	
59 ○ ⇄	Thompson > Pedersen
59 ○ ⇄	Blake > Nafti
61 ○ ⊕	Blake / RF / OP / IA
67 ○ ⇄	Tugay > Johansson
76 ○ ⇄	Gallagher > Emerton
76 ○ ■	Heskey
80 ○ ⊕	Heskey / LF / OP / OA
84 ○ ⇄	Morrison > Pandiani
90 ○ ■	Morrison
Full time 2-1	

Blues leapfrogged Blackburn Rovers with a vital victory in the battle between former Manchester United team-mates turned managers.

Jonathan Stead made no mistake with a close range header from Brett Emerton's cross to put the visitors into an interval lead. However the introduction of Robbie Blake in the second half proved to be an inspired substitution as Blues drew level just 60 seconds later.

Stan Lazaridis started the move with Emile Heskey touching it on for Blake who made no mistake with a clinical finish past Friedel.

'There's only one Robbie' was the chant from the Tilton Road with a cheeky reference to the departure of former favourite Robbie Savage to Blackburn four months earlier.

Blake was involved again as Emile Heskey fired the winner just ten minutes from time. The ex-Burnley man's tenacity led to an error by the Rovers defence allowing Heskey the chance to finish with another thunderbolt strike from 20 yards – his second in as many games to clinch a first victory in six matches for Blues.

Quote	Premiership Milestone
● **Steve Bruce**	➤ **100**
Emile Heskey has had his critics, but he has done fantastically well for us.	Damien Johnson made his 100th Premiership appearance in the colours of Birmingham.

Venue:	St Andrew's	Referee:	B.Knight - 04/05	Birmingham City
Attendance:	28,621	Matches:	16	Blackburn Rovers
Capacity:	30,016	Yellow Cards:	27	
Occupancy:	95%	Red Cards:	3	

Form Coming into Fixture

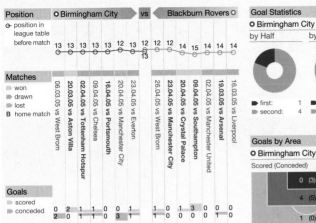

Position
- ⊙ position in league table before match

Birmingham City vs **Blackburn Rovers**

13 13 13 13 13 12 13 12 12 12 14 15 14 14 14
13

Matches
- 🡆 won
- 🡆 drawn
- 🡆 lost
- B home match

06.03.05 vs West Brom
20.03.05 vs Aston Villa
02.04.05 vs Tottenham Hotspur
09.04.05 vs Chelsea
16.04.05 vs Portsmouth
20.04.05 vs Manchester City
23.04.05 vs Everton
26.04.05 vs West Brom
23.04.05 vs Manchester City
20.04.05 vs Crystal Palace
09.04.05 vs Southampton
02.04.05 vs Manchester United
19.03.05 vs Arsenal
16.03.05 vs Liverpool

Goals
- 🡆 scored
- 🡆 conceded

scored	0	2	1	1	0	0	1		1	0	1	3	0	0	0
conceded	2	0	1	1	0	3	1		1	0	0	0	0	1	0

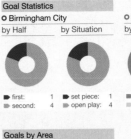

Goal Statistics

⊙ Birmingham City

by Half		by Situation	
🡆 first:	1	🡆 set piece:	1
🡆 second:	4	🡆 open play:	4

⊙ Blackburn Rovers

by Half		by Situation	
🡆 first:	2	🡆 set piece:	2
🡆 second:	3	🡆 open play:	2
		🡆 own goals:	1

Goals by Area

⊙ Birmingham City
Scored (Conceded)

0 (3)	
4 (5)	
1 (0)	

⊙ Blackburn Rovers
Scored (Conceded)

2 (1)	
3 (0)	
0 (1)	

Team Statistics

Starting Line-Ups

Lazaridis, Anderton Clemence, Emerton Gallagher, Neill

Flitcroft

Upson, Nafti Blake, Todd

Taylor Maik, Pandiani Morrison, Stead, Mokoena, Friedel

Cunningham, Johnson, Heskey, Nelson

Reid

Melchiot, Pennant, Pedersen Thompson, Johansson Tugay

🡆 **4/4/2**   🡆 **4/5/1**

Unused Sub: Vaesen, Taylor Martin   Unused Sub: Enckelman, Short

Premiership Totals

	⊙ Birmingham	Blackburn ⊙
Premiership Appearances	1,953	1,296
Team Appearances	692	1,011
Goals Scored	171	74
Assists	254	94
Clean Sheets (goalkeepers)	35	50
Yellow Cards	191	198
Red Cards	8	12

Age/Height

Birmingham City Age	Blackburn Rovers Age
🡆 **28 yrs, 8 mo**	🡆 **27 yrs, 2 mo**
Birmingham City Height	Blackburn Rovers Height
🡆 **5'11"**	🡆 **6'**

Match Statistics

League Table after Fixture

		Played	Won	Drawn	Lost	For	Against	Pts
● 5	Liverpool	36	16	7	13	49	37	55
● 6	Bolton	36	15	9	12	45	41	54
● 7	Middlesbrough	36	13	12	11	51	45	51
↑ 8	Man City	36	12	12	12	44	37	48
↓ 9	Tottenham	35	13	9	13	42	39	48
↓ 10	Aston Villa	35	12	11	12	42	43	47
● 11	Charlton	35	12	9	14	40	51	45
↑ 12	Birmingham	36	10	12	14	38	44	42
↓ 13	Blackburn	36	9	14	13	31	40	41

Statistics

	⊙ Birmingham	Blackburn ⊙
Goals	2	1
Shots on Target	6	1
Shots off Target	4	4
Hit Woodwork	1	0
Possession %	57	43
Corners	6	1
Offsides	1	2
Fouls	15	16
Disciplinary Points	8	4

2-1

Birmingham City ○
Arsenal ○

▶ Mehdi Nafti puts Freddie Ljungberg under pressure

Event Line
Half time 0-0

62 ○ ⇄ Morrison > Carter
68 ○ ⇄ Edu > Ljungberg
68 ○ ⇄ Aliadiere > van Persie
75 ○ ⇄ Flamini > Fabregas
78 ○ ⇄ Tebily > Melchiot
80 ○ ⊕ Pandiani / LF / C / IA
81 ○ ▮ Pandiani
88 ○ ⊕ Bergkamp / LF / OP / IA
      Assist: Viera
90 ○ ⊕ Heskey / RF / OP / IA
      Assist: Pandiani
90 ○ ⇄ Taylor Martin > Pandiani

Full time 2-1

Blues beat FA Cup Finalists Arsenal on the final day of the season in a game that was decided by an amazing three goals in the last ten minutes.

Walter Pandiani gave Blues the lead after Jermaine Pennant's corner had been cleared to Stephen Clemence who lobbed the ball back into the area. The Uruguayan striker prodded it home and proceeded to celebrate wildly by ripping his shirt off to earn himself a booking.

Arsenal's minds looked firmly on the following week's Millennium Stadium date with Manchester United but they still managed to draw level just two minutes from time. Blues went to sleep as Patrick Viera chipped the ball through to Dennis Bergkamp, who looked suspiciously offside. Despite Maik Taylor's desperate attempts, the ball rolled into the net.

But incredibly Blues were back in front just 60 seconds later. Emile Heskey made no mistake with a tremendous shot from just inside the box to cap a tremendous first season at St. Andrew's.

Blues held on for their first victory against Arsenal in 22 years to finish the season on a high.

Quote

● **Steve Bruce**

It is always nice to beat Arsenal and a great way to finish off the season. We deserved the win, although I didn't think we would get it when Dennis Bergkamp equalised.

Venue:	St Andrew's	Referee:	D.J.Gallagher - 04/05	Birmingham City
Attendance:	29,302	Matches:	35	Arsenal
Capacity:	30,016	Yellow Cards:	80	
Occupancy:	98%	Red Cards:	5	

Form Coming into Fixture

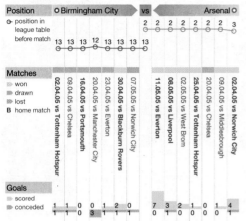

Position	O Birmingham City	vs	Arsenal O

position in league table before match

Birmingham City: 13 13 13 12 13 13 13
Arsenal: 2 2 2 2 2 2 2 3

Matches
- won
- drawn
- lost
- B home match

02.04.05 vs Tottenham Hotspur
09.04.05 vs Chelsea
16.04.05 vs Portsmouth
20.04.05 vs Manchester City
23.04.05 vs Everton
30.04.05 vs Blackburn Rovers
07.05.05 vs Norwich City
11.05.05 vs Everton
08.05.05 vs Liverpool
02.05.05 vs West Brom
25.04.05 vs Tottenham Hotspur
20.04.05 vs Chelsea
09.04.05 vs Middlesbrough
02.04.05 vs Norwich City

Goals
- scored
- conceded

| scored | 1 | 1 | 0 | 0 | 1 | 2 | 0 | | 7 | 3 | 2 | 1 | 0 | 1 | 4 |
| conceded | 1 | 1 | 0 | 3 | 1 | 1 | 1 | | 0 | 1 | 0 | 0 | 0 | 0 | 1 |

Goal Statistics

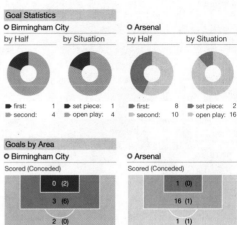

O Birmingham City

by Half	by Situation
first: 1	set piece: 1
second: 4	open play: 4

O Arsenal

by Half	by Situation
first: 8	set piece: 2
second: 10	open play: 16

Goals by Area

O Birmingham City
Scored (Conceded)

0 (2)
3 (6)
2 (0)

O Arsenal
Scored (Conceded)

1 (0)
16 (1)
1 (1)

Team Statistics

Starting Line-Ups

Clapham / Carter / Morrison
Upson / Clemence / Pandiani (Taylor Martin) / van Persie (Aliadiere)
Taylor Maik
Cunningham / Nafti / Heskey / Bergkamp
Melchiot / Pennant / Tebily
Fabregas / Toure / Flamini
Gilberto Silva / Senderos
Lehmann
Vieira / Campbell
Ljungberg / Cole / Edu

4/4/2 (Birmingham City)
Unused Sub: Vaesen, Blake

4/4/2 (Arsenal)
Unused Sub: Almunia, Eboue

	O Birmingham	Arsenal O
Premiership Appearances	1,626	1,678
Team Appearances	676	1,423
Goals Scored	126	205
Assists	132	238
Clean Sheets (goalkeepers)	35	26
Yellow Cards	149	206
Red Cards	7	16

Age/Height

Birmingham City Age	Arsenal Age
27 yrs, 7 mo	**26 yrs, 2 mo**
Birmingham City Height	Arsenal Height
6'	**6'**

Match Statistics

League Table after Fixture

	Played	Won	Drawn	Lost	For	Against	Pts
● 2 Arsenal	38	25	8	5	87	36	83
...	...	...	...	...	...	...	...
↑ 12 Birmingham	38	11	12	15	40	46	45
↑ 13 Fulham	38	12	8	18	52	60	44
↓ 14 Newcastle	38	10	14	14	47	57	44
↓ 15 Blackburn	38	9	15	14	32	43	42
● 16 Portsmouth	38	10	9	19	43	59	39
↑ 17 West Brom	38	6	16	16	36	61	34
↑ 18 Crystal Palace	38	7	12	19	41	62	33

Statistics	O Birmingham	Arsenal O
Goals	2	1
Shots on Target	4	5
Shots off Target	5	6
Hit Woodwork	0	1
Possession %	48	52
Corners	3	2
Offsides	6	3
Fouls	10	8
Disciplinary Points	4	0

2-3

West Bromwich Albion ⚪
Birmingham City ⚪

▶ Mikael Forssell gets a shot away

Event Line	
10 ⚪ ⊕ Heskey / H / OP / IA	
	Assist: Clapham
12 ⚪ ⊕ Horsfield / RF / C / IA	
	Assist: Gaardsoe
26 ⚪ ⊕ Jarosik / H / IFK / 6Y	
	Assist: Pennant
33 ⚪ ⊕ Heskey / H / OP / IA	
	Assist: Pennant
34 ⚪ ■ Clement	
40 ⚪ ■ Clapham	
Half time 1-3	
46 ⚪ ⇄ Albrechtsen > Watson	
56 ⚪ ⇄ Ellington > Campbell	
63 ⚪ ⇄ Pandiani > Heskey	
64 ⚪ ⊕ Horsfield / RF / OP / IA	
72 ⚪ ⇄ Izzet > Forssell	
76 ⚪ ⇄ Earnshaw > Carter	
81 ⚪ ■ Jarosik	
81 ⚪ ⇄ Clemence > Johnson	
82 ⚪ ■ Upson	
Full time 2-3	

Blues' first away win of 2005 finally arrived with a narrow victory over West Brom.

An Emile Heskey brace either side of Jiri Jarosik's first goal for the club gave Blues their first maximum points haul of 2005/06. The Baggies didn't give up easily though with former Blues favourite Geoff Horsfield grabbing both goals for the home side.

Blues broke the deadlock on ten minutes when Heskey headed home from Jamie Clapham's cross.

The good work was undone just two minutes later as Horsfield made no mistake from close range after a comedy of errors in the visitors' defence.

Blues were back in front when Jermaine Pennant's curling free-kick found the giant figure of Jarosik, who headed past Chris Kirkland.

Pennant was the provider again as Heskey made it 3-1 to Blues.

Horsfield then latched on to a poor attempted clearance by Damien Johnson to shoot past Maik Taylor and set up a nervy finish but Blues held on.

Quote	Premiership Milestone
● Steve Bruce	▶ First Goal
We needed that first win of the season and deserved it after our first-half performance.	Jiri Jarosik netted his first Premiership goal.

Venue:	The Hawthorns	Referee:	G.Poll - 05/06	**West Bromwich Albion**
Attendance:	23,993	Matches:	3	**Birmingham City**
Capacity:	28,003	Yellow Cards:	13	
Occupancy:	86%	Red Cards:	1	

Form Coming into Fixture

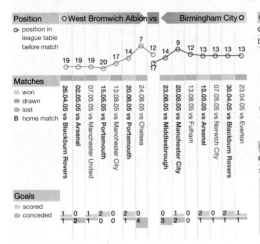

Position	○ West Bromwich Albion vs	Birmingham City ○

G- position in league table before match

Matches
- won
- drawn
- lost
- B home match

Goals
- scored
- conceded

Goal Statistics

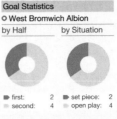

○ West Bromwich Albion

by Half	by Situation
first: 2	set piece: 2
second: 4	open play: 4

○ Birmingham City

by Half	by Situation
first: 2	set piece: 1
second: 4	open play: 5

Goals by Area

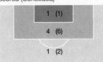

○ West Bromwich Albion
Scored (Conceded)

| 1 (1) |
| 4 (6) |
| 1 (2) |

○ Birmingham City
Scored (Conceded)

| 0 (3) |
| 4 (6) |
| 2 (0) |

Team Statistics

Starting Line-Ups

West Brom: Robinson, Greening, Clement, Carter, Earnshaw, Horsfield, Gaardsoe, Wallwork, Campbell, Ellington, Watson, Albrechtsen, Gera — Kirkland

Birmingham: Pennant, Melchiot, Butt, Cunningham, Heskey, Pandiani, Forssell, Izzet, Jarosik, Upson, Johnson, Clemence, Clapham — Taylor Maik

▶ 4/4/2   ▶ 4/4/2

Unused Sub: Kuszczak, Moore   Unused Sub: Vaesen, Gray

Premiership Totals	○ West Brom	Birmingham ○
Premiership Appearances	1,257	2,138
Team Appearances	378	669
Goals Scored	146	191
Assists	110	211
Clean Sheets (goalkeepers)	9	36
Yellow Cards	104	244
Red Cards	6	14
Full Internationals	4	11

Age/Height

West Bromwich Albion Age	Birmingham City Age
▶ **27 yrs, 1 mo**	▶ **28 yrs, 7 mo**
West Bromwich Albion Height	Birmingham City Height
▶ **6'**	▶ **6'**

Match Statistics

League Table after Fixture

		Played	Won	Drawn	Lost	For	Against	Pts
↓ 7	Man Utd	2	2	0	0	3	0	6
↑ 8	Aston Villa	4	1	2	1	4	4	5
↓ 9	West Ham	3	1	1	1	4	3	4
↓ 10	Middlesbrough	3	1	1	1	3	2	4
↓ 11	Liverpool	2	1	1	0	1	0	4
↓ 12	Blackburn	4	1	1	2	3	5	4
↑ 13	Birmingham	4	1	1	2	4	7	4
↑ 14	Fulham	4	1	1	2	3	6	4
↓ 15	West Brom	4	1	1	2	4	8	4

Statistics	○ West Brom	Birmingham ○
Goals	2	3
Shots on Target	8	7
Shots off Target	7	1
Hit Woodwork	1	0
Possession %	54	46
Corners	3	2
Offsides	5	2
Fouls	11	24
Disciplinary Points	4	12

0-1

Sunderland ○
Birmingham City ○

► Julian Gray is the hero for Birmingham

Steve Bruce's inspired substitutions saw Blues reap the rewards as we came away from the Stadium of Light with a massive victory against fellow strugglers Sunderland.

Julian Gray's second half strike was enough to secure a crucial win and gain ground on the other early strugglers in the Premiership table.

It took only five minutes for Blues to create their first chance with a trademark long range effort from Jiri Jarosik that keeper Ben Alnwick collected comfortably. A minute later Black Cats striker Jonathan Stead tried his luck from a similar distance at the other end which forced Nico Vaesen into his first save.

Bruce played his last card with the introduction of Gray midway through the second half and it paid dividends just three minutes later.

All three substitutes were involved with Jermaine Pennant providing a pin-point cross which was met by a bullet Pandiani header.

Alnwick could only parry the ball away and Gray was in the right place to secure a vital victory.

Quote

● **Steve Bruce**

When you've got Julian Gray, Jermaine Pennant and Walter Pandiani on the bench, then of course you can change the game.

Venue:	Stadium of Light	Referee:	U.D.Rennie - 05/06	**Sunderland**
Attendance:	32,442	Matches:	14	**Birmingham City**
Capacity:	48,300	Yellow Cards:	25	
Occupancy:	67%	Red Cards:	2	

Form Coming into Fixture

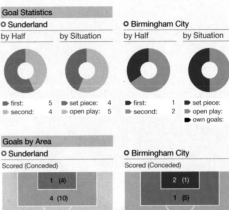

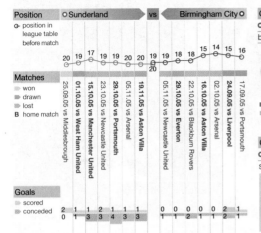

Position
G- position in
league table
before match

| | 20 | 19 | 17 | 19 | 19 | 20 | 20 | 19 | 19 | 18 | 18 | | 15 | 14 | 15 | 16 |
| | | | | | | | | 20 | | | | | | | | |

Matches
- won
- drawn
- lost
- B home match

25.09.05 vs Middlesbrough
01.10.05 vs West Ham United
15.10.05 vs Manchester United
23.10.05 vs Newcastle United
29.10.05 vs Portsmouth
05.11.05 vs Arsenal
19.11.05 vs Aston Villa
05.11.05 vs Newcastle United
29.10.05 vs Everton
22.10.05 vs Blackburn Rovers
16.10.05 vs Aston Villa
02.10.05 vs Arsenal
24.09.05 vs Liverpool
17.09.05 vs Portsmouth

Goals
- scored
- conceded

| scored | 2 | 1 | 1 | 2 | 1 | 1 | 1 | 0 | 0 | 0 | 0 | 0 | 2 | 1 |
| conceded | 0 | 1 | 3 | 3 | 4 | 3 | 3 | 1 | 1 | 2 | 1 | 1 | 2 | 1 |

Goal Statistics

O Sunderland
by Half | by Situation

- first: 5 — set piece: 4
- second: 4 — open play: 5

O Birmingham City
by Half | by Situation

- first: 1 — set piece: 1
- second: 2 — open play: 1
- — own goals: 1

Goals by Area

O Sunderland
Scored (Conceded)

| 1 (4) |
| 4 (10) |
| 4 (3) |

O Birmingham City
Scored (Conceded)

| 2 (1) |
| 1 (5) |
| 0 (3) |

Team Statistics

Starting Line-Ups

Hoyte, Welsh Lawrence, Johnson, Melchiot
Kilkenny Pennant
Collins D, Bassila Gray, Le Tallec Brown, Taylor Martin
Alnwick, Heskey, Jarosik Pandiani, Vaesen
Breen, Whitehead, Stead
Izzet
Cunningham
Nosworthy, Miller, Dunn Gray, Upson

4/4/2

Unused Sub: Davis, Caldwell

4/5/1

Unused Sub: Taylor Maik, Clemence

Premiership Totals

	O Sunderland	Birmingham O
Premiership Appearances	354	1,689
Team Appearances	117	598
Goals Scored	18	166
Assists	15	177
Clean Sheets (goalkeepers)	0	5
Yellow Cards	35	188
Red Cards	2	9
Full Internationals	3	9

Age/Height

Sunderland Age	Birmingham City Age
24 yrs, 3 mo	**27 yrs, 11 mo**
Sunderland Height	Birmingham City Height
6'	**6'**

Match Statistics

League Table after Fixture

	Played	Won	Drawn	Lost	For	Against	Pts
↑ 12 Newcastle	13	5	3	5	12	13	18
↓ 13 Blackburn	14	5	3	6	15	18	18
↑ 14 Aston Villa	14	4	3	7	14	22	15
↓ 15 Fulham	13	3	3	7	14	19	12
• 16 West Brom	13	3	2	8	13	22	11
• 17 Portsmouth	14	2	4	8	11	20	10
• 18 Everton	12	3	1	8	4	16	10
• 19 Birmingham	13	2	3	8	8	17	9
• 20 Sunderland	14	1	2	11	12	28	5

Statistics

	O Sunderland	Birmingham O
Goals	0	1
Shots on Target	3	7
Shots off Target	1	3
Hit Woodwork	0	0
Possession %	51	49
Corners	6	2
Offsides	1	2
Fouls	7	10
Disciplinary Points	0	0

1-0

Birmingham City ○
Fulham ○

➡ Jamie Clapham makes a last-ditch challenge

Event Line
Half time 0-0
53 ○ ⇄ Pennant > Lazaridis
69 ○ ⇄ Jarosik > Tebily
74 ○ ⇄ Clapham > Dunn
84 ○ ⊕ Butt / H / OP / IA
Assist: Heskey
Full time 1-0

Blues' season-long wait for a home win finally ended at St. Andrew's as Nicky Butt's late goal secured a dramatic and vital win against Fulham.

After a very scrappy and uneventful first half, Blues dominated the second period and created numerous chances that they failed to convert.

Blues' pressure was relentless in the closing stages but it looked like being another frustrating day for the home faithful until the 84th minute when the visitors' rugged resistance was finally broken.

Emile Heskey did brilliantly to nod Jamie Clapham's deep cross into the path of Butt and the former England man dived full length to send his header beyond the despairing dive of Mark Crossley.

The goal sparked scenes of wild celebration around St. Andrew's as the players, management and fans were finally able to release some of the pent-up anxiety that had built up during a nail-biting afternoon.

Quote

⬤ **Steve Bruce**

It wasn't pretty in the first half, but we showed what we were about in the second.

Premiership Milestone

➡ **Debut**

Marcos Painter made his Premiership debut.

Venue:	St Andrew's	Referee:	U.D.Rennie - 05/06	**Birmingham City**
Attendance:	27,597	Matches:	16	**Fulham**
Capacity:	30,016	Yellow Cards:	28	
Occupancy:	92%	Red Cards:	2	

Form Coming into Fixture

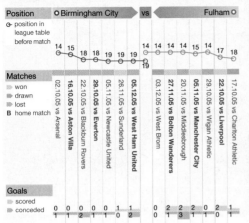

Position — o Birmingham City vs Fulham o

- position in league table before match

14 15 18 18 19 19 19 19 | 14 14 14 14 15 14 17 18 / 19

Matches
- won
- drawn
- lost
- B home match

16.10.05 vs Arsenal
16.10.05 vs Aston Villa
22.10.05 vs Blackburn Rovers
29.10.05 vs Everton
05.11.05 vs Newcastle United
26.11.05 vs Sunderland
05.12.05 vs West Ham United
03.12.05 vs West Brom
27.11.05 vs Bolton Wanderers
20.11.05 vs Middlesbrough
05.11.05 vs Manchester City
29.10.05 vs Wigan Athletic
22.10.05 vs Liverpool
17.10.05 vs Charlton Athletic

Goals
- scored
- conceded

| 0 | 0 | 0 | 0 | 0 | 1 | 1 | | 0 | 2 | 2 | 2 | 0 | 2 | 1 |
| 1 | 1 | 2 | 1 | 1 | 0 | 2 | | 0 | 1 | 3 | 1 | 1 | 0 | 1 |

Goal Statistics

o Birmingham City

by Half | **by Situation**

- first: 1
- second: 1
- set piece: 0
- open play: 2

o Fulham

by Half | **by Situation**

- first: 7
- second: 2
- set piece: 2
- open play: 7

Goals by Area

o Birmingham City — Scored (Conceded)

	1 (2)	
	1 (3)	
	0 (3)	

o Fulham — Scored (Conceded)

	0 (2)	
	9 (5)	
	0 (0)	

Team Statistics

Starting Line-Ups

Painter, Lazaridis / Pennant, John, Rosenior, Malbranque, Upson, Clemence, Heskey, Knight, Vaesen, McBride, Christanval, Crossley, Cunningham, Butt, Dunn / Clapham, Goma, Legwinski, Tebily / Jarosik, Johnson, Radzinski, Bocanegra

▶ 4/4/1/1   ▶ 4/5/1

Unused Sub: Taylor Maik, Pandiani

Unused Sub: Warner, Jensen N, Pearce, Elrich, Helguson

Premiership Totals	o Birmingham	Fulham o
Premiership Appearances	1,965	1,048
Team Appearances	778	731
Goals Scored	158	101
Assists	203	85
Clean Sheets (goalkeepers)	6	50
Yellow Cards	227	91
Red Cards	12	7
Full Internationals	9	8

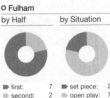

Age/Height

Birmingham City Age	Fulham Age
▶ **28 yrs, 7 mo**	▶ **28 yrs, 6 mo**
Birmingham City Height	Fulham Height
▶ **5'11"**	▶ **5'11"**

Match Statistics

League Table after Fixture

		Played	Won	Drawn	Lost	For	Against	Pts
↑	12 Blackburn	16	6	3	7	18	22	21
↓	13 Middlesbrough	16	5	4	7	20	23	19
↑	14 Aston Villa	16	4	5	7	16	24	17
↓	15 Fulham	16	4	4	8	16	21	16
↑	16 West Brom	16	4	4	8	17	24	16
↓	17 Everton	14	5	1	8	7	16	16
↑	18 Birmingham	15	3	3	9	10	19	12
↓	19 Portsmouth	15	2	4	9	11	23	10
●	20 Sunderland	17	1	2	14	14	35	5

Statistics	o Birmingham	Fulham o
Goals	1	0
Shots on Target	7	0
Shots off Target	4	4
Hit Woodwork	0	0
Possession %	43	57
Corners	2	2
Offsides	9	4
Fouls	12	10
Disciplinary Points	0	0

2-0

Birmingham City ○
Wigan Athletic ○

Premiership
02.01.06

▶ Emile Heskey battles with Arjan De Zeeuw

Event Line

13 ○ ▪ Chimbonda	
19 ○ ▪ McCulloch	
20 ○ ⊕ Pennant / H / OP / IA	
Assist: Jarosik	
33 ○ ⊕ Melchiot / RF / C / 6Y	
Assist: Izzet	

Half time 2-0

46 ○ ⇄ Taylor Martin > Melchiot	
46 ○ ⇄ Teale > Skoko	
47 ○ ▪ Heskey	
71 ○ ⇄ Connolly > McCulloch	
73 ○ ⇄ Kavanagh > Bullard	
74 ○ ⇄ Pandiani > Jarosik	
84 ○ ⇄ Kilkenny > Izzet	

Full time 2-0

Blues produced what was arguably their best performance of the season-to-date to run out comfortable winners against a high-flying Wigan side.

Blues started brightly and the home side's attacking dominance was rewarded on 20 minutes. Jiri Jarosik beat his marker on the left wing before delivering a pinpoint cross towards Jermaine Pennant who headed the ball back across visiting keeper Mike Pollitt into the far corner of the net to the delight and relief of the St. Andrew's crowd.

Blues were brimming with confidence and causing the Wigan defence all sorts of problems so it was no surprise when Steve Bruce's side doubled their advantage on 33 minutes.

Pennant curled in a corner which bounced around the visitors' box before Muzzy Izzet drilled in a low shot from the edge of the box. The midfielder's effort was deflected into the path of Mario Melchiot and the defender rifled the ball home.

Blues never looked like conceding in the second half and saw out the game to start 2006 with a well-deserved win.

Quote

🔵 **Eric Black**

It's a great start to the year and it was vital that we claimed all three points.

Premiership Milestone

▶ **First Goal**

Jermaine Pennant netted his first Premiership goal for Birmingham.

Venue:	St Andrew's	Referee:	P.Walton - 05/06		Birmingham City
Attendance:	29,189	Matches:	23		Wigan Athletic
Capacity:	30,016	Yellow Cards:	73		
Occupancy:	97%	Red Cards:	4		

Form Coming into Fixture

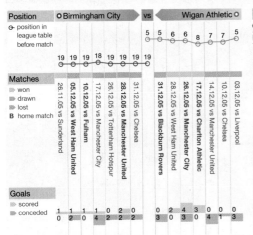

Position	O Birmingham City	vs	Wigan Athletic O

position in league table before match: 5 5 6 6 8 7 7 5

Birmingham City: 19 19 19 18 19 19 19 19

Matches
- won
- drawn
- lost
- B home match

05.11.05 vs Sunderland
05.11.05 vs West Ham United
10.12.05 vs Fulham
17.12.05 vs Manchester City
26.12.05 vs Tottenham Hotspur
28.12.05 vs Manchester United
31.12.05 vs Chelsea

31.12.05 vs Blackburn Rovers
26.12.05 vs West Ham United
17.12.05 vs Charlton Athletic
14.12.05 vs Manchester United
10.12.05 vs Chelsea
03.12.05 vs Liverpool

Goals
- scored
- conceded

| scored | 1 | 1 | 1 | 1 | 0 | 2 | 0 | | 0 | 2 | 4 | 3 | 0 | 0 | 0 |
| conceded | 0 | 2 | 0 | 4 | 2 | 2 | 2 | | 3 | 0 | 3 | 0 | 4 | 1 | 3 |

Goal Statistics

O Birmingham City

by Half | by Situation

- first: 2   set piece: 1
- second: 4   open play: 5

O Wigan Athletic

by Half | by Situation

- first: 6   set piece: 0
- second: 3   open play: 9

Goals by Area

O Birmingham City
Scored (Conceded)

2 (4)
3 (8)
1 (0)

O Wigan Athletic
Scored (Conceded)

1 (3)
8 (9)
0 (2)

Team Statistics

Starting Line-Ups

Birmingham City:
- Lazaridis
- Gray
- Upson
- Izzet / Kilkenny
- Heskey
- Taylor Maik
- Cunningham
- Jarosik / Pandiani
- Johnson
- Camara
- Melchiot
- Pennant
- Taylor Martin

Wigan Athletic:
- Bullard
- Chimbonda / Kavanagh
- Francis
- Henchoz
- Roberts
- Pollitt
- Skoko / Teale
- De Zeeuw
- McCulloch / Connolly
- Wright

4/4/1/1

Unused Sub: Vaesen, Butt

4/4/2

Unused Sub: Filan, Jackson

Premiership Totals

	O Birmingham	Wigan O
Premiership Appearances	1,901	645
Team Appearances	775	201
Goals Scored	157	50
Assists	185	38
Clean Sheets (goalkeepers)	36	3
Yellow Cards	187	81
Red Cards	13	2
Full Internationals	10	8

Age/Height

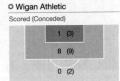

Birmingham City Age: **28 yrs, 5 mo**

Wigan Athletic Age: **29 yrs, 3 mo**

Birmingham City Height: **6'**

Wigan Athletic Height: **6'**

Match Statistics

League Table after Fixture

		Played	Won	Drawn	Lost	For	Against	Pts
● 5	Wigan	21	11	1	9	25	26	34
...		...	...	...	...	...	...	...
↑ 14	Fulham	21	6	5	10	25	30	23
↑ 15	Everton	21	7	2	12	14	31	23
↓ 16	Middlesbrough	20	5	7	8	25	30	22
● 17	West Brom	21	5	4	12	20	31	19
● 18	Portsmouth	21	4	5	12	16	33	17
● 19	Birmingham	20	4	4	12	15	29	16
● 20	Sunderland	20	1	3	16	15	38	6

Statistics

	O Birmingham	Wigan O
Goals	2	0
Shots on Target	4	2
Shots off Target	4	4
Hit Woodwork	0	0
Possession %	58	42
Corners	8	3
Offsides	3	2
Fouls	9	16
Disciplinary Points	4	8

5-0

Birmingham City ○
Portsmouth ○

➡ Mikael Forssell strokes home from the penalty spot

Event Line

5 ○ ⊕	Jarosik / H / OP / 6Y
	Assist: Melchiot
37 ○ ⊕	Pennant / LF / OP / IA
	Assist: Heskey
Half time 2-0	
53 ○ ⇄	Olisadebe > Pericard
55 ○ ⊕	Upson / H / C / IA
	Assist: Pennant
71 ○	Johnson
74 ○ ⇄	Dunn > Jarosik
76 ○	Griffin
78 ○ ⇄	Forssell > Heskey
81 ○ ⇄	Kilkenny > Cunningham
83 ○ ⇄	Priske > Stefanovic
90 ○ ⇄	Karadas > Pamarot
90 ○ ⊕	Dunn / RF / OP / IA
	Assist: Sutton
90 ○ ⊕	Forssell / RF / P / IA
	Assist: Forssell
Full time 5-0	

Blues put in a stunning attacking performance to totally demolish Portsmouth at St. Andrew's.

Goals from Jiri Jarosik, Jermaine Pennant, Matthew Upson, Mikael Forssell and David Dunn saw Blues record their biggest ever Premiership victory and at the same time leapfrog Harry Redknapp's side into 18th place in the table.

With just five minutes on the clock Jarosik sent St. Andrew's into raptures with a well-headed goal from Mario Melchiot's cross.

Benjamin Mwaruwari missed a great chance when he somehow blasted the ball over from just four yards out and he was made to pay just 60 seconds later as Pennant unleashed a low drive past Jamie Ashdown.

Matt Upson burst past his marker to meet Pennant's free-kick with a bullet header to make it 3-0 after the break.

With the game entering injury time Blues added a fourth when substitute Forssell successfully converted from the penalty spot. And the rout was completed when Sutton's back heel found Dunn and the midfielder fired the ball home.

Quote

🔴 **Steve Bruce**

There is no magic formula. We are playing better than a few weeks ago and that has coincided with the return of our better players.

Venue:	St Andrew's	Referee:	C.J.Foy - 05/06		Birmingham City
Attendance:	29,138	Matches:	22		Portsmouth
Capacity:	30,016	Yellow Cards:	51		
Occupancy:	97%	Red Cards:	6		

Form Coming into Fixture

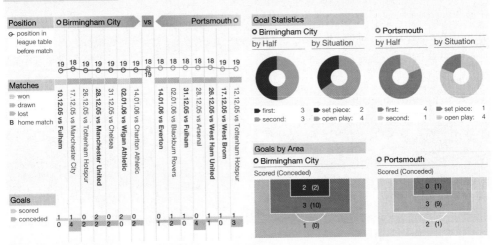

Position ○ Birmingham City vs Portsmouth ○

○ position in league table before match

Goal Statistics

○ Birmingham City — by Half / by Situation

- first: 3
- second: 3
- set piece: 2
- open play: 4

○ Portsmouth — by Half / by Situation

- first: 4
- second: 1
- set piece: 1
- open play: 4

Matches
- won
- drawn
- lost
- B home match

League positions: 19 18 19 19 19 19 19 18 18 18 18 18 19 19 / 19

Matches:
10.12.05 vs Fulham
17.12.05 vs Manchester City
26.12.05 vs Tottenham Hotspur
28.12.05 vs Manchester United
31.12.05 vs Chelsea
02.01.06 vs Wigan Athletic
14.01.06 vs Charlton Athletic
14.01.06 vs Everton
02.01.06 vs Blackburn Rovers
31.12.05 vs Fulham
28.12.05 vs Arsenal
26.12.05 vs West Ham United
17.12.05 vs West Brom
12.12.05 vs Tottenham Hotspur

Goals
- scored
- conceded

Goals scored/conceded:
| scored | 1 | 1 | 0 | 2 | 0 | 2 | 0 | | 0 | 1 | 1 | 0 | 1 | 1 | 1 |
| conceded | 0 | 4 | 2 | 2 | 2 | 0 | 2 | | 1 | 2 | 0 | 4 | 1 | 0 | 3 |

Goals by Area

○ Birmingham City — Scored (Conceded)
- 2 (2)
- 3 (10)
- 1 (0)

○ Portsmouth — Scored (Conceded)
- 0 (1)
- 3 (9)
- 2 (1)

Team Statistics

Starting Line-Ups

Birmingham City:
Taylor / Maik
Lazaridis, Jarosik / Dunn, O'Neil, Pamarot / Karadas
Upson, Izzet, Sutton, Mwaruwari, Mendes, O'Brien
Cunningham / Kilkenny, Johnson, Heskey / Forssell, Pericard / Olisadebe, Davis, Stefanovic / Priske
Melchiot, Pennant, Taylor, Griffin
Ashdown

4/4/2 **4/4/2**

Unused Sub: Vaesen, Gray   Unused Sub: Westerveld, Hughes

Premiership Totals

	○ Birmingham	Portsmouth ○
Premiership Appearances	2,186	813
Team Appearances	785	345
Goals Scored	270	37
Assists	266	33
Clean Sheets (goalkeepers)	37	5
Yellow Cards	244	104
Red Cards	15	6
Full Internationals	12	7

Age/Height

Birmingham City Age: **▶ 28 yrs, 7 mo**   Portsmouth Age: **▶ 26 yrs, 3 mo**

Birmingham City Height: **▶ 6'**   Portsmouth Height: **▶ 6'**

Match Statistics

League Table after Fixture

	Played	Won	Drawn	Lost	For	Against	Pts
↑ 11 Everton	23	9	2	12	16	31	29
↓ 12 Charlton	20	9	1	10	26	30	28
↓ 13 Fulham	22	7	5	10	26	30	26
↓ 14 Newcastle	22	7	5	10	20	25	26
● 15 Aston Villa	23	6	8	9	26	32	26
● 16 West Brom	23	6	4	13	21	32	22
↓ 17 Middlesbrough	22	5	7	10	27	40	22
↑ 18 Birmingham	22	5	4	13	20	31	19
↓ 19 Portsmouth	23	4	5	14	16	39	17

Statistics

	○ Birmingham	Portsmouth ○
Goals	5	0
Shots on Target	7	4
Shots off Target	3	6
Hit Woodwork	0	0
Possession %	53	47
Corners	7	2
Offsides	2	2
Fouls	11	23
Disciplinary Points	4	4

1-0

Birmingham City ○
Sunderland ○

Premiership
25.02.06

➡ Jiri Jarosik only has eyes for the ball

Event Line

25 ○ ⇄ Butt > Johnson	
39 ○ ⬛ Nosworthy	
39 ○ ⊕ Heskey / H / IFK / 6Y	
Assist: Pennant	

Half time 1-0

46 ○ ⇄ Delap > Lawrence	
46 ○ ⇄ Elliott > Murphy D	
46 ○ ⇄ Campbell > Sutton	
54 ○ ⬛ Whitehead	
68 ○ ⬛ Leadbitter	
75 ○ ⇄ Dunn > Izzet	
82 ○ ⇄ Woods > Breen	

Full time 1-0

Blues fought their way to a desperately-needed victory against the Premiership's basement side Sunderland despite a far from sparkling performance.

Emile Heskey headed home the only goal of the game just before the half time break on a bitterly cold afternoon at St. Andrew's.

Excellent interplay between Jiri Jarosik and Heskey ended with the Czech midfielder unleashing a rasping effort from 25 yards which curled just wide of Davis's right hand post.

Jarosik was then fouled on the left of the penalty area to set up a free-kick opportunity from which Blues scored the only goal.

Jermaine Pennant swung in the resultant dead ball to the far post and Heskey leapt above Danny Collins to head home from inside the six yard box.

David Dunn joined the action late on and went desperately close to scoring with two excellent long range efforts but ultimately it didn't matter as Blues held on for victory to move within three points of safety.

Quote

🔴 **Steve Bruce**

There was a lot of nervousness out there today, but sometimes you have to play the match and not the occasion.

Premiership Milestone

 50

Julian Gray made his 50th Premiership appearance.

Venue:	St Andrew's	Referee:	S.G.Bennett - 05/06	**Birmingham City**
Attendance:	29,257	Matches:	29	**Sunderland**
Capacity:	30,016	Yellow Cards:	98	
Occupancy:	97%	Red Cards:	9	

Form Coming into Fixture

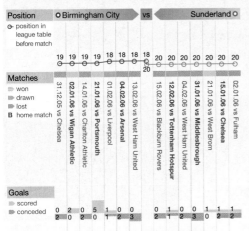

Position ○ Birmingham City vs Sunderland ○

↺ position in league table before match

Matches
- won
- drawn
- lost
- B home match

Goals
- scored
- conceded

Goal Statistics

○ Birmingham City

by Half | by Situation

- first: 4
- second: 4
- set piece: 3
- open play: 4
- own goals: 1

○ Sunderland

by Half | by Situation

- first: 2
- second: 2
- set piece: 0
- open play: 3
- own goals: 1

Goals by Area

○ Birmingham City
Scored (Conceded)

3 (4)
5 (6)
0 (0)

○ Sunderland
Scored (Conceded)

1 (3)
2 (6)
1 (3)

Team Statistics

Starting Line-Ups

Gray — Jarosik
Taylor Martin — Izzet Dunn — Sutton Campbell — Kyle
Latka — Johnson Butt — Heskey — Murphy D Elliott
Melchiot — Pennant
Taylor Maik

Lawrence Delap — Nosworthy
Whitehead — Breen Woods
Leadbitter — Collins D
Arca — Hoyte
Davis

▶ 4/4/2   **▶ 4/4/2**

Unused Sub: Vaesen, Forssell   Unused Sub: Murphy J, Caldwell

Premiership Totals

	○ Birmingham	Sunderland ○
Premiership Appearances	1,953	645
Team Appearances	534	287
Goals Scored	272	32
Assists	244	42
Clean Sheets (goalkeepers)	38	3
Yellow Cards	247	75
Red Cards	18	4
Full Internationals	9	5

Age/Height

Birmingham City Age **▶ 27 yrs, 11 mo**   Sunderland Age **▶ 24 yrs, 9 mo**

Birmingham City Height **▶ 6'1"**   Sunderland Height **▶ 5'11"**

Match Statistics

League Table after Fixture

	Played	Won	Drawn	Lost	For	Against	Pts
↓ 12 Everton	27	11	3	13	19	34	36
↓ 13 Charlton	27	10	5	12	32	37	35
• 14 Fulham	26	9	5	12	36	37	32
• 15 Aston Villa	27	7	10	10	32	35	31
• 16 Middlesbrough	25	7	7	11	33	44	28
• 17 West Brom	26	7	5	14	24	38	26
• 18 Birmingham	26	6	5	15	22	37	23
• 19 Portsmouth	27	4	6	17	18	47	18
• 20 Sunderland	27	2	4	21	18	49	10

Statistics

	○ Birmingham	Sunderland ○
Goals	1	0
Shots on Target	7	4
Shots off Target	7	4
Hit Woodwork	0	0
Possession %	52	48
Corners	6	2
Offsides	3	1
Fouls	13	14
Disciplinary Points	0	12

1-0

Birmingham City ○
Bolton Wanderers ○

▶ Maik Taylor celebrates an important three points

Event Line

8 ○ ⇄ Lazaridis > Clemence
30 ○ ⇄ Forssell > Butt
37 ○ ⊕ Jarosik / LF / OP / OA
　　　　Assist: Johnson
Half time 1-0
46 ○ ⇄ Hunt > O'Brien
68 ○ ⇄ Borgetti > Diouf
77 ○ 　Pennant
86 ○ ⇄ Vaz Te > Nolan
86 ○ ⇄ Dunn > Lazaridis
Full time 1-0

A wonder goal from Jiri Jarosik secured a fantastic victory for Blues in a nerve-tingling encounter against Bolton at St. Andrew's as Steve Bruce's side moved out of the relegation zone for the first time since mid-October.

Jarosik capped off a scintillating performance with a blistering shot on 37 minutes that sent a noisy home crowd into raptures. The big Czech showed fantastic skill to flick the ball past Jay Jay Okocha before unleashing a fabulous shot that swerved into the bottom corner. It was a goal of supreme quality and importance which understandably sparked scenes of unbridled joy amongst the home fans and also ensured that Jarosik would have a 'goal of the season' trophy as a memento of his season-long loan at St. Andrew's.

It was edge of the seat stuff at times in the second half as Blues hung on to their slender advantage.

But hang on to it they did to secure a vital three points that took Bruce's boys above relegation rivals West Brom and Portsmouth and into that elusive 17th spot.

Quote

● **Steve Bruce**

All credit to the players. I hope this win can give a bit of confidence to everybody.

Premiership Milestone

▶ **100**

Maik Taylor made his 100th Premiership appearance in the colours of Birmingham.

Venue:	St Andrew's	Referee:	C.J.Foy - 05/06	**Birmingham City**
Attendance:	26,493	Matches:	35	**Bolton Wanderers**
Capacity:	30,016	Yellow Cards:	82	
Occupancy:	88%	Red Cards:	9	

Form Coming into Fixture

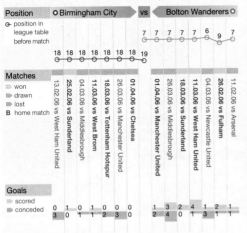

Position
- G- position in league table before match

Matches
- won
- drawn
- lost
- B home match

Goals
- scored
- conceded

0	1	0	1	0	0	0
3	0	1	1	2	3	0

1	3	2	4	1	2	1
2	4	0	1	3	1	1

Goal Statistics

Birmingham City

by Half / by Situation

- first: 1
- second: 1
- set piece: 2
- open play: 0

Bolton Wanderers

by Half / by Situation

- first: 7
- second: 7
- set piece: 5
- open play: 8
- own goals: 1

Goals by Area

Birmingham City

Scored (Conceded)

1 (4)
1 (5)
0 (1)

Bolton Wanderers

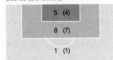

Scored (Conceded)

5 (4)
8 (7)
1 (1)

Team Statistics

Starting Line-Ups

Sadler, Jarosik, Diouf / Borgetti, O'Brien / Hunt, Clemence / Lazaridis, Okocha, Taylor Martin, Ben Haim, Taylor Maik, Butt / Forssell, Heskey, Davies, Diagne-Faye, Jaaskelainen, Cunningham, N'Gotty, Johnson, Nolan / Vaz Te, Tebily, Pennant, Giannakopoulos, Pedersen

▶ 4/5/1   **▶ 4/5/1**

Unused Sub: Vaesen, Campbell   Unused Sub: Walker, Nakata

Premiership Totals

	Birmingham	Bolton
Premiership Appearances	2,101	1,349
Team Appearances	879	1,166
Goals Scored	186	150
Assists	211	129
Clean Sheets (goalkeepers)	40	48
Yellow Cards	223	181
Red Cards	16	8
Full Internationals	10	10

Age/Height

Birmingham City Age	Bolton Wanderers Age
▶ 28 yrs, 6 mo	**▶ 27 yrs, 7 mo**
Birmingham City Height	Bolton Wanderers Height
▶ 6'	**▶ 6'**

Match Statistics

League Table after Fixture

		Played	Won	Drawn	Lost	For	Against	Pts
● 7	Bolton	31	13	9	9	43	35	48
...		...	...	...	...	...	...	...
● 14	Middlesbrough	31	11	7	13	44	52	40
● 15	Fulham	33	10	6	17	41	54	36
● 16	Aston Villa	32	8	11	13	34	46	35
↑ 17	Birmingham	32	7	7	18	24	44	28
↓ 18	West Brom	32	7	6	19	28	49	27
↓ 19	Portsmouth	31	7	6	18	27	52	27
● 20	Sunderland	32	2	5	25	21	57	11

Statistics

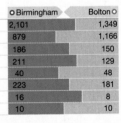

	Birmingham	Bolton
Goals	1	0
Shots on Target	2	1
Shots off Target	5	7
Hit Woodwork	0	0
Possession %	47	53
Corners	5	2
Offsides	1	1
Fouls	12	7
Disciplinary Points	4	0

2-1

Birmingham City ○
Blackburn Rovers ○

Premiership
19.04.06

► Chris Sutton is chopped down when in full flow

Event Line

29 ○ ▢	Cunningham
37 ○ ⇄	Melchiot > Pennant
Half time 0-0	
46 ⇄	Peter > Pedersen
56 ○ ▢	Tebily
62 ○ ⊕	Butt / LF / OP / 6Y
	Assist: Gray
67 ○ ⇄	Forssell > Heskey
71 ○ ⇄	Kuqi > Emerton
74 ○ ⇄	Mokoena > Todd
78 ○ ⊕	Savage / RF / OP / IA
	Assist: Peter
82 ○ ▢	Johnson
87 ○ ⊕	Forssell / LF / C / IA
	Assist: Gray
90 ○ ▢	Gray
90 ○ ▢	Sutton
Full time 2-1	

Blues kept their survival hopes alive thanks to victory over Blackburn Rovers on a night of high drama and driving rain at St. Andrew's.

Nicky Butt opened the scoring for Steve Bruce's side before Robbie Savage scored a somewhat fortuitous equaliser for the visitors.

But with just three minutes remaining, Mikael Forssell showed his scoring touch of old to lift Blues back out of the Premiership's bottom three on goal difference.

Butt broke the deadlock on 62 minutes when he stabbed the ball home from Julian Gray's cross.

But Blackburn equalised totally against the run of play when Maik Taylor palmed Sergio's Peter's shot into Savage's path and the former Blues midfielder directed the ball into the bottom corner.

But with the game seemingly slipping away, Forssell raised the rafters with an excellently-taken winner. Gray swung in a quality pass from the left and Forssell did well to dig the ball out from under his feet and rifle home from eight yards.

Quote

● **Steve Bruce**

The players were terrific and Mikael Forssell came off the bench to score a very important winning goal.

Premiership Milestone

► **25**

Both Nicky Butt and Mikael Forssell netted their 25th Premiership goals.

Venue:	St Andrew's		Referee:	U.D.Rennie - 05/06		**Birmingham City**
Attendance:	25,287		Matches:	40		**Blackburn Rovers**
Capacity:	30,016		Yellow Cards:	83		
Occupancy:	84%		Red Cards:	4		

Form Coming into Fixture

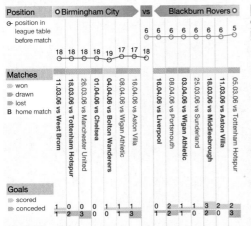

Goal Statistics

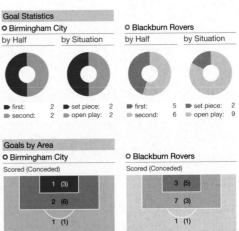

Birmingham City

by Half — by Situation

- first: 2
- second: 2
- set piece: 2
- open play: 2

Blackburn Rovers

by Half — by Situation

- first: 5
- second: 6
- set piece: 2
- open play: 9

Goals by Area

Birmingham City — Scored (Conceded)

| 1 (3) |
| 2 (6) |
| 1 (1) |

Blackburn Rovers — Scored (Conceded)

| 3 (5) |
| 7 (3) |
| 1 (1) |

Team Statistics

Starting Line-Ups

4/4/2

Unused Sub: Vaesen, Bruce, Kilkenny

4/4/1/1

Unused Sub: Enckelman, Dickov

Premiership Totals	Birmingham	Blackburn
Premiership Appearances	2,119	1,378
Team Appearances	774	873
Goals Scored	239	113
Assists	212	112
Clean Sheets (goalkeepers)	41	64
Yellow Cards	239	211
Red Cards	18	10
Full Internationals	9	11

Age/Height

Birmingham City Age: **28 yrs, 7 mo**

Blackburn Rovers Age: **27 yrs, 1 mo**

Birmingham City Height: **6'**

Blackburn Rovers Height: **6'**

Match Statistics

League Table after Fixture

		Played	Won	Drawn	Lost	For	Against	Pts
●	6 Blackburn	35	16	6	13	46	42	54
...		...	...	...	...	...	...	...
●	14 Man City	34	12	4	18	40	41	40
●	15 Aston Villa	35	9	12	14	39	50	39
●	16 Fulham	34	11	6	17	43	55	39
↑	17 Birmingham	35	8	8	19	28	49	32
↓	18 Portsmouth	35	8	8	19	32	57	32
●	19 West Brom	35	7	8	20	29	52	29
●	20 Sunderland	34	2	6	26	22	61	12

Statistics	Birmingham	Blackburn
Goals	2	1
Shots on Target	6	6
Shots off Target	6	5
Hit Woodwork	0	1
Possession %	53	47
Corners	9	11
Offsides	3	1
Fouls	15	12
Disciplinary Points	20	0

Premiership Results Table 2005/06

Legend

Won	Yellow Card	45 Time of Goal
Drawn	Red Card	45 Time of Assist
Lost	Goal	

Match: | Players: | Substitutes:

Date	H/A	Opp.	H/T	F/T	Pos	P1	P2	P3	P4	P5	P6	P7	P8	P9	P10	P11	Sub 1st	Sub 2nd	Sub 3rd
13-08	A	Fulham	0-0	0-0	07	Taylor Maik	Melchiot	Cunningham	Upson⁶⁸	Clapham	Pennant	Butt	Clemence⁸⁷	Gray	Heskey	Pandiani	Forssell	Morrison 71	87
20-08	H	Man City	1-1	1-1	13	Taylor Maik	Melchiot	Cunningham	Upson	Clapham	Pennant	Butt	Clemence⁵⁴	Gray	Pandiani	Forssell	Izzet	Lazaridis 65	77
23-08	H	Middlesbrough	0-2	0-3	13	Taylor Maik	Melchiot	Cunningham	Upson	Lazaridis	Pennant	Butt	Tebily	Clemence	Pandiani	Forssell	Forssell	Jarosik 46	Gray
27-08	A	West Brom	3-1	3-2	13	Taylor Maik	Melchiot	Cunningham	Upson⁸²	Clapham	Pennant	Butt	Jarosik⁶⁸¹	Johnson	Forssell	Pandiani	Pandiani	Izzet 63	Clemence
10-09	H	Charlton	1-1	1-1	16	Taylor Maik	Melchiot	Cunningham	Upson	Clapham	Pennant	Butt	Jarosik	Johnson	Forssell	Pandiani	Pandiani	Gray 10	Izzet 46
17-09	A	Portsmouth	1-1	1-1	15	Taylor Maik	Tebily	Cunningham⁸⁷	Upson	Gray	Pennant	Butt⁴⁵	Jarosik⁰⁶	Johnson	Heskey⁰⁶	Izzet⁴²	Izzet 42	Clapham	Pandiani
24-09	H	Liverpool	0-0	2-2	14	Taylor Maik	Tebily	Cunningham⁸⁷	Upson	Clapham	Pennant	Johnson	Kilkenny⁷⁸⁴	Gray²	Heskey⁰⁶	Pandiani⁷⁵	Pandiani 75	Tebily	90
02-10	A	Arsenal	0-0	0-1	15	Taylor Maik	Tebily	Cunningham²⁴	Upson	Clapham	Pennant	Johnson	Clemence⁷⁸	Gray	Heskey	Pandiani	Lazaridis	Forssell 55	87
16-10	H	Aston Villa	0-1	0-1	15	Taylor Maik	Tebily	Taylor Martin	Upson	Clapham	Pennant	Johnson⁸⁷	Johnson	Gray	Heskey	Pandiani	Jarosik 39	Forssell⁸⁴	Dunn
22-10	A	Blackburn	0-2	1-2	17	Taylor Maik	Tebily	Cunningham⁴⁸	Upson	Lazaridis	Pennant⁶⁹	Johnson	Butt	Clapham	Heskey⁰³	Forssell	Jarosik	Forssell 70	Dunn 67
29-10	H	Everton	0-1	0-1	19	Taylor Maik	Cunningham	Taylor Martin	Upson	Clapham	Pennant	Jarosik	Butt	Johnson	Heskey	Forssell	Kilkenny	Pandiani 34	75
05-11	A	Newcastle	0-0	0-1	19	Taylor Maik	Cunningham	Taylor Martin	Upson	Clapham	Pennant	Kilkenny	Jarosik	Izzet⁴¹	Heskey⁴²	Lazaridis⁴²	Pandiani	Forssell 86	73
26-11	H	Sunderland	1-0	1-0	19	Melchiot	Taylor Martin	Cunningham	Upson	Painter	Johnson	Johnson	Jarosik	Clemence	Izzet⁴¹	Heskey 190	Pandiani⁶⁸	Pennant 46	Gray⁸ 59
05-12	H	West Ham	1-2	1-2	19	Vaesen	Melchiot	Taylor Martin	Cunningham	Upson	Johnson	Johnson	Clemence⁶⁵	Izzet	Dunn¹¹	Heskey	Lazaridis	Jarosik 08	Gray⁸ 23
10-12	A	Fulham	0-0	0-0	18	Vaesen⁹⁰	Tebily	Cunningham	Upson	Painter	Johnson	Pennant	Clemence	Lazaridis	Dunn⁻	Pennant⁸⁴	Pennant	Jarosik 53	Clapham 69
17-12	A	Man City	0-3	1-4	19	Vaesen⁹⁰	Cunningham	Taylor Martin	Cunningham	Painter	Johnson	Butt	Clemence⁶⁵	Clapham	Pandiani⁻	Heskey	Forssell	Pennant⁷⁶ 23	Gray⁸ 35
26-12	H	Tottenham	1-2	2-2	19	Tebily⁻	Cunningham	Taylor Martin	Lazaridis	Pennant⁻	Kilkenny	Butt⁴⁴	Izzet⁶⁵	Gray	Dunn	Heskey⁸	Dunn	Pandiani 72	Painter 83
28-12	A	Man Utd	2-2	2-3	19	Cunningham	Cunningham	Taylor Martin	Clapham⁸	Pennant⁷⁸	Johnson⁷⁸	Clemence⁻	Butt	Pennant	Kilkenny	Heskey⁷⁸	Kilkenny	Painter 69	Birley 60
31-12	A	Chelsea	0-2	0-2	19	Melchiot	Cunningham	Taylor Martin	Gray	Pennant	Butt	Johnson	Pandiani	Clemence⁻	Pandiani	Heskey⁴⁷	Tebily	Kilkenny 12	65
02-01	H	Wigan	2-0	2-0	19	Melchiot⁶³	Cunningham	Cunningham⁻	Lazaridis	Pennant⁰	Johnson	Izzet⁶³	Johnson	Gray	Jarosik²⁰	Heskey⁴⁷	Taylor Martin⁴⁶	Pandiani 74	Kilkenny
14-01	A	Charlton	2-0	5-0	19	Melchiot⁰⁵	Tebily	Cunningham⁻	Upson⁶⁵	Pennant⁷⁵⁵	Pennant	Izzet	Johnson	Jarosik⁻	Heskey	Sutton	Dunn	Pandiani 76	76
21-01	H	Portsmouth	2-0	5-0	18	Melchiot	Cunningham	Latka	Upson	Pennant	Johnson⁷¹	Izzet	Jarosik⁰⁶	Heskey³⁷	Sutton⁰⁰	Dunn³⁰	Forssell⁹⁹⁰	Forssell⁹⁹⁰ 78	Kilkenny 81
01-02	A	Liverpool	0-1	1-1	18	Melchiot	Cunningham	Latka	Upson	Pennant	Johnson²⁸	Kilkenny	Johnson³⁰	Sutton	Heskey⁸⁸	Lazaridis⁻	Lazaridis 34	Tebily	Bruce 90
04-02	A	Arsenal	0-1	0-2	18	Melchiot	Cunningham	Latka	Gray	Pennant	Butt	Izzet⁻	Jarosik⁻	Jarosik⁻	Heskey⁸³	Forssell	Forssell 69	Campbell 70	Bruce 88
13-02	H	West Ham	0-3	0-3	18	Melchiot	Cunningham	Latka⁸²⁻	Gray	Pennant	Bruce⁴⁵	Clemence	Jarosik	Jarosik⁻	Sutton⁻	Painter 67	Campbell 67	Clapham 71
25-02	A	Sunderland	1-0	1-0	18	Melchiot	Cunningham⁻	Latka²⁵	Gray	Pennant⁸⁹	Johnson⁻	Jarosik	Jarosik	Johnson³⁰	Butt	Heskey³⁹	Sutton⁻ 25	Butt 46	Dunn 75
04-03	A	Middlesbrough	0-0	0-0	18	Melchiot⁻	Bruce	Taylor Martin	Gray	Pennant⁻	Kilkenny⁻	Butt	Johnson⁻	Butt	Dunn⁻	Campbell⁻	Campbell 56	Jarosik 56	Forssell 78
11-03	H	West Brom	0-1	1-1	18	Melchiot²⁶	Cunningham	Latka	Clapham	Pennant⁻	Butt⁸⁸	Johnson	Dunn⁻	Johnson⁴⁹⁴⁹	Forssell⁴⁹⁴⁹	Izzet⁶⁷	Izzet⁶⁷ 56	Campbell 77	Kilkenny 80
18-03	H	Tottenham	0-1	1-2	18	Tebily⁵⁷	Taylor Martin	Cunningham⁸¹	Pennant	Izzet⁻	Butt⁸¹	Johnson	Heskey⁻	Campbell	Forssell 08	Kilkenny 81
26-03	A	Man Utd	1-3	1-3	18	Tebily⁸⁶	Cunningham²⁹	Taylor Martin	Pennant⁴⁵	Johnson³⁰	Johnson	Clemence	Campbell	Tebily	Kilkenny 82	Lazaridis 79
01-04	H	Chelsea	0-0	0-0	18	Melchiot⁵⁶	Cunningham²⁹	Taylor Martin	Sadler	Pennant⁻	Johnson⁸²	Butt⁻	Clemence⁻	Campbell⁻	Forssell 57	Kilkenny 88
04-04	H	Bolton	1-0	1-0	17	Tebily	Cunningham	Taylor Martin	Sadler	Pennant⁷⁷	Johnson³⁷	Johnson	Butt⁻	Clemence⁶⁷	Lazaridis⁻ 08	Forssell 77	Dunn 86
08-04	A	Wigan	1-1	1-1	17	Tebily⁸⁶	Cunningham	Taylor Martin	Sadler	Pennant⁶⁰	Izzet*	Jarosik	Sutton⁻	Johnson	Forssell 08	Kilkenny 81	Dunn 65
16-04	H	Aston Villa	1-1	1-3	17	Tebily⁸⁶	Cunningham⁻	Taylor Martin	Sadler	Pennant	Johnson⁸⁴	Butt⁸⁰	Dunn⁻	Sutton⁰⁵	Forssell 17	Lazaridis 79
19-04	A	Blackburn	0-1	1-2	17	Tebily⁶⁶	Melchiot	Taylor Martin²⁹	Sadler	Pennant⁻	Johnson⁸²	Butt⁸²	Sutton⁰⁰	Gray⁶²⁸⁷⁹⁰	Melchiot⁻	Forssell⁸⁷ 37	Campbell 68	Bruce 87
22-04	H	Everton	0-0	0-0	18	Melchiot⁸³	Cunningham⁷⁰	Sadler⁹⁰	Pennant⁻	Johnson	Johnson⁷⁵	Butt⁸²	Gray	Forssell 68	Campbell 68
29-04	A	Newcastle	0-0	0-0	18	Melchiot⁷⁴	Cunningham	Sadler	Pennant⁻	Johnson⁷⁵	Johnson	Forssell	Campbell	Clemence 72	Campbell 87
07-05	A	Bolton	0-1	0-1	18	Melchiot	Bruce	Taylor Martin⁷²	Pennant	Butt	Naffti*	Johnson	Campbell	Heskey	Kilkenny 71

Premiership Results Table 2004/05

Match: | Players: | Substitutes:

Date	H/A	Opponent	H/T	F/T	Pos	First String											Subs 1st	2nd	3rd
14-08	H	Portsmouth	1-1	1-1	05	Taylor Maik	Melchiot	Cunningham	Taylor Martin25	Lazaridis80	Gronkjaer	Savage 1018	Izzet70	Johnson10	Forssell	Heskey	Gray 67	Morrison 90	–
21-08	H	Chelsea	0-0	0-1	19	Taylor Maik	Melchiot	Cunningham	Upson	Lazaridis	Gronkjaer	Savage	Izzet	Johnson	Gray	Heskey	John 76	–	–
24-08	A	Man City	1-0	1-0	07	Taylor Maik	Melchiot	Cunningham	Lazaridis108	Gronkjaer	Izzet69	Johnson	Gray	Forssell↔	Heskey09↔		Clemence 54	Tebily 59	–
28-08	A	Tottenham	0-1	0-1	13	Taylor Maik	Melchiot	Cunningham	Upson	Gray	Izzet69	Clemence↔	Heskey85	Johnson	Morrison		Morrison 72	John 79	–
11-09	A	Middlesbrough	1-1	1-2	14	Taylor Maik	Melchiot	Cunningham	Upson	Gray	Gronkjaer	Izzet77	Yorke79	Heskey14290	Morrison↔		John 75	–	–
18-09	H	Charlton	0-0	1-1	14	Taylor Maik	Melchiot	Cunningham	Upson	Gray	Johnson57	Izzet68	Savage84	Gronkjaer85	Heskey↔		Yorke 68	–	–
25-09	A	Bolton	0-1	1-1	15	Taylor Maik	Melchiot	Cunningham	Upson	Clapham	Johnson	Izzet49↔	Savage27	Dunn↔	Morrison↔		Gray 77	–	–
03-10	H	Newcastle	1-1	2-2	15	Taylor Maik	Melchiot	Cunningham	Upson57	Johnson	Savage5790	Izzet↔	Gronkjaer	Dunn2353↔	Heskey↔		Clemence69 36	Gray 88	–
16-10	A	Man Utd	0-0	0-0	14	Taylor Maik	Melchiot	Cunningham	Johnson	Savage6749↔	Gronkjaer	Dunn	Yorke↔	Heskey↔			Dunn 77	Gray 88	–
24-10	H	Southampton	0-0	0-0	14	Taylor Maik	Melchiot	Cunningham	Johnson→71	Savage951	Dunn→	Gronkjaer	Heskey↔				Yorke 46	Tebily 90	Clapham 90
30-10	A	Crystal Palace	0-0	0-0	16	Taylor Maik	Melchiot	Cunningham	Lazaridis→	Gronkjaer	Johnson→	Dunn→	Yorke→				Anderton 60	Clapham 82	Clemence 85
06-11	H	Liverpool	0-0	1-0	14	Taylor Maik	Melchiot	Cunningham	Upson74	Gray	Johnson22	Savage	Clemence↔	Dunn→	Heskey		Lazaridis 63	Clapham 88	–
13-11	H	Everton	0-0	0-1	15	Taylor Maik	Melchiot	Cunningham	Upson77	Gray	Johnson	Savage	Izzet68	Yorke→	Heskey		Yorke 61	Anderton 73	Clapham 81
21-11	A	Blackburn	3-1	3-3	14	Taylor Maik	Melchiot	Cunningham	Upson60	Lazaridis→	Johnson→	Savage38	Anderton 17↔	Gronkjaer	Heskey		Anderton77 60	Clemence 74	Clapham 80
27-11	H	Norwich	1-0	1-0	13	Taylor Maik	Melchiot	Cunningham	Upson	Clapham	Johnson22	Savage	Anderton	Gronkjaer	Dunn88↔	Heskey09	Yorke 76	Clemence 82	–
04-12	A	Arsenal	0-1	0-3	15	Taylor Maik	Melchiot33↔45	Cunningham	Upson60	Clapham	Savage	Anderton	Dunn 1345↔	Gray	Heskey09		Taylor Martin81 67	Clapham 90	–
12-12	H	Aston Villa	2-0	2-1	14	Taylor Maik	Melchiot↔	Cunningham	Clapham	Savage	Anderton→	Carter77	Dunn30	Heskey↔			Morrison 57	Anderton 83	Clapham 87
18-12	A	West Brom	3-0	4-0	12	Taylor Maik	Tebily66	Cunningham	Lazaridis↔	Savage04↔	Carter23	Dunn	Gray45	Heskey1042↔			Gray 50	Clapham 54	Melchiot 60
26-12	A	Middlesbrough	2-0	2-0	12	Taylor Maik	Tebily	Cunningham	Lazaridis	Savage45	Carter	Dunn42↔	Heskey2541↔				Clemence 75	Anderton 82	Yorke 84
28-12	H	Fulham	2-1	3-2	09	Taylor Maik	Melchiot	Cunningham	Tebily	Savage35↔	Carter41	Clapham	Dunn	Heskey1044↔			Gray 79	Clemence 82	Anderton 86
01-01	H	Newcastle	0-2	1-2	12	Taylor Maik	Melchiot	Cunningham↔	Tebily↔	Savage935	Carter↔	Lazaridis	Dunn	Heskey4264			Morrison25↔ 75	Yorke 80	Clapham 84
04-01	A	Bolton	0-1	1-3	14	Taylor Maik	Melchiot	Cunningham↔	Upson35	Clemence↔	Carter↔	Lazaridis	Morrison64	Heskey39			Gray 64	Yorke 73	Clapham 77
15-01	H	Charlton	0-1	1-2	15	Taylor Maik	Melchiot	Cunningham	Tebily	Johnson60	Clemence↔	Anderton	Lazaridis	Morrison66↔	Heskey→		Gray 70	Yorke 77	Blake 77
22-01	H	Fulham	0-0	0-0	14	Taylor Maik	Melchiot55	Cunningham	Taylor Martin↔	Johnson82↔	Carter	Anderton55↔	Morrison→	Heskey51			Anderton 69	Blake 77	Yorke 86
02-02	A	Southampton	2-0	2-1	14	Taylor Maik	Melchiot	Cunningham	Diao	Johnson	Carter	Gray	Blake 41↔	Morrison→			Tebily 76	Morrison 90	Carter 90
05-02	A	Liverpool	0-1	0-1	14	Taylor Maik	Melchiot41	Cunningham	Pennant 12↔	Johnson↔	Carter	Gray	Pandiani 12↔	Morrison→			Carter 72	Morrison 81	Tebily 90
12-02	H	Man City	2-0	2-0	12	Taylor Maik	Taylor Martin→	Cunningham	Pennant90	Johnson45	Nafti65↔	Gray45	Pandiani	Heskey3871			Carter 72	Morrison 84	Blake 89
26-02	A	Crystal Palace	0-1	0-2	12	Taylor Maik	Melchiot↔	Cunningham	Pennant45↔	Johnson	Clemence	Gray	Blake→	Pandiani39↔			Natti 18	Blake 84	–
06-03	A	West Brom	0-0	0-0	13	Taylor Maik	Tebily→	Cunningham	Pennant27	Johnson	Clemence	Gray	Pandiani32	Morrison60→			Anderton 63	Blake 68	–
20-03	H	Aston Villa	2-0	2-0	13	Taylor Maik	Melchiot30	Cunningham	Diao28↔	Johnson	Clemence	Gray	Pandiani52↔	Blake			Anderton 73	Yorke 68	Blake 66
02-04	H	Tottenham	0-0	1-1	13	Taylor Maik	Cunningham	Johnson41	Clemence↔	Gray	Pandiani66↔	Natti	Blake				Natti 37	Morrison 80	–
09-04	A	Chelsea	0-0	0-1	13	Taylor Maik	Cunningham	Pennant21	Johnson↔	Carter 66	Lazaridis↔	Pandiani52↔	Heskey				Natti 76	Morrison 88	–
16-04	H	Portsmouth	0-0	0-0	13	Taylor Maik	Cunningham↔	Pennant	Johnson	Carter↔	Lazaridis	Pandiani66↔	Heskey				Gray89 56	Morrison 67	Natti 71
20-04	A	Man City	0-0	0-0	13	Taylor Maik	Cunningham	Pennant	Johnson	Nafti70↔	Lazaridis↔	Heskey					Gray 67	Morrison 80	Natti 88
23-04	A	Everton	1-0	1-1	13	Taylor Maik	Cunningham	Pennant↔	Anderton↔	Carter	Pandiani85	Heskey					Lazaridis 66	Pandiani 76	Carter 76
30-04	A	Blackburn	0-1	2-1	12	Taylor Maik	Cunningham32	Pennant05↔	Anderton↔	Carter	Heskey05						Blake 68	Clemence81 79	Morrison88 89
07-05	A	Norwich	1-0	1-1	12	Taylor Maik	Cunningham45↔	Pennant	Johnson	Pandiani↔	Heskey7680						Blake 46	Morrison90 84	Taylor Martin 89
15-05	H	Arsenal	0-0	0-0	12	Taylor Maik	Cunningham	Pennant	Natti	Clemence	Carter↔	Pandiani 808190↔	Morrison				Clemence71 19	Blake 46	Taylor Martin 90

99

Premiership Results Table 2003/04

Legend:

Won	Yellow Card	45 Time of 1st Sub — 45 Time of Goal
Drawn	Red Card	45 Time of 2nd Sub — 45 Time of Assist
Lost	Goal	45 Time of 3rd Sub

Match: | Players: | Substitutes:

Date	H/A	Opponent	H/T	F/T	Pos	First String											→1st	→2nd	→3rd
16-08	H	Tottenham	1-0	1-0	06	Taylor Maik	Kenna	Cunningham	Purse	Clapham	Johnson→	Savage25/36	Clemence31	Dunn3/38	Horsfield→	Dugarry→	John 69	Devlin 80	Tebily 72 · 90
23-08	A	Southampton	0-0	0-0	06	Taylor Maik	Kenna	Cunningham	Upson	Clapham	Johnson→	Savage78	Clemence	Dunn	Horsfield→	John→	Lazaridis 59	Morrison 80	Devlin · 88
30-08	A	Newcastle	0-0	1-0	06	Taylor Maik	Kenna84	Cunningham	Upson	Clapham	Johnson61	Savage	Clemence→	Lazaridis→	Dunn61←	John→	Horsfield 71	Cisse 79	Tebily · 88
14-09	H	Fulham	1-1	2-2	08	Taylor Maik	Kenna→	Purse82	Upson82	Clapham	Johnson11/45	Savage	Clemence→	Dunn	Forssell45/82	John→	Tebily 46	Lazaridis 64	Morrison · 70
20-09	A	Leeds	0-0	2-0	07	Taylor Maik	Johnson	Cunningham	Upson	Clapham	Dunn84←	Savage45/79	Clemence	Lazaridis	Forssell79/8←	Dugarry70←	Cisse 85	Tebily 88	Morrison · 90
27-09	H	Portsmouth	1-0	2-0	04	Taylor Maik	Johnson	Cunningham	Upson	Clapham	Dunn	Savage	Clemence2/50	Lazaridis2/50	Forssell→	Dugarry→	Cisse74 71	Tebily 84	Figueroa · 87
04-10	A	Man Utd	0-1	0-3	05	Taylor Maik34	Johnson	Cunningham	Upson	Clapham	Johnson→	Cisse35	Clemence→	Lazaridis→	Forssell→	Dugarry→	Bennett 35	Carter 66	Tebily · 79
14-10	H	Chelsea	0-0	0-0	04	Taylor Maik	Tebily	Cunningham	Upson	Clapham	Johnson→	Cisse83	Clemence36	Lazaridis→	Dunn	Dugarry56←	Hughes 78	John · 85	—
19-10	H	Aston Villa	0-0	0-0	04	Bennett	Forssell	Cunningham	Upson	Clapham	Dunn34	Savage45	Clemence36	Lazaridis→	Dunn	Dugarry→	Morrison 76	Cisse 76	Tebily · 78
25-10	H	Bolton	0-1	1-2	04	Taylor Maik	Tebily44←	Cunningham	Upson	Clapham	Dunn→	Cisse→	Clemence	Lazaridis64←	Forssell31	Dugarry→/84	Kenna 58	Hughes 77	Morrison · 88
03-11	H	Charlton	0-1	1-2	04	Taylor Maik	Tebily→	Cunningham	Upson	Clapham	Hughes→	Savage	Clemence	Lazaridis64←	Forssell	Dugarry/84/83	Kenna 55	Morrison 77	John · 89
08-11	A	Wolverhampton	0-0	1-1	05	Taylor Maik	Johnson	Cunningham	Upson	Clapham	Clemence	Savage	Dunn	Lazaridis→	Forssell49	Dugarry/83	Lazaridis 80	John · 88	—
22-11	H	Arsenal	0-1	0-3	05	Taylor Maik	Johnson26	Cunningham	Upson→	Clapham	Clemence	Savage	Cisse9←	Lazaridis→	Dunn	Forssell→	John 64	Hughes 85	Morrison · 87
30-11	L	Liverpool	1-1	1-3	08	Bennett	Tebily	Cunningham	Upson→	Clapham	Dunn	Savage33	Clemence→	Lazaridis	Forssell33	Dugarry→	Tebily 73	Kirovski 80	Morrison · 80
06-12	H	Blackburn	0-0	0-4	08	Taylor Maik	Kenna→	Cunningham→	Tebily	Clapham	Johnson	Savage→	Dunn	Lazaridis	Forssell	Dugarry72	Morrison 73	Cisse 79	Clemence · 83
13-12	A	Leicester	1-0	2-0	08	Taylor Maik	Kenna81	Cunningham	Upson68	Clapham42	Johnson32	Savage66←	Clemence44←	Dunn	Forssell66←	Morrison42	Lazaridis 66	Cisse 72	John · 83
26-12	H	Man City	0-1	2-1	08	Taylor Maik	Kenna	Cunningham	Upson	Lazaridis	Johnson	Savage11/81	Clemence→	Hughes→	Forssell87	Morrison→	Kirovski 61	John 61	Cisse · 89
28-12	A	Everton	0-3	1-4	10	Taylor Maik	Kenna	Cunningham	Upson	Carter	Johnson	Savage68	Clemence→	Dunn68	Forssell	John→	Morrison 54	Cisse 67	Kirovski · 78
07-01	A	Tottenham	0-3	1-4	10	Taylor Maik	Tebily	Cunningham	Purse	Carter	Johnson	Hughes16	Clemence16	Dunn→	Morrison	Morrison67←	Tebily 46	John 80	Kirovski · 83
10-01	H	Southampton	1-1	2-1	08	Taylor Maik	Tebily71	Cunningham	Purse	Kenna67	Johnson	Savage46	Clemence	Dunn→	Morrison67←	Morrison→	Kirovski 90	Carter · 90	—
18-01	A	Chelsea	0-0	0-0	09	Taylor Maik	Tebily→	Cunningham	Purse	Kenna	Johnson→	Savage81	Clemence	Hughes→	John→	Morrison→	Lazaridis 66	Kirovski 81	Carter · 89
31-01	H	Newcastle	0-0	1-1	09	Taylor Maik	Tebily39	Cunningham90	Purse	Kenna→	Johnson→	Savage	Clemence	Hughes	Forssell→	Morrison	John90 76	—	—
08-02	A	Man City	0-0	0-0	10	Taylor Maik	Tebily63	Cunningham	Purse	Kenna→	Johnson→	Savage	Hughes	Lazaridis	Forssell49←	John→	Dugarry 63	Clapham 70	Morrison · 79
11-02	H	Everton	2-0	3-0	09	Taylor Maik	Tebily	Cunningham	Purse	Kenna→	Johnson35	Savage4←	Hughes	Lazaridis39←	Forssell60	Morrison	Dugarry 63	John 76	Taylor Martin · 80
22-02	A	Aston Villa	2-0	2-2	08	Taylor Maik	Tebily	Cunningham	Purse	Kenna→	Johnson79	Savage19/57	Clemence57	Hughes	Forssell23/80←	Dugarry→	Morrison60/96/85	Dunn 55	John90 · 83
03-03	H	Middlesbrough	1-0	3-1	07	Bennett	Tebily	Cunningham	Taylor Martin 23	Upson	Johnson79	Savage19/57	Clemence→	Hughes	Forssell23/80←	Morrison86←	John 83	Carter 88	Kenna · 90
06-03	A	Bolton	1-0	2-0	05	Taylor Maik	Tebily	Cunningham	Taylor Martin	Upson	Johnson69←	Savage84	Clemence→	Hughes69	Forssell24←	Morrison24	John 76	Carter 86	Kenna · 88
13-03	H	Leicester	0-0	0-1	06	Taylor Maik	Tebily	Cunningham55←	Taylor Martin	Lazaridis→	Hughes	Savage	Clemence→	Lazaridis	Forssell	Morrison	John 68	Barrowman 87	—
20-03	H	Middlesbrough	2-4	3-5	07	Taylor Martin	Tebily	Cunningham59	Upson	Grainger59	Johnson→	Hughes	Clemence	Lazaridis23	Forssell23/4559	Morrison45	John 46	—	—
27-03	L	Leeds	1-1	4-1	06	Taylor Martin	Tebily	Cunningham69	Upson	Grainger→	Johnson	Hughes 12/67	Clemence	Lazaridis23	Forssell69/83←	Morrison83←	Clemence 39	Tebily 84	—
03-04	A	Fulham	0-0	0-0	06	Taylor Martin	Tebily	Cunningham	Upson77	Grainger→	Johnson	Savage50	Clemence	Lazaridis	Forssell→	Morrison	Clemence 39	Clapham 69	Grainger39 · 14
10-04	H	Man Utd	1-0	1-2	06	Taylor Martin	Tebily→	Cunningham46←	Upson	Lazaridis→	Johnson	Savage39	Hughes	Clapham	Forssell→	Morrison	Bennett 45	Clapham 46	John · 78
12-04	A	Portsmouth	0-0	1-1	08	Taylor Maik45	Tebily→	Cunningham46←	Upson	Upson	Johnson67	Savage→	Hughes	Clapham	Forssell→	John67	Clemence65 58	Clemence · 58	Morrison · 78
17-04	A	Charlton	0-0	1-1	09	Taylor Martin	Tebily	Cunningham	Upson84	Clapham	Johnson	Savage→	Clemence	Hughes	Forssell→	Morrison84←	Morrison 84	Kenna 90	—
25-04	H	Wolverhampton	2-1	2-2	09	Taylor Martin→	Tebily	Cunningham55←	Lazaridis→	Clapham	Johnson	Savage28	Clemence→	Lazaridis→	Forssell3441	Morrison3441	Morrison 34/41	Barrowman 87	—
01-05	H	Arsenal	0-0	0-0	09	Bennett	Tebily	Cunningham	Upson	Clapham	Johnson16	Savage49	Clemence→	Lazaridis→	Forssell→	Morrison	Hughes 61	Hughes 72	John · 76
08-05	L	Liverpool	0-1	1-3	10	Bennett	Tebily	Cunningham64←	Upson	Clapham	Johnson55	Savage	Clemence→	Lazaridis	Dunn→	Morrison	John 59	Cisse68 · 59	John · 83
15-05	A	Blackburn	0-1	1-1	10	Taylor Maik	Tebily→	Taylor Martin	Upson	Clapham	Johnson83	Savage	Clemence→	Lazaridis	Forssell	Morrison	Hughes 57	Cisse68 · 83	John · 60

Premiership Results Table 2002/03

Legend:
- Won
- Drawn
- Lost
- Yellow Card
- Red Card
- Goal
- 45 — Time of 1st Sub
- 45 — Time of 2nd Sub
- 45 — Time of 3rd Sub
- 45 — Time of Goal
- 45 — Time of Assist

Match: | Players: | Substitutes:

Date	H/A	Opponent	H/T	F/T	Pos	First String											←1st	←2nd	←3rd
18-08	A	Arsenal	0-2	0-2	18	Vaesen	Kenna	Cunningham	Purse24	Tebily→	Johnson	Hughes	Cisse74	Johnson	Horsfield→	John	Carter 60	Lazaridis 71	
24-08	H	Blackburn	0-1	0-1	19	Vaesen	Tebily	Cunningham	Purse37	Grainger→	Carter	Hughes	Cisse	Hughes→	Horsfield→	John	Mooney 85		
28-08	A	Everton	0-0	1-1	18	Vaesen	Tebily→	Cunningham	Purse	Grainger	Savage39	Savage39	Cisse	Hughes58→	Kenna	John5050	Kenna 36	Carter 70	Morrison 81
31-08	H	Leeds	1-0	0-1	14	Vaesen	Kenna	Cunningham	Purse	Grainger3272	Devlin21→	Johnson→	Cisse	Powell0→	Morrison→	John55→	Hughes 74	Horsfield 84	Lazaridis 89
11-09	A	Liverpool	0-1	2-2	15	Vaesen	Kenna	Cunningham	Purse34	Devlin→	Johnson→	Cisse	Savage89	Johnson→	Morrison6190	John6→	Carter 75	Horsfield 76	Lazaridis90
16-09	A	Aston Villa	1-0	3-0	09	Vaesen	Kenna	Cunningham	Purse	Devlin→	Grainger13	Savage31→	Cisse67	Johnson→	Morrison3	John→	Powell 69	Horsfield 88	
21-09	H	Middlesbrough	0-1	0-1	10	Vaesen	Kenna-	Cunningham	Purse27	Grainger→	Carter→	Savage37	Cisse70	Johnson	Morrison26	John→	Horsfield 66	Kirovski 81	Powell
28-09	H	Newcastle	0-1	0-2	14	Vaesen	Kenna	Cunningham	Purse70→	Carter→	Devlin	Savage28	Cisse88	Johnson	Morrison	John→	Horsfield 79	Powell	
05-10	A	West Ham	2-1	2-1	12	Vaesen	Kenna	Cunningham	Purse	Johnson	Devlin	Savage04	Cisse11	Lazaridis43→	Kirovski	John044→	Powell 82	Horsfield 83	
19-10	H	West Brom	0-1	1-1	12	Vaesen	Kenna	Vickers→	Carter	Savage	Powell06	Cisse	Lazaridis	Morrison	Horsfield	John52→	Woodhouse 83	Hughes	
26-10	H	Man City	0-1	0-2	13	Vaesen	Kenna→	Tebily81	Johnson	Savage	Cisse	Lazaridis	Morrison	Horsfield	John	Hughes	Woodhouse 83	Hughes 87	Kirovski
02-11	A	Bolton	0-0	3-1	12	Vaesen	Kenna→	Tebily73	Sadler	Powell→	Cisse62	Lazaridis	Morrison45	John→	Horsfield 83	Powell 77	Hughes	
09-11	H	Chelsea	0-3	0-3	14	Vaesen	Kenna	Cunningham	Devlin61	Sadler→	Cisse	Lazaridis	Morrison	John 72→	Horsfield 60	Powell 77	Hughes	
17-11	H	Sunderland	0-0	1-0	13	Vaesen	Tebily	Cunningham	Devlin21	Kenna	Cisse79→	Lazaridis89	Powell09→	John→	Horsfield 83	Horsfield 63	Hughes	Kirovski
23-11	A	Fulham	0-1	0-1	13	Vaesen	Tebily,83	Purse	Devlin→	Kenna	Cisse29	Lazaridis	Morrison 89	John→	Powell→	Hughes 60	Kirovski 80	Johnson
30-11	H	Tottenham	0-0	1-1	11	Vaesen	Tebily	Cunningham	Kenna 68	Hughes→	Cisse→	Lazaridis	Morrison	John→	Powell→	Hughes 83	Kirovski	
07-12	A	Southampton	0-0	0-2	13	Vaesen	Cunningham	Purse	Johnson23→	Kenna	Cisse90	Kirovski 0→59→	Morrison07	John→	Carter 71	Kirovski 81	
15-12	A	Fulham	1-0	1-0	13	Vaesen	Cunningham	Purse70	Kenna→	Hughes→	Cisse 6774	Johnson→	Morrison.55	John→	Powell78	Woodhouse 75	Hughes	
21-12	H	Charlton	0-1	1-1	13	Vaesen	Cunningham	Vickers	Kirovski	Savage87	Cisse90	Johnson→	Kirovski 45→	Devlin→	Lazaridis45	Morrison,84	Hughes	
26-12	H	Everton	1-1	1-1	13	Kenna→	Cunningham	Vickers	Devlin	Savage	Cisse	Johnson→	Morrison	Horsfield	Lazaridis	Morrison,84	Hughes	Woodhouse
28-12	A	Man Utd	0-1	0-2	15	Kenna80	Cunningham→	Johnson M→	Devlin	Savage30	Cisse	Lazaridis	Morrison	Horsfield	Powell	Hughes 77	Kirovski 68	
01-01	H	Leeds	0-2	0-4	15	Kenna	Hutchinson	Johnson M→	Savage39	Cisse90	Lazaridis	Morrison	Horsfield	Powell 63	Kirovski	
12-01	H	Arsenal	0-2	0-4	15	Coly22→	Vickers	Kenna	Savage	Clemence→	Clapham	John	Kirovski	Grainger 68		
18-01	A	Blackburn	1-1	1-1	15	Vaesen	Johnson M→	Clapham23	Savage	Clemence→	Lazaridis7083	Dugarry→	Devlin	Grainger 35	Kirovski 65	John 83
01-02	A	Bolton	1-1	2-4	16	Kenna→	Clapham→	Devlin→	Savage 44	Clemence 60	Lazaridis 44	Morrison 190	John	Kirovski 67	Kirovski 78	
04-02	H	Man Utd	0-0	0-1	16	Kenna→	Clapham	Johnson M→	Savage	Clemence49	Lazaridis	Morrison	Horsfield→	Devlin 35	Kirovski 84	Devlin
08-02	H	Chelsea	1-3	1-3	16	Kenna→	Clapham	Johnson84	Savage 87	Clemence 3→	Lazaridis 68	Horsfield→	John→	Grainger 68	Kirovski 78	Devlin
23-02	A	Liverpool	1-0	2-1	16	Kenna 74	Upson,63	Johnson	Savage34	Clemence	Lazaridis 7→	Dugarry	Morrison87	Carter 79	Morrison 87	Devlin
03-03	A	Aston Villa	0-0	2-0	16	Kenna→	Upson	Johnson→	Savage→	Clemence	Lazaridis 74→	Dugarry	John→	Horsfield 77	Fagan 83	Devlin
08-03	H	Man City	1-0	1-0	16	Cunningham35	Upson	Johnson→	Savage30	Clemence	Lazaridis	Dugarry	Morrison→	Horsfield 81	Carter 84	John
16-03	A	West Brom	0-0	1-0	16	Bennett	Kenna→	Upson	Johnson→	Savage	Clemence	Johnson	Morrison→	Horsfield 59	Devlin 74	John
22-03	H	Tottenham	0-0	1-0	16	Bennett	Marriott	Kenna→	Upson	Clapham	Savage	Clemence	Johnson	Morrison→	Horsfield 90	Carter 68	John90
05-04	A	Sunderland	0-1	1-2	16	Bennett	Kenna→	Upson	Clapham	Devlin 77	Johnson7→	Dugarry7→	Horsfield	Lazaridis 56	Kirovski 86	Carter
12-04	H	Sunderland	1-0	2-0	16	Bennett	Kenna 60	Clapham	Devlin→	Hughes 43→	Clemence 68	Lazaridis	Dugarry 20→	Horsfield 59	John 64	Carter
19-04	A	Charlton	1-0	2-0	15	Bennett	Kenna→	Cunningham	Clapham	Savage 5555	Clemence→	Hughes 79	Dugarry 20→	Horsfield 56	Carter 68	Kirovski
21-04	H	Southampton	1-0	3-2	15	Bennett	Kenna→	Cunningham 75	Clapham	Savage80	Clemence 1840	Hughes 63→	Dugarry 7582	Horsfield 79	Devlin 54	John→82
26-04	A	Middlesbrough	2-0	3-0	16	Bennett	Kenna→	Cunningham	Clapham	Savage	Clemence→	Hughes→	Dugarry 1840→	Horsfield 80	Devlin 64	John
03-05	A	Newcastle	0-1	1-3	16	Bennett	Kenna→	Upson41	Johnson→	Savage	Clemence	Hughes 54	Dugarry 36→	Johnson M 46	John 70	John 81
11-05	H	West Ham	0-0	2-2	13	Bennett	Kennat→	Purse	Upson	Johnson	Savage 88	Clemence57	Lazaridis→	John 88	Lazaridis 63	Devlin 73

101

1
Maik Taylor
Goalkeeper

The Northern Ireland international goalkeeper initially joined Blues on a season-long loan in the summer of 2003 from Fulham. Following some impressive performances, the move was made permanent in a £1.5 million deal in March 2004. He went on to make more than 100 Premiership appearances for Blues, prior to the club's relegation in 2006 and was widely regarded as one of the top division's leading keepers.

Taylor began his career at non-league Farnborough Town before moving into the Football League with Barnet. After impressing in the lower divisions with the Bees, he earned a move to the Premiership with Southampton before switching to Fulham.

Player Details:

Date of Birth:	04.09.1971
Place of Birth:	Hildeshein
Nationality:	Northern Irish
Height:	6'4"
Weight:	13st 9lb
Foot:	Right

Player Performance 05/06

League Performance

Percentage of total possible time player was on pitch   ⊙ position in league table at end of month

Month:	Aug	Sep	Oct	Nov	Dec	Jan	Feb	Mar	Apr	May	Total
	100%	100%	100%	50%	50%	100%	100%	100%	100%	100%	89%
	13	14	19	19	19	18	18	18	18	18	
Team Pts:	4/12	2/9	0/12	3/6	4/18	6/9	4/12	1/12	10/21	0/3	34/114
Team Gls F:	4	3	0	1	5	7	2	1	5	0	28
Team Gls A:	7	4	5	1	12	2	6	7	5	1	50
Total mins:	360	270	360	90	270	270	360	360	630	90	3,060
Starts (sub):	4	3	4	1	3	3	4	4	7	1	34
Goals:	0	0	0	0	0	0	0	0	0	0	0
Assists:	0	0	0	0	0	0	0	0	0	0	0
Clean sheets:	1	0	0	0	0	2	1	0	4	0	8
Cards (Y/R):	0	0	0	0	0	0	0	0	0	0	0

League Performance Totals

Clean Sheets

- Taylor: 8
- Team-mates: 2
- **Total: 10**

Assists

- Taylor: 0
- Team-mates: 28
- **Total: 28**

Cards

- Taylor: 0
- Team-mates: 57
- **Total: 57**

Cup Games

	Apps	CS	Cards
FA Cup	6	3	0
Carling Cup	1	0	0
Total	**7**	**3**	**0**

Career History

Career Milestones

Club Debut:
vs Tottenham (H), W 1-0, Premiership

 16.08.03

Time Spent at the Club:

▶ **3 Seasons**

First Goal Scored for the Club:
—

▶ —

Full International:

▶ **N. Ireland**

Premiership Totals

92-06

Appearances	144
Clean Sheets	43
Assists	0
Yellow Cards	1
Red Cards	3

Clubs

Year	Club	Apps	CS
03-06	Birmingham	122	36
97-04	Fulham	235	94
96-97	Southampton	18	7
95-96	Barnet	83	
94-95	Farnborough T		

Off the Pitch

Age:

- Taylor: 34 years, 8 months
- Team: 27 years, 8 months
- League: 26 years, 11 months

Height:

- Taylor: 6'4"
- Team: 5'11"
- League: 5'11"

Weight:

- Taylor: 13st 9lb
- Team: 11st 12lb
- League: 12st

18 Nico Vaesen
Goalkeeper

Season Review 05/06

Nico Vaesen joined Blues in the summer of 2001 from Huddersfield and just 12 months later the Belgian-born shot stopper played an instrumental role in helping the club gain promotion.

He was a regular during the side's inaugural Premiership season until he was cruelly sidelined with a knee injury in the local derby against Aston Villa at Villa Park in March 2003. He returned to full fitness during the latter stages of 2003 and spent periods on loan at Gillingham, Bradford and Crystal Palace, helping the latter to play-off final success at the Millennium Stadium in May 2004. But Vaesen made just seven first team appearances in his final two years at St. Andrew's and was allowed to leave the club when his contract expired in the summer of 2006.

Player Details:

Date of Birth:	28.09.1969
Place of Birth:	Hasselt
Nationality:	Belgian
Height:	6'3"
Weight:	13st 1lb
Foot:	Left

Player Performance 05/06

League Performance

Percentage of total possible time player was on pitch   ⊙ position in league table at end of month

Month:	Aug	Sep	Oct	Nov	Dec	Jan	Feb	Mar	Apr	May	Total
	13	14	19	50% 19	50% 19	18	18	18	18	18	11%
	0%	0%	0%			0%	0%	0%	0%	0%	
Team Pts:	4/12	2/9	0/12	3/6	4/18	6/9	4/12	1/12	10/21	0/3	34/114
Team Gls F:	4	3	0	1	4	5	2	1	5	0	28
Team Gls A:	7	4	5	1	12	2	6	7	5	1	50
Total mins:	0	0	0	90	270	0	0	0	0	0	360
Starts (sub):	0	0	0	1	3	0	0	0	0	0	4
Goals:	0	0	0	0	0	0	0	0	0	0	0
Assists:	0	0	0	0	0	0	0	0	0	0	0
Clean sheets:	0	0	0	1	1	0	0	0	0	0	2
Cards (Y/R):	0	0	0	0	0/1	0	0	0	0	0	0/1

League Performance Totals

Clean Sheets

▶ Vaesen:	2
▷ Team-mates:	8
Total:	**10**

Assists

▶ Vaesen:	0
▷ Team-mates:	28
Total:	**28**

Cards

▶ Vaesen:	1
▷ Team-mates:	56
Total:	**57**

Cup Games

	Apps	CS	Cards
FA Cup	0	0	0
Carling Cup	3	1	0
Total	**3**	**1**	**0**

Career History

Career Milestones

Club Debut:

vs MK Dons (A), L 3-1, Championship

11.08.01

Time Spent at the Club:

▶ **5 Seasons**

First Goal Scored for the Club:

—

▶ —

Full International:

▶ —

Premiership Totals

92-06

Appearances	31
Clean Sheets	7
Assists	0
Yellow Cards	0
Red Cards	1

Clubs

Year	Club	Apps	CS
04-04	Crystal Palace	13	6
04-04	Bradford City	6	2
03-04	Gillingham	5	2
01-06	Birmingham	63	18
98-01	Huddersfield	154	45
	Eendracht Aalst		

Off the Pitch

Age:

▶ Vaesen:	36 years, 8 months
▷ Team:	27 years, 8 months
∣ League:	26 years, 11 months

Height:

▶ Vaesen:	6'3"
▷ Team:	5'11"
∣ League:	5'11"

Weight:

▶ Vaesen:	13st 1lb
▷ Team:	11st 12lb
∣ League:	12st

24 Alex Bruce
Defence

Defender Alex Bruce, the son of Blues boss Steve, moved to Birmingham during the January 2005 transfer window from Blackburn Rovers.

The former Ewood Park trainee spent periods on loan at League One sides Oldham Athletic and Sheffield Wednesday during the 2004/05 campaign, helping the latter to promotion via the play-offs. Bruce went out on a further loan spell to League One side Tranmere Rovers during the first part of the 2005/06 season before returning to St. Andrew's to make his Blues first team breakthrough, appearing in 12 games.

Bruce has now opted to represent the Republic of Ireland under-21s, despite a similar offer from Northern Ireland.

Player Details:

Date of Birth:	28.09.1984
Place of Birth:	Norwich
Nationality:	Irish
Height:	5'11"
Weight:	11st 6lb
Foot:	Right

Player Performance 05/06

League Performance

Percentage of total possible time player was on pitch   ⊖ position in league table at end of month

Month:	Aug	Sep	Oct	Nov	Dec	Jan	Feb	Mar	Apr	May	Total
	0% 13	0% 14	0% 19	0% 19	0% 19	0% 18	26% 18	26% 18	0% 18	100% 18	8%
Team Pts:	4/12	2/9	0/12	3/6	4/18	6/9	4/12	1/12	10/21	0/3	34/114
Team Gls F:	4	3	0	1	5	7	2	1	5	0	28
Team Gls A:	7	4	5	1	12	2	6	7	5	1	50
Total mins:	0	0	0	0	0	0	92	93	0	90	275
Starts (sub):	0	0	0	0	0	0	1 (2)	1 (1)	0	1	3 (3)
Goals:	0	0	0	0	0	0	0	0	0	0	0
Assists:	0	0	0	0	0	0	0	0	0	0	0
Clean sheets:	0	0	0	0	0	0	0	0	0	0	0
Cards (Y/R):	0	0	0	0	0	0	1	0	0	0	1

League Performance Totals

Goals

▶ Bruce:	0
▦ Team-mates:	26
Total:	**26**
● own goals:	2

Assists

▶ Bruce:	0
▦ Team-mates:	28
Total:	**28**

Cards

▶ Bruce:	1
▦ Team-mates:	56
Total:	**57**

Cup Games

	Apps	Goals	Cards
FA Cup	6	0	1
Carling Cup	0	0	0
Total	**6**	**0**	**1**

Career History

Career Milestones

Club Debut:
vs Torquay (A), D 0-0, FA Cup
▶ **07.01.06**

Time Spent at the Club:
▶ **2 Seasons**

First Goal Scored for the Club:
▶ —

Full International:
▶ —

Premiership Totals
92-06

Appearances	6
Goals	0
Assists	0
Yellow Cards	1
Red Cards	0

Clubs

Year	Club	Apps	Gls
05-05	Tranmere	12	0
05-05	Sheff Wed	9	0
04-05	Oldham Ath	16	0
04-06	Birmingham	12	0

Off the Pitch

Age:

- ▶ Bruce: 21 years, 8 months
- ▦ Team: 27 years, 8 months
- | League: 26 years, 11 months

Height:
- ▶ Bruce: 5'11"
- ▦ Team: 5'11"
- | League: 5'11"

Weight:
- ▶ Bruce: 11st 6lb
- ▦ Team: 11st 12lb
- | League: 12st

106

30 Samuel Oji
Defence

Central defender Sam Oji was signed from Arsenal at the age of 18.

He is a strong and powerful player who is good in the air and comfortable on the ball.

During the 2005/06 season he spent two months on loan League One side Doncaster Rovers where he played five games, including a late substitute appearance in the Carling Cup quarter-final against his former club Arsenal.

Oji's only first team appearance for Blues during 2005/06 came in the FA Cup replay victory over Reading.

Player Details:

Date of Birth:	09.10.1985
Place of Birth:	Westminster
Nationality:	English
Height:	6'
Weight:	14st 5lb
Foot:	Right

Player Performance 05/06

League Performance

Percentage of total possible time player was on pitch   ⊙ position in league table at end of month

Month:	Aug	Sep	Oct	Nov	Dec	Jan	Feb	Mar	Apr	May	Total
	13	14	19	19	19	18	18	18	18	18	
	0%	0%	0%	0%	0%	0%	0%	0%	0%	0%	0%
Team Pts:	4/12	2/9	0/12	3/6	4/18	6/9	4/12	1/12	10/21	0/3	34/114
Team Gls F:	4	3	0	1	5	7	2	1	5	0	28
Team Gls A:	7	4	5	1	12	2	6	7	5	1	50
Total mins:	0	0	0	0	0	0	0	0	0	0	
Starts (sub):	0	0	0	0	0	0	0	0	0	0	0
Goals:	0	0	0	0	0	0	0	0	0	0	0
Assists:	0	0	0	0	0	0	0	0	0	0	0
Clean sheets:	0	0	0	0	0	0	0	0	0	0	0
Cards (Y/R):	0	0	0	0	0	0	0	0	0	0	0

League Performance Totals

Goals
- ▶ Oji: 0
- ▷ Team-mates: 26
- **Total: 26**
- ▶ own goals: 2

Assists
- ▶ Oji: 0
- ▷ Team-mates: 28
- **Total: 28**

Cards
- ▶ Oji: 0
- ▷ Team-mates: 57
- **Total: 57**

Cup Games

	Apps	Goals	Cards
FA Cup	1	0	0
Carling Cup	0	0	0
Total	**1**	**0**	**0**

Career History

Career Milestones

Club Debut:
vs Reading (H), W 2-1, FA Cup
▶ **07.02.06**

Time Spent at the Club:
▶ **2 Seasons**

First Goal Scored for the Club:
—
▶ —

Full International:
▶ —

Premiership Totals
92-06

Appearances	0
Goals	0
Assists	0
Yellow Cards	0
Red Cards	0

Clubs

Year	Club	Apps	Gls
05-06	Doncaster	5	0
04-06	Birmingham	1	0

Off the Pitch

Age:
- ▶ Oji: 20 years, 7 months
- ▷ Team: 27 years, 8 months
- | League: 26 years, 11 months

Height:
- ▶ Oji: 6'
- ▷ Team: 5'11"
- | League: 5'11"

Weight:
- ▶ Oji: 14st 5lb
- ▷ Team: 11st 12lb
- | League: 12st

31 Marcos Painter
Defence

Season Review 05/06

Marcos Painter is a local lad and another product of the club's Academy system. The tough-tackling defender made his Blues first team debut against Scunthorpe United in the Carling Cup in September 2005. He had to wait a little longer for his first chance to shine in the Premiership but when it duly arrived he grasped it with relish. Painter came into the back four for the Premiership clash with Fulham at St. Andrew's in December 2005 and produced an accomplished display to ensure a clean sheet and three crucial points in a 1-0 home win. He went on to start five games for the club as well as being introduced as a substitute in four others.

The Republic of Ireland under 21 international signed a new three-year contract in the summer of 2006.

Player Details:

Date of Birth:	17.08.1986
Place of Birth:	Birmingham
Nationality:	Irish
Height:	6'
Weight:	11st 6lb
Foot:	Left

Player Performance 05/06

League Performance

Percentage of total possible time player was on pitch   ⊖ position in league table at end of month

Month:	Aug	Sep	Oct	Nov	Dec	Jan	Feb	Mar	Apr	May	Total
	13 0%	14 0%	19 0%	19 0%	34% 19	18 0%	18 5%	18 0%	18 0%	18 0%	6%
Team Pts:	4/12	2/9	0/12	3/6	4/18	6/9	4/12	1/12	10/21	0/3	34/114
Team Gls F:	4	3	0	1	5	7	2	1	5	0	28
Team Gls A:	7	4	5	1	12	2	6	7	5	1	50
Total mins:	0	0	0	0	186	0	19	0	0	0	205
Starts (sub):	0	0	0	0	2 (1)	0	0 (1)	0	0	0	2 (2)
Goals:	0	0	0	0	0	0	0	0	0	0	0
Assists:	0	0	0	0	0	0	0	0	0	0	0
Clean sheets:	0	0	0	0	1	0	0	0	0	0	1
Cards (Y/R):	0	0	0	0	0	0	0	0	0	0	0

League Performance Totals

Goals
- ▶ Painter: 0
- ▶ Team-mates: 26
- **Total: 26**
- ▶ own goals: 2

Assists
- ▶ Painter: 0
- ▶ Team-mates: 28
- **Total: 28**

Cards
- ▶ Painter: 0
- ▶ Team-mates: 57
- **Total: 57**

Cup Games

	Apps	Goals	Cards
FA Cup	3	0	0
Carling Cup	2	0	0
Total	**5**	**0**	**0**

Career History

Career Milestones

Club Debut:
vs Scunthorpe (A), W 0-2, League Cup
▶ **20.09.05**

Time Spent at the Club:
▶ **1 Season**

First Goal Scored for the Club:
–
▶ **—**

Full International:
▶ **—**

Premiership Totals

92-06

Appearances	4
Goals	0
Assists	0
Yellow Cards	0
Red Cards	0

Clubs

Year	Club	Apps	Gls
05-06	Birmingham	9	0

Off the Pitch

Age:
- ▶ Painter: 19 years, 9 months
- ▶ Team: 27 years, 8 months
- | League: 26 years, 11 months

Height:
- ▶ Painter: 6'
- ▶ Team: 5'11"
- | League: 5'11"

Weight:
- ▶ Painter: 11st 6lb
- ▶ Team: 11st 12lb
- | League: 12st

23 Mathew Sadler
Defence

Another product of the club's flourishing Academy set-up, Mathew Sadler made his first team debut in a League Cup-tie at Leyton Orient in October 2002.

A very skilful and cultured defender, Sadler has represented England youth at several age groups. He made his Premiership bow in the home game against Bolton a month later and made his second league appearance at, of all places, Old Trafford. Sadler missed several seasons due to reoccurring injuries but he fought back to earn a recall towards the end of the 2005/06 season and made the left back position his own.

Sadler put pen to paper on a new two-year contract in the summer of 2006.

Player Details:

Date of Birth:	26.02.1985
Place of Birth:	Birmingham
Nationality:	English
Height:	5'11"
Weight:	11st 5lb
Foot:	Left

Player Performance 05/06

League Performance

Percentage of total possible time player was on pitch   ⊖ position in league table at end of month

Month:	Aug	Sep	Oct	Nov	Dec	Jan	Feb	Mar	Apr	May	Total
									100%	100%	
	13	14	19	19	19	18	18	18	18	18	21%
	0%	0%	0%	0%	0%	0%	0%	0%			
Team Pts:	4/12	2/9	0/12	3/6	4/18	6/9	4/12	1/12	10/21	0/3	34/114
Team Gls F:	4	3	0	1	5	7	2	1	5	0	28
Team Gls A:	7	4	5	1	12	2	6	7	5	1	50
Total mins:	0	0	0	0	0	0	0	0	630	90	720
Starts (sub):	0	0	0	0	0	0	0	0	7	1	8
Goals:	0	0	0	0	0	0	0	0	0	0	0
Assists:	0	0	0	0	0	0	0	0	0	0	0
Clean sheets:	0	0	0	0	0	0	0	0	4	0	4
Cards (Y/R):	0	0	0	0	0	0	0	0	1	0	1

League Performance Totals

Goals

- Sadler: 0
- Team-mates: 26
- **Total: 26**
- own goals: 2

Assists

- Sadler: 0
- Team-mates: 28
- **Total: 28**

Cards

- Sadler: 1
- Team-mates: 56
- **Total: 57**

Cup Games

	Apps	Goals	Cards
FA Cup	1	0	0
Carling Cup	0	0	0
Total	1	0	0

Career History

Career Milestones

Club Debut:

vs Leyton Orient (A), W 3-2, Lge Cup

02.10.02

Time Spent at the Club:

▶ **4 Seasons**

First Goal Scored for the Club:

—

▶ —

Full International:

▶ —

Premiership Totals

92-06

Appearances	10
Goals	0
Assists	0
Yellow Cards	1
Red Cards	0

Clubs

Year	Club	Apps	Gls
03-04	Northampton T	8	0
02-06	Birmingham	13	0

Off the Pitch

Age:

- Sadler: 21 years, 3 months
- Team: 27 years, 8 months
- League: 26 years, 11 months

Height:

- Sadler: 5'11"
- Team: 5'11"
- League: 5'11"

Weight:

- Sadler: 11st 5lb
- Team: 11st 12lb
- League: 12st

26 Olivier Tebily
Defence

Season Review 05/06

Olivier Tebily moved to Blues from Celtic in March 2002 and played a significant role in the club's successful promotion bid, playing mainly at centre-half but also in midfield in the play-off final against Norwich.

Ivory Coast international Tebily joined the Glasgow outfit in July 1999 following a five-month stint with Blues boss Steve Bruce's former club Sheffield United. Since joining the club, Tebily has been used in a variety of positions in defence and midfield. He was particular instrumental during the latter stages of the 2005/06 season after displacing Mario Melchiot at right-back.

His incredible strength and enthusiasm endeared him to the St. Andrew's faithful during a difficult campaign for the club.

Player Details:

Date of Birth:	19.12.1975
Place of Birth:	Abidjan
Nationality:	Ivorian
Height:	6'
Weight:	13st
Foot:	Right

Player Performance 05/06

League Performance

Percentage of total possible time player was on pitch

⊙- position in league table at end of month

Month:	Aug	Sep	Oct	Nov	Dec	Jan	Feb	Mar	Apr	May	Total
	13%	33%	71%	0%	31%	0%	7%	2%	71%	0%	31%
	13	14	19	19	19	18	18	18	18	18	
Team Pts:	4/12	2/9	0/12	3/6	4/18	6/9	4/12	1/12	10/21	0/3	34/114
Team Gls F:	4	3	0	1	5	7	2	1	5	0	28
Team Gls A:	7	4	5	1	12	2	6	7	5	1	50
Total mins:	46	90	255	0	170	0	26	8	450	0	1,045
Starts (sub):	1	1 (1)	3	0	2 (1)	0	0 (1)	0 (1)	5	0	12 (4)
Goals:	0	0	0	0	0	0	0	0	0	0	0
Assists:	0	0	0	0	0	0	0	0	0	0	0
Clean sheets:	0	0	0	0	0	0	0	0	0	0	0
Cards (Y/R):	0	0	0	0	0	0	0	0	2	0	2
									3	0	3

League Performance Totals

Goals

- ▶ Tebily: 0
- ▶ Team-mates: 26
- **Total: 26**
- ▶ own goals: 2

Assists

- ▶ Tebily: 0
- ▶ Team-mates: 28
- **Total: 28**

Cards

- ▶ Tebily: 3
- ▶ Team-mates: 54
- **Total: 57**

Cup Games

	Apps	Goals	Cards
FA Cup	2	0	1
Carling Cup	1	0	0
Total	**3**	**0**	**1**

Career History

Career Milestones

Club Debut:

vs Coventry (A), D 1-1, Championship

▶ **24.03.02**

Time Spent at the Club:

▶ **4.5 Seasons**

First Goal Scored for the Club:

—

▶ **—**

Full International:

▶ **Ivory Coast**

Premiership Totals

92-06

Appearances	70
Goals	0
Assists	0
Yellow Cards	13
Red Cards	1

Clubs

Year	Club	Apps	Gls
02-06	Birmingham	88	0
99-02	Celtic		
99-99	Sheff Utd	8	0
	Chateauroux		

Off the Pitch

Age:

- ▶ Tebily: 30 years, 5 months
- ▶ Team: 27 years, 8 months
- | League: 26 years, 11 months

Height:

- ▶ Tebily: 6'
- ▶ Team: 5'11"
- | League: 5'11"

Weight:

- ▶ Tebily: 13st
- ▶ Team: 11st 12lb
- | League: 12st

29 Mario Melchiot
Defence

Season Review 05/06

Mario Melchiot became an instant favourite with the fans in his first season at Blues following his free transfer move from Chelsea in the summer of 2004. He was a regular at right back and entertained the crowd with his neat skills and explosive overlapping runs. Melchiot's shameless showboating in the home win over Aston Villa also won him the 'Moment of the Season' award, voted for by the fans at the End of Season Dinner.

Unfortunately the Amsterdam-born defender, who was a product of Ajax's highly-regarded youth system, failed to live up to those high standards in his second term at St. Andrew's. He was allowed to leave when his contract expired at the end of the 2005/06 campaign having clocked up 66 appearances and scored two goals.

Player Details:

Date of Birth:	04.11.1976
Place of Birth:	Amsterdam
Nationality:	Dutch
Height:	6'2"
Weight:	11st 11lb
Foot:	Right/Left

Player Performance 05/06

League Performance

Percentage of total possible time player was on pitch   ⊙ position in league table at end of month

Month:	Aug	Sep	Oct	Nov	Dec	Jan	Feb	Mar	Apr	May	Total
	100%	50%	0%	50%	1%	84%	100%	98%	37%	100%	54%
Team Pts:	4/12	2/9	0/12	3/6	4/18	6/9	4/12	1/12	10/21	0/3	34/114
Team Gls F:	4	3	0	1	5	7	2	1	5	0	28
Team Gls A:	7	4	5	1	12	2	6	7	5	1	50
Total mins:	360	136	0	90	8	226	360	352	233	90	1,855
Starts (sub):	4	2	0	1	1	3	4	4	2 (1)	1	22 (1)
Goals:	0	0	0	0	0	1	0	0	0	0	1
Assists:	0	0	0	0	0	1	0	0	0	0	1
Clean sheets:	1	0	0	1	0	1	1	0	2	0	6
Cards (Y/R):	0	0	0	0	0	0	0	1	2	0	3

League Performance Totals

Goals

- ▶ Melchiot: 1
- ▷ Team-mates: 25
- **Total: 26**
- ▶ own goals: 2

Assists

- ▶ Melchiot: 1
- ▷ Team-mates: 27
- **Total: 28**

Cards

- ▶ Melchiot: 3
- ▷ Team-mates: 54
- **Total: 57**

Cup Games

	Apps	Goals	Cards
FA Cup	5	0	0
Carling Cup	1	0	0
Total	**6**	**0**	**0**

Career History

Career Milestones

Club Debut:
vs Portsmouth (A), D 1-1, Premiership

▶ **14.08.04**

Time Spent at the Club:

▶ **2 Seasons**

First Goal Scored for the Club:
vs Charlton (A), L 3-1, Premiership

▶ **15.01.05**

Full International:

▶ **Netherlands**

Premiership Totals

92-06

Appearances	187
Goals	6
Assists	7
Yellow Cards	17
Red Cards	0

Clubs

Year	Club	Apps	Gls
04-06	Birmingham	67	2
99-04	Chelsea	165	5
	Ajax		

Off the Pitch

Age:

- ▶ Melchiot: 29 years, 6 months
- ▷ Team: 27 years, 8 months
- | League: 26 years, 11 months

Height:

- ▶ Melchiot: 6'2"
- ▷ Team: 5'11"
- | League: 5'11"

Weight:

- ▶ Melchiot: 11st 11lb
- ▷ Team: 11st 12lb
- | League: 12st

4 Kenny Cunningham
Defence

One of Steve Bruce's first moves after Blues' promotion to the Premiership was to sign the experienced defender Kenny Cunningham on a four-year deal at St. Andrew's. The free transfer from Wimbledon proved to be an excellent acquisition and the Republic of Ireland international played a pivotal role in the centre of defence throughout the club's four-year Premiership adventure.

Cunningham clocked up nearly 70 caps for his country, for which he was the captain for several years, before deciding to retire from international action after Ireland's failure to qualify for the 2006 World Cup finals.

Cunningham clocked up 144 appearances for Blues before his departure in the summer of 2006 when his contract expired.

Player Details:

Date of Birth:	28.06.1971
Place of Birth:	Dublin
Nationality:	Irish
Height:	6'
Weight:	11st 2lb
Foot:	Right

Player Performance 05/06

League Performance

Percentage of total possible time player was on pitch   ⊙ position in league table at end of month

Month:	Aug	Sep	Oct	Nov	Dec	Jan	Feb	Mar	Apr	May	Total
% on pitch	100%	100%	52%	100%	100%	91%	25%	50%	98%	0%	80%
Position	13	14	19	19	19	18	18	18	18	18	
Team Pts:	4/12	2/9	0/12	3/6	4/18	6/9	4/12	1/12	10/21	0/3	34/114
Team Gls F:	4	3	0	1	5	7	2	1	5	0	28
Team Gls A:	7	4	5	1	12	2	6	7	5	1	50
Total mins:	360	270	187	180	540	247	90	180	616	0	2,670
Starts (sub):	4	3	3	2	6	3	1	2	7	0	31
Goals:	0	0	0	0	0	0	0	0	0	0	0
Assists:	0	0	0	0	0	0	0	0	0	0	0
Clean sheets:	1	0	0	1	1	2	0	0	4	0	9
Cards (Y/R):	0	1	1/1	0	0	0	0	1	2	0	5/1

League Performance Totals

Goals

- Cunningham: 0
- Team-mates: 26
- **Total: 26**
- own goals: 2

Assists

- Cunningham: 0
- Team-mates: 28
- **Total: 28**

Cards

- Cunningham: 6
- Team-mates: 51
- **Total: 57**

Cup Games

	Apps	Goals	Cards
FA Cup	2	0	0
Carling Cup	0	0	0
Total	**2**	**0**	**0**

Career History

Career Milestones

Club Debut:

vs Arsenal (A), L 2-0, Premiership

 **18.08.02**

Time Spent at the Club:

 **4 Seasons**

First Goal Scored for the Club:

—

 —

Full International:

 **Rep. Ireland**

Premiership Totals

92-06

Appearances	335
Goals	0
Assists	17
Yellow Cards	29
Red Cards	2

Clubs

Year	Club	Apps	Gls
02-06	Birmingham	144	0
94-02	Wimbledon	306	0
89-94	Millwall	153	2
	Tolka Rovers		

Off the Pitch

Age:

- Cunningham: 34 years, 11 months
- Team: 27 years, 8 months
- League: 26 years, 11 months

Height:

- Cunningham: 6'
- Team: 5'11"
- League: 5'11"

Weight:

- Cunningham: 11st 2lb
- Team: 11st 12lb
- League: 12st

3 Jamie Clapham
Defence

Jamie Clapham joined Blues in the January transfer window of 2003 from Ipswich Town and played a key role in the club's successful survival bid in our first season in the Premiership.

He missed a large bulk of the 2003/04 season due to a combination of injury and a nasty bout of Shingles but returned to make the left-back slot his own during the following campaign. In his final season at St. Andrew's, Clapham registered his first goal for the club in memorable fashion as he grabbed a first half equaliser against Manchester United in a game that Blues went on to draw 2-2.

He was just three short of clocking up a century of appearances for the club when he left in the summer of 2006 at the end of his contract.

Player Details:

Date of Birth:	07.12.1975
Place of Birth:	Lincoln
Nationality:	English
Height:	5'9"
Weight:	11st 8lb
Foot:	Left

Player Performance 05/06

League Performance

Percentage of total possible time player was on pitch   ⊖ position in league table at end of month

Month:	Aug	Sep	Oct	Nov	Dec	Jan	Feb	Mar	Apr	May	Total
	71%	83%	93%	50%	35%	0%	5%	25%	0%	0%	35%
	13	14	19	19	19	18	18	18	18	18	
Team Pts:	4/12	2/9	0/12	3/6	4/18	6/9	4/12	1/12	10/21	0/3	34/114
Team Gls F:	4	3	0	1	5	7	2	1	5	0	28
Team Gls A:	7	4	5	1	12	2	6	7	5	1	50
Total mins:	257	224	334	90	190	0	19	90	0	0	1,204
Starts (sub):	3	2 (1)	4	1	2 (1)	0	0 (1)	1	0	0	13 (3)
Goals:	0	0	0	0	1	0	0	0	0	0	1
Assists:	1	0	0	0	0	0	0	0	0	0	1
Clean sheets:	1	0	0	0	0	0	0	0	0	0	1
Cards (Y/R):	1	1	0	0	0	0	0	0	0	0	2

League Performance Totals

Goals

▶ Clapham:	1	
▷ Team-mates:	25	
Total:	**26**	
▶ own goals:	2	

Assists

▶ Clapham:	1
▷ Team-mates:	27
Total:	**28**

Cards

▶ Clapham:	2
▷ Team-mates:	55
Total:	**57**

Cup Games

	Apps	Goals	Cards
FA Cup	3	0	0
Carling Cup	4	0	0
Total	**7**	**0**	**0**

Career History

Career Milestones

Club Debut:

vs Arsenal (H), L 0-4, Premiership

▶ **12.01.03**

Time Spent at the Club:

▶ **3.5 Seasons**

First Goal Scored for the Club:

vs Man Utd (H), D 2-2, Premiership

▶ **28.12.05**

Full International:

▶ —

Premiership Totals

92-06

Appearances	152
Goals	5
Assists	9
Yellow Cards	5
Red Cards	0

Clubs

Year	Club	Apps	Gls
03-06	Birmingham	97	1
98-03	Ipswich	252	14
97-97	Bristol R	5	0
97-97	Leyton Orient	6	0
94-98	Tottenham	1	0

Off the Pitch

Age:

▶ Clapham:	30 years, 5 months
▷ Team:	27 years, 8 months
│ League:	26 years, 11 months

Height:

▶ Clapham:	5'9"
▷ Team:	5'11"
│ League:	5'11"

Weight:

▶ Clapham:	11st 8lb
▷ Team:	11st 12lb
│ League:	12st

8

Martin Latka
Defence

Czech Republic under-21 international Martin Latka arrived at Blues during the January 2006 transfer window to help in the club's bid to avoid relegation. The 6'4" centre half joined on loan from Slavia Prague until the end of the season and made an encouraging debut as Blues picked up an impressive away point at Liverpool.

Unfortunately that was as good as it got for the big Czech as he gave away a ridiculous penalty in only his third game to gift West Ham a decisive second goal in a 3-0 defeat at Upton Park.

Latka went on to make just four more appearances and the club's demotion to the Championship ended any chance of the defender making a permanent switch to St. Andrew's.

Player Details:

Date of Birth:	28.09.1984
Place of Birth:	Ceske Budejovice
Nationality:	Czech
Height:	6'4"
Weight:	13st 1lb
Foot:	Right

Player Performance 05/06

League Performance

Percentage of total possible time player was on pitch ⊖ position in league table at end of month

Month:	Aug	Sep	Oct	Nov	Dec	Jan	Feb	Mar	Apr	May	Total
							95%	50%			
	0%	0%	0%	0%	0%	0%			0%	0%	15%
	13	14	19	19	19	18	18	18	18	18	
Team Pts:	4/12	2/9	0/12	3/6	4/18	6/9	4/12	1/12	10/21	0/3	34/114
Team Gls F:	4	3	0	1	5	7	2	1	5	0	28
Team Gls A:	7	4	5	1	12	2	6	7	5	1	50
Total mins:	0	0	0	0	0	0	341	180	0	0	521
Starts (sub):	0	0	0	0	0	0	4	2	0	0	6
Goals:	0	0	0	0	0	0	0	0	0	0	0
Assists:	0	0	0	0	0	0	0	0	0	0	0
Clean sheets:	0	0	0	0	0	0	1	0	0	0	1
Cards (Y/R):	0	0	0	0	0	0	1	1	0	0	2

League Performance Totals

Goals

▶ Latka: 0
▶ Team-mates: 26
Total: 26
▶ own goals: 2

Assists

▶ Latka: 0
▶ Team-mates: 28
Total: 28

Cards

▶ Latka: 2
▶ Team-mates: 55
Total: 57

Cup Games

	Apps	Goals	Cards
FA Cup	1	0	1
Carling Cup	0	0	0
Total	**1**	**0**	**1**

Career History

Career Milestones

Club Debut:
vs Liverpool (A), D 1-1, Premiership
▶ **01.02.06**

Time Spent at the Club:
▶ **0.5 Seasons**

First Goal Scored for the Club:
—
▶ —

Full International:
▶ —

Premiership Totals

92-06

Appearances	6
Goals	0
Assists	0
Yellow Cards	2
Red Cards	0

Clubs

Year	Club	Apps	Gls
06-06	Birmingham	7	0
	Slavia Prague		

Off the Pitch

Age:

▶ Latka: 21 years, 8 months
▶ Team: 27 years, 8 months
| League: 26 years, 11 months

Height:

▶ Latka: 6'4"
▶ Team: 5'11"
| League: 5'11"

Weight:

▶ Latka: 13st 1lb
▶ Team: 11st 12lb
| League: 12st

2 Martin Taylor
Defence

Season Review 05/06

Versatile defender Martin Taylor joined Blues in January 2004 from Blackburn Rovers in a £1.25 million deal.

The 6'4" player was a product of Rovers' youth Academy system. Born in Ashington, Northumberland, he has a single England under-21 cap to his name. Nicknamed 'Tiny' by his former Blackburn colleagues, Taylor made his Premiership debut for Rovers back in March 1999. His preferred position is centre-back, but he can also play at full-back.

Since joining Blues, Taylor's first team chances have been limited by the impressive central defensive partnership of Matthew Upson and Kenny Cunningham, but when called upon to deputise, Tiny has slotted in well.

Player Details:

Date of Birth:	09.11.1979
Place of Birth:	Ashington
Nationality:	English
Height:	6'4"
Weight:	14st 9lb
Foot:	Right

Player Performance 05/06

League Performance

Percentage of total possible time player was on pitch   ⊙ position in league table at end of month

Month:	Aug	Sep	Oct	Nov	Dec	Jan	Feb	Mar	Apr	May	Total
	0%	0%	50%	100%	59%	16%	25%	75%	100%	100%	53%
	13	14	19	19	19	18	18	18	18	18	
Team Pts:	4/12	2/9	0/12	3/6	4/18	6/9	4/12	1/12	10/21	0/3	34/114
Team Gls F:	4	3	0	1	5	7	2	1	5	0	28
Team Gls A:	7	4	5	1	12	2	6	7	5	1	50
Total mins:	0	0	180	180	316	44	90	270	630	90	1,800
Starts (sub):	0	0	2	2	4	0 (1)	1	3	7	1	20 (1)
Goals:	0	0	0	0	0	0	0	0	0	0	0
Assists:	0	0	0	0	0	0	0	0	0	0	0
Clean sheets:	0	0	0	1	0	0	1	0	4	0	6
Cards (Y/R):	0	0	0	0	0	0	0	0	0	1	1

League Performance Totals

Goals

- ▶ Taylor: 0
- ▷ Team-mates: 26

Total: 26

- ▶ own goals: 2

Assists

- ▶ Taylor: 0
- ▷ Team-mates: 28

Total: 28

Cards

- ▶ Taylor: 1
- ▷ Team-mates: 56

Total: 57

Cup Games

	Apps	Goals	Cards
FA Cup	3	0	1
Carling Cup	4	0	0
Total	**7**	**0**	**1**

Career History

Career Milestones

Club Debut:
vs Everton (H), W 3-0, Premiership

▶ **11.02.04**

Time Spent at the Club:

▶ **2.5 Seasons**

First Goal Scored for the Club:
vs Middlesbrough (H), W 3-1, Prem.

▶ **03.03.04**

Full International:

▶ **—**

Premiership Totals

92-06

Appearances	106
Goals	3
Assists	0
Yellow Cards	3
Red Cards	0

Clubs

Year	Club	Apps	Gls
04-06	Birmingham	49	1
00-00	Stockport	7	0
00-00	Darlington	4	0
97-04	Blackburn	124	6

Off the Pitch

Age:

- ▶ Taylor: 26 years, 6 months
- ▷ Team: 27 years, 8 months
- | League: 26 years, 11 months

Height:

- ▶ Taylor: 6'4"
- ▷ Team: 5'11"
- | League: 5'11"

Weight:

- ▶ Taylor: 14st 9lb
- ▷ Team: 11st 12lb
- | League: 12st

5 Matthew Upson
Defence

Season Review 05/06

The highly-rated centre half joined Blues from Arsenal in January 2003, in a package totalling a possible £2.5 million. Upson had joined Arsenal in 1997 in a £1 million deal from Luton Town and ironically made his debut for the Gunners against Blues in the League Cup. He made a total of 57 appearances for the North London side, before making the switch to St. Andrew's. Upson made an immediate impact at Blues and his impressive performances in the centre of defence earned him a call-up to the England squad. The defender became the first Blues player since Trevor Francis in 1978 to win an England cap when he made his international debut in a friendly against South Africa in May 2003. Upson was given a new two-year contract at the start of 2006, but his season ended miserably when he tore his Achilles tendon in April – an injury that is expected to keep him out of action for a number of months.

Player Details:

Date of Birth:	18.04.1979
Place of Birth:	Eye
Nationality:	English
Height:	6'1"
Weight:	11st 5lb
Foot:	Left

Player Performance 05/06

League Performance

Percentage of total possible time player was on pitch   ⊖ position in league table at end of month

Month:	Aug	Sep	Oct	Nov	Dec	Jan	Feb	Mar	Apr	May	Total
	100%	100%	100%	100%	86%	100%	49%	0%	0%	0%	61%
position	13	14	19	19	19	18	18	18	18	18	
Team Pts:	4/12	2/9	0/12	3/6	4/18	6/9	4/12	1/12	10/21	0/3	34/114
Team Gls F:	4	3	0	1	5	7	2	1	5	0	28
Team Gls A:	7	4	5	1	12	2	6	7	5	1	50
Total mins:	360	270	360	180	462	270	178	0	0	0	2,080
Starts (sub):	4	3	4	2	6	3	2	0	0	0	24
Goals:	0	0	0	0	0	1	0	0	0	0	1
Assists:	0	0	0	0	0	0	0	0	0	0	0
Clean sheets:	1	0	0	1	1	2	0	0	0	0	5
Cards (Y/R):	2	0	0	0	0	0	0	0	0	0	2

League Performance Totals

Goals
- Upson: 1
- Team-mates: 25
- **Total: 26**
- own goals: 2

Assists
- Upson: 0
- Team-mates: 28
- **Total: 28**

Cards
- Upson: 2
- Team-mates: 55
- **Total: 57**

Cup Games

	Apps	Goals	Cards
FA Cup	1	0	1
Carling Cup	4	0	2
Total	**5**	**0**	**3**

Career History

Career Milestones

Club Debut:
vs Bolton (A), L 4-2, Premiership
▶ **01.02.03**

Time Spent at the Club:
▶ **3.5 Seasons**

First Goal Scored for the Club:
vs Newcastle (H), D 2-2, Premiership
▶ **03.10.04**

Full International:
▶ **England**

Premiership Totals

92-06

Appearances	138
Goals	3
Assists	4
Yellow Cards	13
Red Cards	1

Clubs

Year	Club	Apps	Gls
03-06	Birmingham	116	3
02-02	Reading	15	1
01-01	Crystal Palace	7	0
00-00	Nottm Forest	1	0
97-03	Arsenal	57	0
94-97	Luton Town	2	0

Off the Pitch

Age:

- Upson: 27 years, 1 month
- Team: 27 years, 8 months
- League: 26 years, 11 months

Height:
- Upson: 6'1"
- Team: 5'11"
- League: 5'11"

Weight:
- Upson: 11st 5lb
- Team: 11st 12lb
- League: 12st

11 Stan Lazaridis
Midfield

Season Review 05/06

Long serving winger Stan Lazaridis was a firm favourite with the fans during his seven years at St. Andrew's.

The Australian international signed from West Ham in 1999 and made a great start to his Blues career by scoring a spectacular free-kick on his debut against Fulham.

Lazaridis was often used as a substitute by Steve Bruce as Blues won promotion to the top flight in 2002 and he went on to become a consistently good performer in the Premiership. He was disappointed not to be offered a new deal when his contract expired in the summer of 2006 but he could at least find solace in Germany where he was part of the first Australian squad to compete in the World Cup finals for over three decades.

Player Details:

Date of Birth:	16.08.1972
Place of Birth:	Perth
Nationality:	Australian
Height:	5'9"
Weight:	12st
Foot:	Left

Player Performance 05/06

League Performance

Percentage of total possible time player was on pitch   ⊖ position in league table at end of month

Month:	Aug	Sep	Oct	Nov	Dec	Jan	Feb	Mar	Apr	May	Total
	29%	14	29% 19	48% 19	38% 19	100% 18	18 16%	72% 18	18 15%	18 0%	34%
	13	0%									
Team Pts:	4/12	2/9	0/12	3/6	4/18	6/9	4/12	1/12	10/21	0/3	34/114
Team Gls F:	4	3	0	1	5	7	2	1	5	0	28
Team Gls A:	7	4	5	1	12	2	6	7	5	1	50
Total mins:	103	0	105	86	207	270	56	258	93	0	1,178
Starts (sub):	1 (1)	0	1 (1)	1	2 (1)	3	0 (1)	3	0 (2)	0	11 (6)
Goals:	0	0	0	0	0	0	0	0	0	0	0
Assists:	0	0	0	0	0	0	0	0	0	0	0
Clean sheets:	0	0	0	0	0	2	0	0	1	0	3
Cards (Y/R):	0	0	0	1	0	0	0	0	0	0	1

League Performance Totals

Goals
- ▶ Lazaridis: 0
- ▶ Team-mates: 26
- **Total: 26**
- ▶ own goals: 2

Assists
- ▶ Lazaridis: 0
- ▶ Team-mates: 28
- **Total: 28**

Cards
- ▶ Lazaridis: 1
- ▶ Team-mates: 56
- **Total: 57**

Cup Games

	Apps	Goals	Cards
FA Cup	2	0	0
Carling Cup	1	0	0
Total	**3**	**0**	**0**

Career History

Career Milestones

Club Debut:
vs Fulham (H), D 2-2, Championship

 07.08.99

Time Spent at the Club:

▶ **7 Seasons**

First Goal Scored for the Club:
vs Fulham (H), D 2-2, Championship

 07.08.99

Full International:

▶ **Australia**

Premiership Totals

92-06

Appearances	166
Goals	7
Assists	25
Yellow Cards	10
Red Cards	0

Clubs

Year	Club	Apps	Gls
99-06	Birmingham	222	8
95-99	West Ham	87	3
	West Adelaide		

Off the Pitch

Age:
- ▶ Lazaridis: 33 years, 9 months
- ▶ Team: 27 years, 8 months
- | League: 26 years, 11 months

Height:
- ▶ Lazaridis: 5'9"
- ▶ Team: 5'11"
- | League: 5'11"

Weight:
- ▶ Lazaridis: 12st
- ▶ Team: 11st 12lb
- | League: 12st

36 Mathew Birley
Midfield

Season Review 05/06

Local born midfielder Mathew Birley came through the club's Academy set-up to earn a one-year professional contract in the summer of 2005. The deal was extended for a further 12 months in 2006.

The skilful winger, who can operate on either side of the pitch, made his first team debut in the League Cup against Norwich in October 2005. He went on to make his Premiership bow at the home of champions Chelsea on the final day of 2005 after playing the final 25 minutes at Stamford Bridge. Birley was then handed his full debut in the FA Cup win over Reading to take his final tally of appearances for the season to three – one in each of the major top flight competitions.

Player Details:

Date of Birth:	26.07.1986
Place of Birth:	Birmingham
Nationality:	English
Height:	5'10"
Weight:	11st 5lb
Foot:	Right/Left

Player Performance 05/06

League Performance

Percentage of total possible time player was on pitch   ⊖ position in league table at end of month

Month:	Aug	Sep	Oct	Nov	Dec	Jan	Feb	Mar	Apr	May	Total
	0%	0%	0%	0%	5%	0%	0%	0%	0%	0%	1%
	13	14	19	19	19	18	18	18	18	18	
Team Pts:	4/12	2/9	0/12	3/6	4/18	6/9	4/12	1/12	10/21	0/3	34/114
Team Gls F:	4	3	0	1	5	7	2	1	5	0	28
Team Gls A:	7	4	5	1	12	2	6	7	5	1	50
Total mins:	0	0	0	0	25	0	0	0	0	0	25
Starts (sub):	0	0	0	0	0 (1)	0	0	0	0	0	0 (1)
Goals:	0	0	0	0	0	0	0	0	0	0	0
Assists:	0	0	0	0	0	0	0	0	0	0	0
Clean sheets:	0	0	0	0	0	0	0	0	0	0	0
Cards (Y/R):	0	0	0	0	0	0	0	0	0	0	0

League Performance Totals

Goals

▶ Birley:	0
▷ Team-mates:	26
Total:	**26**
▶ own goals:	2

Assists

▶ Birley:	0
▷ Team-mates:	28
Total:	**28**

Cards

▶ Birley:	0
▷ Team-mates:	57
Total:	**57**

Cup Games

	Apps	Goals	Cards
FA Cup	1	0	0
Carling Cup	1	0	0
Total	**2**	**0**	**0**

Career History

Career Milestones

Club Debut:
vs Norwich (H), W 2-1, League Cup
▶ **26.10.05**

Time Spent at the Club:
▶ **5.5 Seasons**

First Goal Scored for the Club:
–
▶ —

Full International:
▶ —

Premiership Totals

92-06

Appearances	1
Goals	0
Assists	0
Yellow Cards	0
Red Cards	0

Clubs

Year	Club	Apps	Gls
05-06	Birmingham	3	0

Off the Pitch

Age:

▶ Birley: 19 years, 10 months
▷ Team: 27 years, 8 months
| League: 26 years, 11 months

Height:

▶ Birley: 5'10"
▷ Team: 5'11"
| League: 5'11"

Weight:

▶ Birley: 11st 5lb
▷ Team: 11st 12lb
| League: 12st

25
Stephen Clemence
Midfield

Season Review 05/06

Stephen Clemence joined Blues from Tottenham Hotspur during the January 2003 transfer window after making 108 appearances for the White Hart Lane club.

The son of ex-England goalkeeper Ray Clemence, he is a product of the FA's School of Excellence who represented England up to under 21 level.

Clemence is a quality passer of the ball and a reliable midfielder who rarely puts in a bad performance when called upon.

The Liverpool-born player clocked up a century of games for Blues in his final appearance of the 2005/06 season against Newcastle.

Player Details:

Date of Birth:	31.03.1978
Place of Birth:	Liverpool
Nationality:	English
Height:	5'11"
Weight:	11st 7lb
Foot:	Left

Player Performance 05/06

League Performance

Percentage of total possible time player was on pitch — position in league table at end of month

Month:	Aug	Sep	Oct	Nov	Dec	Jan	Feb	Mar	Apr	May	Total
% on pitch	65%	0%	36%	0%	57%	0%	25%	25%	16%	0%	28%
Position	13	14	19	19	19	18	18	18	18	18	
Team Pts:	4/12	2/9	0/12	3/6	4/18	6/9	4/12	1/12	10/21	0/3	34/114
Team Gls F:	4	3	0	1	5	7	2	1	5	0	28
Team Gls A:	7	4	5	1	12	2	6	7	5	1	50
Total mins:	235	0	129	0	309	0	90	90	101	0	954
Starts (sub):	3 (1)	0	2	0	4	0	1	1	2 (1)	0	13 (2)
Goals:	0	0	0	0	0	0	0	0	0	0	0
Assists:	0	0	0	0	0	0	0	0	0	0	0
Clean sheets:	1	0	0	0	1	0	0	0	1	0	3
Cards (Y/R):	2	0	1	0	1	0	0	0	0	0	4

League Performance Totals

Goals

- Clemence: 0
- Team-mates: 26
- **Total: 26**
- own goals: 2

Assists

- Clemence: 0
- Team-mates: 28
- **Total: 28**

Cards

- Clemence: 4
- Team-mates: 53
- **Total: 57**

Cup Games

	Apps	Goals	Cards
FA Cup	4	0	2
Carling Cup	2	0	0
Total	**6**	**0**	**2**

Career History

Career Milestones

Club Debut:
vs Arsenal (H), L 0-4, Premiership
▶ 12.01.03

Time Spent at the Club:
▶ 3.5 Seasons

First Goal Scored for the Club:
vs Liverpool (H), W 2-1, Premiership
▶ 23.02.03

Full International:
▶ —

Premiership Totals
92-06

Appearances	177
Goals	6
Assists	14
Yellow Cards	25
Red Cards	0

Clubs

Year	Club	Apps	Gls
03-06	Birmingham	100	5
94-03	Tottenham	108	3

Off the Pitch

Age:
- Clemence: 28 years, 2 months
- Team: 27 years, 8 months
- League: 26 years, 11 months

Height:
- Clemence: 5'11"
- Team: 5'11"
- League: 5'11"

Weight:
- Clemence: 11st 7lb
- Team: 11st 12lb
- League: 12st

10 David Dunn
Midfield

Season Review 05/06

David Dunn joined Blues on a four-year-deal from Blackburn Rovers in the summer of 2003. He made an immediate impression at St. Andrew's, scoring twice in his first three games, but they proved to be his only goals of the 2003/04 season. A hamstring injury plagued the second half of that campaign, and the problem reoccurred twice during the 2004/05 season limiting him to just 11 appearances.

Dunn, who has one senior England cap to his name, underwent a back operation that it was hoped would resolve the problem once and for all and the midfielder returned to action in the local derby with Aston Villa in October 2005. Unfortunately much of Dunn's 2006/07 season was blighted by niggling injuries.

Player Details:

Date of Birth:	27.12.1979
Place of Birth:	Blackburn
Nationality:	English
Height:	5'9"
Weight:	12st
Foot:	Right/Left

Player Performance 05/06

League Performance

Percentage of total possible time player was on pitch   ⊖ position in league table at end of month

Month:	Aug	Sep	Oct	Nov	Dec	Jan	Feb	Mar	Apr	May	Total
	13 0%	14 0%	19 6%	36% 19	40% 19	11% 18	14% 18	38% 18	7% 18	0% 18	17%
Team Pts:	4/12	2/9	0/12	3/6	4/18	6/9	4/12	1/12	10/21	0/3	34/114
Team Gls F:	4	3	0	1	5	7	2	1	5	0	28
Team Gls A:	7	4	5	1	12	2	6	7	5	1	50
Total mins:	0	0	23	65	217	30	49	136	46	0	566
Starts (sub):	0	0	0 (1)	1	3 (1)	0 (2)	1 (1)	2	1 (2)	0	8 (7)
Goals:	0	0	0	0	0	1	0	0	1	0	2
Assists:	0	0	0	0	1	0	0	0	0	0	1
Clean sheets:	0	0	0	0	0	0	0	0	0	0	0
Cards (Y/R):	0	0	0	0	0	0	0	0	0	0	0

League Performance Totals

Goals

- ▶ Dunn: 2
- ▷ Team-mates: 24
- **Total: 26**
- ▶ own goals: 2

Assists

- ▶ Dunn: 1
- ▷ Team-mates: 27
- **Total: 28**

Cards

- ▶ Dunn: 0
- ▷ Team-mates: 57
- **Total: 57**

Cup Games

	Apps	Goals	Cards
FA Cup	3	1	0
Carling Cup	2	0	0
Total	**5**	**1**	**0**

Career History

Career Milestones

Club Debut:
vs Tottenham (H), W 1-0, Premiership
▶ **16.08.03**

Time Spent at the Club:
▶ **3 Seasons**

First Goal Scored for the Club:
vs Tottenham (H), W 1-0, Premiership
▶ **16.08.03**

Full International:
▶ **England**

Premiership Totals

92-06

Appearances	119
Goals	22
Assists	23
Yellow Cards	13
Red Cards	0

Clubs

Year	Club	Apps	Gls
03-06	Birmingham	57	7
97-03	Blackburn	169	38

Off the Pitch

Age:
- ▶ Dunn: 26 years, 5 months
- ▷ Team: 27 years, 8 months
- | League: 26 years, 11 months

Height:
- ▶ Dunn: 5'9"
- ▷ Team: 5'11"
- | League: 5'11"

Weight:
- ▶ Dunn: 12st
- ▷ Team: 11st 12lb
- | League: 12st

21 Julian Gray
Midfield

Season Review 05/06

Julian Gray arrived at St. Andrew's in July 2004 from Crystal Palace on a Bosman free transfer and signed a three-year deal, which will keep him at Blues until 2007.

The 6'1" left-sided midfielder is a former Arsenal trainee who came through the youth ranks at Highbury, but made just one substitute appearance in the Premiership for the Gunners against Newcastle on the final day of the 1999/2000 season. Gray moved to Palace that summer and was a regular in the Eagles line-up. In his four years at Selhurst Park he clocked up 144 appearances and scored 14 goals.

The pacy and skilful left winger, Gray is always a threat down the flank but has also operated at left back during his time so far at St. Andrew's.

Player Details:

Date of Birth:	21.09.1979
Place of Birth:	Lewisham
Nationality:	English
Height:	6'1"
Weight:	11st
Foot:	Left

Player Performance 05/06

League Performance

Percentage of total possible time player was on pitch   ⟲ position in league table at end of month

Month:	Aug	Sep	Oct	Nov	Dec	Jan	Feb	Mar	Apr	May	Total
%	56%	83%	50%	14%	50%	33%	100%	25%	40%	0%	50%
Position	13	14	19	19	18	18	18	18	18	18	
Team Pts:	4/12	2/9	0/12	3/6	4/18	6/9	4/12	1/12	10/21	0/3	34/114
Team Gls F:	4	3	0	1	5	7	2	1	5	0	28
Team Gls A:	7	4	5	1	12	2	6	7	5	1	50
Total mins:	202	224	180	25	270	90	360	90	252	0	1,693
Starts (sub):	2 (1)	2 (1)	2	0 (1)	3	1	4	1	3	0	18 (3)
Goals:	0	0	0	1	0	0	0	0	0	0	1
Assists:	0	1	0	0	0	0	0	0	2	0	3
Clean sheets:	1	0	0	0	0	1	1	0	1	0	4
Cards (Y/R):	0	0	0	0	0	1	1	0	1	0	1

League Performance Totals

Goals

- ▶ Gray: 1
- ▶ Team-mates: 25

Total: 26

▶ own goals: 2

Assists

- ▶ Gray: 3
- ▶ Team-mates: 25

Total: 28

Cards

- ▶ Gray: 1
- ▶ Team-mates: 56

Total: 57

Cup Games

	Apps	Goals	Cards
FA Cup	4	1	0
Carling Cup	2	1	1
Total	6	2	1

Career History

Career Milestones

Club Debut:
vs Portsmouth (A), D 1-1, Premiership

 14.08.04

Time Spent at the Club:

▶ **2 Seasons**

First Goal Scored for the Club:
vs Liverpool (H), W 2-0, Premiership

▶ **12.02.05**

Full International:

▶ —

Premiership Totals

92-06

Appearances	54
Goals	3
Assists	3
Yellow Cards	1
Red Cards	0

Clubs

Year	Club	Apps	Gls
04-06	Birmingham	63	5
03-03	Cardiff	9	0
00-04	Crystal Palace	144	14
96-00	Arsenal	1	0

Off the Pitch

Age:

- ▶ Gray: 26 years, 8 months
- ▶ Team: 27 years, 8 months
- | League: 26 years, 11 months

Height:

- ▶ Gray: 6'1"
- ▶ Team: 5'11"
- | League: 5'11"

Weight:

- ▶ Gray: 11st
- ▶ Team: 11st 12lb
- | League: 12st

22 Damien Johnson
Midfield

Season Review 05/06

Northern Ireland international Damien Johnson joined Blues in March 2002 for a fee of just £50,000 from Blackburn Rovers, having made over 100 appearances for the Lancashire club after progressing through their Academy ranks.

Johnson, who can also operate in defence when called upon, has been described by Steve Bruce as the best ever signing of his time at the Blues managerial helm.

Johnson's battling performances and never-say-die attitude earned him both the Player of the Year and Players' Player of the Year awards at the end of the 2005/06 season.

Player Details:

Date of Birth:	18.11.1978
Place of Birth:	Lisburn
Nationality:	Northern Irish
Height:	5'9"
Weight:	11st 2lb
Foot:	Right/Left

Player Performance 05/06

League Performance

Percentage of total possible time player was on pitch   ⊖ position in league table at end of month

Month:	Aug	Sep	Oct	Nov	Dec	Jan	Feb	Mar	Apr	May	Total
	23%	100%	100%	50%		83%	100%		97%	100%	100%	79%
Team Pts:	4/12	2/9	0/12	3/6	4/18	6/9	4/12	1/12	10/21	0/3	34/114
Team Gls F:	4	3	0	1	5	7	2	1	5	0	28
Team Gls A:	7	4	5	1	12	2	6	7	5	1	50
Total mins:	81	270	360	90	450	270	53	348	630	90	2,642
Starts (sub):	1	3	4	1	5	3	2	4	7	1	31
Goals:	0	0	0	0	0	0	0	0	0	0	0
Assists:	0	0	0	0	1	0	0	0	1	0	2
Clean sheets:	0	0	0	1	1	2	0	0	4	0	8
Cards (Y/R):	0	0	1	0	0	1	0/1	0	3	0	5/1

League table position: Aug 13, Sep 14, Oct 19, Nov 19, Dec 19, Jan 18, Feb 15, Mar 18, Apr 18, May 18

League Performance Totals

Goals

- ► Johnson: 0
- ⟩ Team-mates: 26
- **Total: 26**
- ► own goals: 2

Assists

- ► Johnson: 2
- ⟩ Team-mates: 26
- **Total: 28**

Cards

- ► Johnson: 6
- ⟩ Team-mates: 51
- **Total: 57**

Cup Games

	Apps	Goals	Cards
FA Cup	4	0	1
Carling Cup	3	0	1
Total	**7**	**0**	**2**

Career History

Career Milestones

Club Debut:
vs Bradford (A), W 1-3, Championship
► **12.03.02**

Time Spent at the Club:
► **4.5 Seasons**

First Goal Scored for the Club:
vs Grimsby (H), W 4-0, Championship
► **30.03.02**

Full International:
► **N. Ireland**

Premiership Totals
92-06

Appearances	161
Goals	4
Assists	14
Yellow Cards	29
Red Cards	3

Clubs

Year	Club	Apps	Gls
02-06	Birmingham	156	3
98-98	Nottm Forest	7	0
97-02	Blackburn	81	4

Off the Pitch

Age:

- ► Johnson: 27 years, 6 months
- ⟩ Team: 27 years, 8 months
- | League: 26 years, 11 months

Height:

- ► Johnson: 5'9"
- ⟩ Team: 5'11"
- | League: 5'11"

Weight:

- ► Johnson: 11st 2lb
- ⟩ Team: 11st 12lb
- | League: 12st

15

Neil Kilkenny
Midfield

Season Review 05/06

Midfielder Neil Kilkenny moved to St. Andrew's from Arsenal in January 2004 on a two-and-a-half year professional contract after coming through the Highbury youth set-up. Blues fought off interest from a number of clubs to sign the talented midfielder, who has made several appearances for England at youth level.

Kilkenny spent six months on loan at League One side Oldham Athletic in 2004/05 and made a favourable impression at the Lancashire club, scoring five goals in 34 games to help Brian Talbot's Latics avoid relegation to the bottom division. He made his breakthrough into the Blues first team during 2005/06 and ended the season with a total of 25 appearances to his name.

Player Details:

Date of Birth:	19.12.1985
Place of Birth:	Enfield
Nationality:	English
Height:	5'8"
Weight:	10st 8lb
Foot:	Right

Player Performance 05/06

League Performance

Percentage of total possible time player was on pitch

↻ position in league table at end of month

Month:	Aug	Sep	Oct	Nov	Dec	Jan	Feb	Mar	Apr	May	Total
	0%	31%	20%	83%	34%	6%	18%	22%	0%	21%	20%
(position)	13	14	19	19	19	18	18	18	18	18	
Team Pts:	4/12	2/9	0/12	3/6	4/18	6/9	4/12	1/12	10/21	0/3	34/114
Team Gls F:	4	3	0	1	5	7	2	1	5	0	28
Team Gls A:	7	4	5	1	12	2	6	7	5	1	50
Total mins:	0	84	71	149	185	15	64	79	2	19	668
Starts (sub):	0	1	0 (2)	2	1 (3)	0 (2)	1	1 (3)	0 (1)	0 (1)	6 (12)
Goals:	0	0	0	0	0	0	0	0	0	0	0
Assists:	0	1	0	0	0	0	0	0	0	0	1
Clean sheets:	0	0	0	0	0	0	0	0	0	0	0
Cards (Y/R):	0	0/1	0	0	0	0	0	0	0	0	0/1

League Performance Totals

Goals
- ▶ Kilkenny: 0
- ▷ Team-mates: 26
- **Total: 26**
- ▶ own goals: 2

Assists
- ▶ Kilkenny: 1
- ▷ Team-mates: 27
- **Total: 28**

Cards
- ▶ Kilkenny: 1
- ▷ Team-mates: 56
- **Total: 57**

Cup Games

	Apps	Goals	Cards
FA Cup	4	0	0
Carling Cup	3	0	0
Total	**7**	**0**	**0**

Career History

Career Milestones

Club Debut:
vs Scunthorpe (A), W 0-2, League Cup

20.09.05

First Goal Scored for the Club:
▶ —

Time Spent at the Club:
▶ **2.5 Seasons**

Full International:
▶ —

Premiership Totals
92-06

Appearances	18
Goals	0
Assists	1
Yellow Cards	0
Red Cards	1

Clubs

Year	Club	Apps	Gls
04-05	Oldham	34	5
04-06	Birmingham	25	0

Off the Pitch

Age:
- ▶ Kilkenny: 20 years, 5 months
- ▷ Team: 27 years, 8 months
- | League: 26 years, 11 months

Height:
- ▶ Kilkenny: 5'8"
- ▷ Team: 5'11"
- | League: 5'11"

Weight:
- ▶ Kilkenny: 10st 8lb
- ▷ Team: 11st 12lb
- | League: 12st

12 Mehdi Nafti
Midfield

Season Review 05/06

The combative midfielder joined Blues on loan from Spanish La Liga side Racing Santander on the final day of the January 2005 transfer window. He went on to make ten appearances before the end of the season and impressed sufficiently to earn a permanent contract at St. Andrew's in the summer of 2005, signing a three-year contract.

Unfortunately Nafti snapped his cruciate ligament during a pre-season game against Deportivo and was forced to sit out much of the 2005/06 season.

The Tunisian international is the proud owner of an African Nations Cup winners' medal after his country's 2-1 success over Morocco in the 2004 final and travelled with the squad to Germany for the World Cup finals in the summer of 2006.

Player Details:

Date of Birth:	28.11.1978
Place of Birth:	Toulouse
Nationality:	Tunisian
Height:	5'10"
Weight:	11st 3lb
Foot:	Right

Player Performance 05/06

League Performance

Percentage of total possible time player was on pitch   ⊕ position in league table at end of month

Month:	Aug	Sep	Oct	Nov	Dec	Jan	Feb	Mar	Apr	May	Total
	0%	0%	0%	0%	0%	0%	0%	0%	0%	79%	2%
Team Pts:	4/12	2/9	0/12	3/6	4/18	6/9	4/12	1/12	10/21	0/3	34/114
Team Gls F:	4	3	0	1	5	7	2	1	5	0	28
Team Gls A:	7	4	5	1	12	2	6	7	5	1	50
Total mins:	0	0	0	0	0	0	0	0	0	71	71
Starts (sub):	0	0	0	0	0	0	0	0	0	1	1
Goals:	0	0	0	0	0	0	0	0	0	0	0
Assists:	0	0	0	0	0	0	0	0	0	0	0
Clean sheets:	0	0	0	0	0	0	0	0	0	0	0
Cards (Y/R):	0	0	0	0	0	0	0	0	0	0	0

Position numbers on chart: 13, 14, 19, 19, 19, 18, 18, 18, 18, 18

League Performance Totals

Goals
- ▶ Nafti: 0
- ▷ Team-mates: 26
- **Total: 26**
- ▶ own goals: 2

Assists
- ▶ Nafti: 0
- ▷ Team-mates: 28
- **Total: 28**

Cards
- ▶ Nafti: 0
- ▷ Team-mates: 57
- **Total: 57**

Cup Games

	Apps	Goals	Cards
FA Cup	0	0	0
Carling Cup	0	0	0
Total	**0**	**0**	**0**

Career History

Career Milestones

Club Debut:
vs Man Utd (A), L 2-0, Premiership

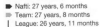
▶ **05.02.05**

Time Spent at the Club:

▶ **1.5 Seasons**

First Goal Scored for the Club:
—

▶ **—**

Full International:

▶ **Tunisia**

Premiership Totals

92-06

Appearances	11
Goals	0
Assists	0
Yellow Cards	4
Red Cards	0

Clubs

Year	Club	Apps	Gls
05-06	Birmingham	11	0
	Racing Santander		
	Toulouse		

Off the Pitch

Age:

- ▶ Nafti: 27 years, 6 months
- ▷ Team: 27 years, 8 months
- | League: 26 years, 11 months

Height:

- ▶ Nafti: 5'10"
- ▷ Team: 5'11"
- | League: 5'11"

Weight:

- ▶ Nafti: 11st 3lb
- ▷ Team: 11st 12lb
- | League: 12st

7 Jermaine Pennant
Midfield

Blues completed the loan signing of Arsenal winger Jermaine Pennant on the final day of the January 2005 transfer window. The switch to Blues was then made permanent during the summer of 2005.

Pennant joined the Gunners as a 15-year-old for a fee of £2 million. During his time at Highbury the England under 21 international had spells on loan at both Watford and Leeds. He remained at Elland Road throughout the 2003/04 season where he made 34 appearances and scored two goals before returning to Highbury in the summer after United were relegated.

Pennant possesses great pace and skill and is an excellent crosser of the ball.

Player Details:

Date of Birth:	15.01.1983
Place of Birth:	Nottingham
Nationality:	English
Height:	5'8"
Weight:	10st 1lb
Foot:	Right

Player Performance 05/06

League Performance

Percentage of total possible time player was on pitch   ⊖ position in league table at end of month

Month:	Aug	Sep	Oct	Nov	Dec	Jan	Feb	Mar	Apr	May	Total
	100%	100%	100%	67%	80%	100%	100%	91%	88%	100%	92%
	13	14	19	19	19	18	18	18	18	18	
Team Pts:	4/12	2/9	0/12	3/6	4/18	6/9	4/12	1/12	10/21	0/3	34/114
Team Gls F:	4	3	0	1	5	7	2	1	5	0	28
Team Gls A:	7	4	5	1	12	2	6	7	5	1	50
Total mins:	360	270	360	121	430	270	360	326	555	90	3,142
Starts (sub):	4	3	4	1 (1)	4 (2)	3	4	4	7	1	35 (3)
Goals:	0	0	0	0	0	2	0	0	0	0	2
Assists:	2	0	0	0	1	1	1	0	0	0	5
Clean sheets:	1	0	0	0	0	2	1	0	3	0	7
Cards (Y/R):	0	0	1	0	0	0	0	1	2	0	4

League Performance Totals

Goals

▶ Pennant:	2
▦ Team-mates:	24
Total:	**26**
▶ own goals:	2

Assists

▶ Pennant:	5
▦ Team-mates:	23
Total:	**28**

Cards

▶ Pennant:	4
▦ Team-mates:	53
Total:	**57**

Cup Games

	Apps	Goals	Cards
FA Cup	6	0	0
Carling Cup	4	1	0
Total	**10**	**1**	**0**

Career History

Career Milestones

Club Debut:

vs Southampton (H), W 2-1, Prem.

▶ **02.02.05**

Time Spent at the Club:

▶ **1.5 Seasons**

First Goal Scored for the Club:

vs Norwich (H), W 2-1, League Cup

▶ **26.10.05**

Full International:

▶ **—**

Premiership Totals

92-06

Appearances	98
Goals	7
Assists	16
Yellow Cards	12
Red Cards	0

Clubs

Year	Club	Apps	Gls
05-06	Birmingham	60	3
03-04	Leeds	36	2
02-03	Watford	23	3
99-05	Arsenal	26	3
98-99	Notts County	2	0

Off the Pitch

Age:

- ▶ Pennant: 23 years, 4 months
- ▦ Team: 27 years, 8 months
- | League: 26 years, 11 months

Height:

- ▶ Pennant: 5'8"
- ▦ Team: 5'11"
- | League: 5'11"

Weight:

- ▶ Pennant: 10st 1lb
- ▦ Team: 11st 12lb
- | League: 12st

37 Peter Till
Midfield

Season Review 05/06

Peter Till joined the club as a schoolboy and progressed through the Academy ranks. He earned a two-year professional contract in the summer of 2005. He operates primarily as a right winger but he can also play up front.

Till made his Blues first team debut during the 2005/06 season in the League Cup win over Scunthorpe United and went on to join the League One side on a three-month loan. He played ten games for the Iron before joining their League Two neighbours Boston United on a similar temporary deal until the end of the season.

Till opened his league goal-scoring account by netting in the 3-1 defeat of Bury and went on to appear in 16 games for the Pilgrims.

Player Details:

Date of Birth:	07.09.1985
Place of Birth:	Birmingham
Nationality:	English
Height:	5'11"
Weight:	11st 4lb
Foot:	Right

Player Performance 05/06

League Performance

Percentage of total possible time player was on pitch   Ꝺ position in league table at end of month

Month:	Aug	Sep	Oct	Nov	Dec	Jan	Feb	Mar	Apr	May	Total
	13	14	19	19	19	18	18	18	18	18	
	0%	0%	0%	0%	0%	0%	0%	0%	0%	0%	0%
Team Pts:	4/12	2/9	0/12	3/6	4/18	6/9	4/12	1/12	10/21	0/3	34/114
Team Gls F:	4	3	0	1	5	7	2	1	5	0	28
Team Gls A:	7	4	5	1	12	2	6	7	5	1	50
Total mins:	0	0	0	0	0	0	0	0	0	0	0
Starts (sub):	0	0	0	0	0	0	0	0	0	0	0
Goals:	0	0	0	0	0	0	0	0	0	0	0
Assists:	0	0	0	0	0	0	0	0	0	0	0
Clean sheets:	0	0	0	0	0	0	0	0	0	0	0
Cards (Y/R):	0	0	0	0	0	0	0	0	0	0	0

League Performance Totals

Goals
- ▶ Till: 0
- ▷ Team-mates: 26
- **Total: 26**
- ▶ own goals: 2

Assists
- ▶ Till: 0
- ▷ Team-mates: 28
- **Total: 28**

Cards
- ▶ Till: 0
- ▷ Team-mates: 57
- **Total: 57**

Cup Games

	Apps	Goals	Cards
FA Cup	0	0	0
Carling Cup	1	0	0
Total	**1**	**0**	**0**

Career History

Career Milestones

Club Debut:

vs Scunthorpe (A), W 0-2, Lge Cup

 **20.09.05**

Time Spent at the Club:

▶ **2 Seasons**

First Goal Scored for the Club:

▶ —

Full International:

▶ —

Premiership Totals

92-06

Appearances	0
Goals	0
Assists	0
Yellow Cards	0
Red Cards	0

Clubs

Year	Club	Apps	Gls
06-06	Boston Utd	16	1
05-06	Scunthorpe	10	0
04-06	Birmingham	1	0

Off the Pitch

Age:
- ▶ Till: 20 years, 8 months
- ▷ Team: 27 years, 8 months
- | League: 26 years, 11 months

Height:
- ▶ Till: 5'11"
- ▷ Team: 5'11"
- | League: 5'11"

Weight:
- ▶ Till: 11st 4lb
- ▷ Team: 11st 12lb
- | League: 12st

6

Muzzy Izzet
Midfield

Player Details:

Date of Birth:	31.10.1974
Place of Birth:	Mile End
Nationality:	Turkish
Height:	5'10"
Weight:	11st 2lb
Foot:	Right

Season Review 05/06

Muzzy Izzet joined Blues on a Bosman free transfer from Leicester City in the summer of 2004.

But the 29-year-old Turkish international midfielder was plagued by injury in his two seasons at St. Andrew's. He opened his goal-scoring account in the 1-1 draw at Bolton in September 2004 but his inaugural Blues campaign was brought to a premature close just two months later when he underwent knee surgery. He returned to action at the start of the 2005/06 season but his injury problems continued and limited the former Chelsea trainee to just 18 games taking his total of appearances for the club to 28.

Due to injury, Izzet announced his retirement from the game in the summer of 2006.

Player Performance 05/06

League Performance

Percentage of total possible time player was on pitch

⊖ position in league table at end of month

Month:	Aug	Sep	Oct	Nov	Dec	Jan	Feb	Mar	Apr	May	Total
	24%	23%	0%	98%	16%	98%	40%	9%	10%	0%	28%
	13	14	19	19	19	18	18	18	18	18	
Team Pts:	4/12	2/9	0/12	3/6	4/18	6/9	4/12	1/12	10/21	0/3	34/114
Team Gls F:	4	3	0	1	5	7	2	1	5	0	28
Team Gls A:	7	4	5	1	12	2	6	7	5	1	50
Total mins:	87	62	0	176	88	264	145	34	65	0	921
Starts (sub):	0 (3)	0 (2)	0	2	2	3	2	0 (1)	1	0	10 (6)
Goals:	0	0	0	0	0	0	0	0	0	0	0
Assists:	0	0	0	0	0	1	0	0	0	0	1
Clean sheets:	0	0	0	1	0	2	1	0	0	0	4
Cards (Y/R):	0	0	0	1	0/1	0	0	0	0	0	1/1

League Performance Totals

Goals

- ▶ Izzet: 0
- ▷ Team-mates: 26
- **Total:** 26
- ▶ own goals: 2

Assists
- ▶ Izzet: 1
- ▷ Team-mates: 27
- **Total:** 28

Cards
- ▶ Izzet: 2
- ▷ Team-mates: 55
- **Total:** 57

Cup Games

	Apps	Goals	Cards
FA Cup	1	0	0
Carling Cup	1	0	0
Total	**2**	**0**	**0**

Career History

Career Milestones

Club Debut:
vs Portsmouth (A), D 1-1, Premiership
▶ **14.08.04**

First Goal Scored for the Club:
vs Bolton (A), D 1-1, Premiership
▶ **25.09.04**

Time Spent at the Club:
▶ **2 Seasons**

Full International:
▶ **Turkey**

Premiership Totals

92-06
Appearances	248
Goals	34
Assists	41
Yellow Cards	42
Red Cards	3

Clubs

Year	Club	Apps	Gls
04-06	Birmingham	28	1
96-04	Leicester	323	47
93-96	Chelsea	0	0

Off the Pitch

Age:
- ▶ Izzet: 31 years, 7 months
- ▷ Team: 27 years, 8 months
- | League: 26 years, 11 months

Height:
- ▶ Izzet: 5'10"
- ▷ Team: 5'11"
- | League: 5'11"

Weight:
- ▶ Izzet: 11st 2lb
- ▷ Team: 11st 12lb
- | League: 12st

14 Jiri Jarosik
Midfield

The performances and goals of Jiri Jarosik provided a few of the high spots in an otherwise depressing 2005/06 campaign at St. Andrew's.

The Czech international arrived on a year-long loan from Chelsea a few games into the season and made an immediate impact, scoring in only his second match in the away win at West Brom. Jarosik went on to prove an excellent acquisition and showed his adaptability by featuring in a number of different positions in the side.

The Czech chipped in with a good ratio of goals, including a cracking strike which beat Bolton in April and clinched the Goal of the Season award. Jarosik ended the campaign as the club's joint top scorer with eight goals from 32 appearances.

Player Details:

Date of Birth:	27.10.1977
Place of Birth:	Usti Nad Labem
Nationality:	Czech
Height:	6'4"
Weight:	13st 3lb
Foot:	Right/Left

Player Performance 05/06

League Performance

Percentage of total possible time player was on pitch   ⊕ position in league table at end of month

Month:	Aug	Sep	Oct	Nov	Dec	Jan	Feb	Mar	Apr	May	Total
	50% 13	44% 14	45% 19	76% 19	40% 19	83% 18	64% 18	34% 18	43% 18	18 0%	49%
Team Pts:	4/12	2/9	0/12	3/6	4/18	6/9	4/12	1/12	10/21	0/3	34/114
Team Gls F:	4	3	0	1	5	7	2	1	5	0	28
Team Gls A:	7	4	5	1	12	2	6	7	5	1	50
Total mins:	180	118	161	136	218	224	230	123	270	0	1,660
Starts (sub):	2	2	1 (2)	2	2 (2)	3	3	1 (1)	3	0	19 (5)
Goals:	1	1	0	0	1	1	0	0	1	0	5
Assists:	0	0	0	0	0	1	0	0	0	0	1
Clean sheets:	0	0	0	0	0	0	1	0	2	0	3
Cards (Y/R):	1	0	0	0	0	0	0	1	0	0	2

League Performance Totals

Goals
- Jarosik: 5
- Team-mates: 21
- **Total: 26**
- own goals: 2

Assists
- Jarosik: 1
- Team-mates: 27
- **Total: 28**

Cards
- Jarosik: 2
- Team-mates: 55
- **Total: 57**

Cup Games

	Apps	Goals	Cards
FA Cup	5	1	0
Carling Cup	3	2	0
Total	**8**	**3**	**0**

Career History

Career Milestones

Club Debut:
vs Middlesbrough (H), L 0-3, Prem.

 23.08.05

Time Spent at the Club:

 **1 Season**

First Goal Scored for the Club:
vs West Brom (A), W 2-3, Premiership

27.08.05

Full International:

Czech Rep.

Premiership Totals

92-06

Appearances	38
Goals	5
Assists	1
Yellow Cards	3
Red Cards	0

Clubs

Year	Club	Apps	Gls
05-06	Birmingham	32	8
05-06	Chelsea	20	0
	CSKA Moscow		
	Slovan Liberec		
	Sparta Prague		

Off the Pitch

Age:

- Jarosik: 28 years, 7 months
- Team: 27 years, 8 months
- League: 26 years, 11 months

Height:
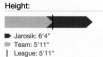
- Jarosik: 6'4"
- Team: 5'11"
- League: 5'11"

Weight:
- Jarosik: 13st 3lb
- Team: 11st 12lb
- League: 12st

20 Nicky Butt
Midfield

Season Review 05/06

Thirty-nine capped England midfielder Nicky Butt arrived at Blues from Newcastle on a season-long loan in the summer of 2005. Prior to joining the Magpies, Butt had spent almost 12 years at Manchester United where he played alongside Blues boss Steve Bruce in Alex Ferguson's all-conquering side of the 1990's. Unfortunately he suffered a stop-start first half of the season at Blues with a sending off early in the campaign at Portsmouth resulting in a four-game ban and then a subsequent injury lay-off. He scored a vital winner against Fulham in December but Blues only really started to see the best of the midfielder towards the end of the season when he also scored a crucial goal in the win over Blackburn. But the club's relegation brought to an end Butt's spell at St. Andrew's, in which he made 29 appearances and scored three goals.

Player Details:

Date of Birth:	21.01.1975
Place of Birth:	Manchester
Nationality:	English
Height:	5'10"
Weight:	11st 5lb
Foot:	Right

Player Performance 05/06

League Performance

Percentage of total possible time player was on pitch   ⊖ position in league table at end of month

Month:	Aug	Sep	Oct	Nov	Dec	Jan	Feb	Mar	Apr	May	Total
	93%	50%	34%	0%	79%	0%	43%	75%	62%	100%	58%
	13	14	19	19	19	18	18	18	18	18	
Team Pts:	4/12	2/9	0/12	3/6	4/18	6/9	4/12	1/12	10/21	0/3	34/114
Team Gls F:	4	3	0	1	5	7	2	1	5	0	28
Team Gls A:	7	4	5	1	12	2	6	7	5	1	50
Total mins:	335	135	124	0	427	0	155	270	388	90	1,924
Starts (sub):	4	2	2	0	4 (1)	0	1 (1)	3	5	1	22 (2)
Goals:	1	0	0	0	1	0	0	0	1	0	3
Assists:	0	0	0	0	0	0	0	0	0	0	0
Clean sheets:	1	0	0	0	1	0	0	0	2	0	4
Cards (Y/R):	1	0/1	0	0	0	0	0	2	2	0	5/1

League Performance Totals

Goals

▶ Butt:	3
▶ Team-mates:	23
Total:	**26**
▶ own goals:	2

Assists

▶ Butt:	0
▶ Team-mates:	28
Total:	**28**

Cards

▶ Butt:	6
▶ Team-mates:	51
Total:	**57**

Cup Games

	Apps	Goals	Cards
FA Cup	2	0	0
Carling Cup	3	0	1
Total	**5**	**0**	**1**

Career History

Career Milestones

Club Debut:
vs Fulham (A), D 0-0, Premiership

▶ **13.08.05**

Time Spent at the Club:

▶ **1 Season**

First Goal Scored for the Club:
vs Man City (H), L 1-2, Premiership

▶ **20.08.05**

Full International:

▶ **England**

Premiership Totals

92-06

Appearances	312
Goals	25
Assists	29
Yellow Cards	54
Red Cards	5

Clubs

Year	Club	Apps	Gls
05-06	Birmingham	29	3
04-06	Newcastle	28	1
93-04	Man Utd	389	26

Off the Pitch

Age:

- ▶ Butt: 31 years, 4 months
- ▶ Team: 27 years, 8 months
- | League: 26 years, 11 months

Height:

- ▶ Butt: 5'10"
- ▶ Team: 5'11"
- | League: 5'11"

Weight:

- ▶ Butt: 11st 5lb
- ▶ Team: 11st 12lb
- | League: 12st

16

Emile Heskey
Forward

Emile Heskey became Blues' record signing when he joined in July 2004 in a £6.25 million deal from Liverpool.

The striker finished his first season at St.Andrew's as the club's top scorer with 11 goals in 38 appearances and walked away with a host awards, including the coveted 'Player of the Year' trophy, at the End of Season Dinner.

The Leicester-born forward made his name at his hometown club, notching 46 goals in 197 games at Filbert Street to earn an £11 million move to Anfield in March 2000. Heskey, who has 40 England caps to his name, started in all of Liverpool's five trophy wins of 2001, including a magnificent goal against Bayern Munich during the Super Cup victory in Monaco.

Player Details:

Date of Birth:	11.01.1978
Place of Birth:	Leicester
Nationality:	English
Height:	6'2"
Weight:	13st 12lb
Foot:	Right

Player Performance 05/06

League Performance

Percentage of total possible time player was on pitch   ⊖ position in league table at end of month

Month:	Aug	Sep	Oct	Nov	Dec	Jan	Feb	Mar	Apr	May	Total
	42%	70%	100%	100%	79%	96%	73%	90%	93%	100%	83%
	13	14	19	19	19	18	18	18	18	18	
Team Pts:	4/12	2/9	0/12	3/6	4/18	6/9	4/12	1/12	10/21	0/3	34/114
Team Gls F:	4	3	0	1	5	7	2	1	5	0	28
Team Gls A:	7	4	5	1	12	2	6	7	5	1	50
Total mins:	150	190	360	180	425	258	263	324	585	90	2,825
Starts (sub):	2	3	4	2	5	3	3	4	7	1	34
Goals:	2	0	0	0	1	0	1	0	0	0	4
Assists:	0	1	0	0	2	1	1	0	2	0	7
Clean sheets:	1	0	0	1	1	2	1	0	3	0	9
Cards (Y/R):	0	0	1	0	1	1	0/1	0	0	0	3/1

League Performance Totals

Goals

▶ Heskey: 4
▷ Team-mates: 22
Total: 26
▪ own goals: 2

Assists

▶ Heskey: 7
▷ Team-mates: 21
Total: 28

Cards

▶ Heskey: 4
▷ Team-mates: 53
Total: 57

Cup Games

	Apps	Goals	Cards
FA Cup	3	0	0
Carling Cup	3	1	0
Total	**6**	**1**	**0**

Career History

Career Milestones

Club Debut:
vs Portsmouth (A), D 1-1, Premiership

14.08.04
Time Spent at the Club:
▶ **2 Seasons**

First Goal Scored for the Club:
vs Man City (H), W 1-0, Premiership

24.08.04
Full International:
▶ **England**

Premiership Totals

92-06

Appearances	342
Goals	86
Assists	63
Yellow Cards	41
Red Cards	2

Clubs

Year	Club	Apps	Gls
04-06	Birmingham	78	16
00-04	Liverpool	228	60
94-00	Leicester	197	46

Off the Pitch

Age:

▶ Heskey: 28 years, 4 months
▷ Team: 27 years, 8 months
| League: 26 years, 11 months

Height:

▶ Heskey: 6'2"
▷ Team: 5'11"
| League: 5'11"

Weight:

▶ Heskey: 13st 12lb
▷ Team: 11st 12lb
| League: 12st

28 Dudley Campbell
Forward

Player Details:

Date of Birth:	02.05.1981
Place of Birth:	London
Nationality:	English
Height:	5'8"
Weight:	11st
Foot:	Right

Season Review 05/06

Striker Dudley 'DJ' Campbell was a surprise transfer deadline signing for Blues in January 2006, arriving for an initial sum of £500,000 from Brentford.

Campbell put pen to paper on a three-and-a-half year deal that will tie him to the club until 2009.

Campbell only became a professional after joining the Bees in the summer of 2005 from Ryman League side Yeading, where he had netted an incredible 83 times in just 109 appearances. He hit the back of the net 12 times in 28 games for Brentford, including a brace in a 2-1 FA Cup victory over Sunderland that brought him to the attention of Steve Bruce.

Player Performance 05/06

League Performance

Percentage of total possible time player was on pitch   ⊖ position in league table at end of month

Month:	Aug	Sep	Oct	Nov	Dec	Jan	Feb	Mar	Apr	May	Total
	0%	0%	0%	0%	0%	0%	24%	63%	15%	100%	15%
	13	14	19	19	19	18	18	18	18	18	
Team Pts:	4/12	2/9	0/12	3/6	4/18	6/9	4/12	1/12	10/21	0/3	34/114
Team Gls F:	4	3	0	1	5	7	2	1	5	0	28
Team Gls A:	7	4	5	1	12	2	6	7	5	1	50
Total mins:	0	0	0	0	0	0	87	227	97	90	501
Starts (sub):	0	0	0	0	0	0	0 (3)	2 (2)	1 (2)	1	4 (7)
Goals:	0	0	0	0	0	0	0	0	0	0	0
Assists:	0	0	0	0	0	0	0	0	0	0	0
Clean sheets:	0	0	0	0	0	0	0	0	0	0	0
Cards (Y/R):	0	0	0	0	0	0	0	0	0	0	0

League Performance Totals

Goals

- Campbell: 0
- Team-mates: 26
- **Total: 26**
- own goals: 2

Assists

- Campbell: 0
- Team-mates: 28
- **Total: 28**

Cards

- Campbell: 0
- Team-mates: 57
- **Total: 57**

Cup Games

	Apps	Goals	Cards
FA Cup	0	0	0
Carling Cup	0	0	0
Total	**0**	**0**	**0**

Career History

Career Milestones

Club Debut:

vs Arsenal (H), L 0-2, Premiership

 **04.02.06**

First Goal Scored for the Club:

—

▶ —

Time Spent at the Club:

▶ **0.5 Seasons**

Full International:

▶ —

Premiership Totals

92-06

Appearances	11
Goals	0
Assists	0
Yellow Cards	0
Red Cards	0

Clubs

Year	Club	Apps	Gls
06-06	Birmingham	11	0
05-06	Brentford	28	12
	Yeading		
	Billericay		
	Stevenage B		
	Chesham		

Off the Pitch

Age:

- Campbell: 25 years
- Team: 27 years, 8 months
- League: 26 years, 11 months

Height:

- Campbell: 5'8"
- Team: 5'11"
- League: 5'11"

Weight:

- Campbell: 11st
- Team: 11st 12lb
- League: 12st

40 Chris Sutton
Forward

Blues beat off competition from a host of other Premiership sides to land Celtic striker Chris Sutton on a free transfer during the January 2006 transfer window.

The former Norwich, Chelsea and Blackburn striker had commanded a total of £21 million in transfer fees during his career and won a Premiership winners' medal at Ewood Park. After making an encouraging start to his spell at St. Andrew's, Sutton suffered a string of niggling injuries that restricted him to just 11 appearances in four months. His only goal in Blues colours came in the local derby defeat away to Aston Villa.

Sutton's contract was cancelled by mutual consent after the club's relegation from the Premiership.

Player Details:

Date of Birth:	10.03.1973
Place of Birth:	Nottingham
Nationality:	English
Height:	6'3"
Weight:	13st 7lb
Foot:	Right

Player Performance 05/06

League Performance

Percentage of total possible time player was on pitch   ⊙ position in league table at end of month

Month:	Aug	Sep	Oct	Nov	Dec	Jan	Feb	Mar	Apr	May	Total
	0%	0%	0%	0%	0%	67%	88%	0%	53%	0%	24%
	13	14	19	19	19	18	18	18	18	18	
Team Pts:	4/12	2/9	0/12	3/6	4/18	6/9	4/12	1/12	10/21	0/3	34/114
Team Gls F:	4	3	0	1	5	7	2	1	5	0	28
Team Gls A:	7	4	5	1	12	2	6	7	5	1	50
Total mins:	0	0	0	0	0	180	316	0	335	0	831
Starts (sub):	0	0	0	0	0	2	4	0	4	0	10
Goals:	0	0	0	0	0	0	0	0	1	0	1
Assists:	0	0	0	0	0	1	0	0	0	0	1
Clean sheets:	0	0	0	0	0	1	0	0	1	0	2
Cards (Y/R):	0	0	0	0	0	0	1	0	1	0	2

League Performance Totals

Goals
- ▶ Sutton: 1
- ▷ Team-mates: 25
- **Total: 26**
- ▶ own goals: 2

Assists
- ▶ Sutton: 1
- ▷ Team-mates: 27
- **Total: 28**

Cards
- ▶ Sutton: 2
- ▷ Team-mates: 55
- **Total: 57**

Cup Games

	Apps	Goals	Cards
FA Cup	1	0	0
Carling Cup	0	0	0
Total	**1**	**0**	**0**

Career History

Career Milestones

Club Debut:
vs Charlton (A), L 2-0, Premiership

▶ **14.01.06**
Time Spent at the Club:
▶ **0.5 Seasons**

First Goal Scored for the Club:
vs Aston Villa (A), L 3-1, Premiership

▶ **16.04.06**
Full International:
▶ **England**

Premiership Totals

92-06

Appearances	247
Goals	82
Assists	53
Yellow Cards	47
Red Cards	2

Clubs

Year	Club	Apps	Gls
06-06	Birmingham	11	1
00-06	Celtic		
99-00	Chelsea	39	3
94-99	Blackburn	162	62
91-94	Norwich	128	43

Off the Pitch

Age:

- ▶ Sutton: 33 years, 2 months
- ▷ Team: 27 years, 8 months
- | League: 26 years, 11 months

Height:
- ▶ Sutton: 6'3"
- ▷ Team: 5'11"
- | League: 5'11"

Weight:

- ▶ Sutton: 13st 7lb
- ▷ Team: 11st 12lb
- | League: 12st

9 Mikael Forssell
Forward

Season Review 05/06

Mikael Forssell initially joined Blues from Chelsea on a four-month loan deal in August 2003. This deal was then extended until the end of the 2003/04 campaign, before being extended yet again for a further season in April 2004. The Finnish international became a firm favourite with the St. Andrew's faithful due to his prolific goal-scoring form in the 2003/04 season – he netted 19 times in 37 games. Unfortunately a serious knee injury just four games into the 2004/05 season left him sidelined for the majority of the rest of that campaign and he officially returned to Stamford Bridge in January 2005. He made his comeback for the Premiership champions in the back end of the 2004/05 campaign before returning to St. Andrew's for a third time in the summer of 2005 – this time on a permanent basis for a fee of £3.5 million. But once again he was forced to miss much of the 2005/06 season while he struggled to regain his fitness.

Player Details:

Date of Birth:	15.03.1981
Place of Birth:	Steinfurt
Nationality:	Finnish
Height:	5'10"
Weight:	10st 10lb
Foot:	Right/Left

Player Performance 05/06

League Performance

Percentage of total possible time player was on pitch   ⊖ position in league table at end of month

Month:	Aug	Sep	Oct	Nov	Dec	Jan	Feb	Mar	Apr	May	Total
	63%	77%	63%	2% 19	12% 19	10% 18	24% 18	34% 18	52% 18	0% 18	38%
	13	14	19								
Team Pts:	4/12	2/9	0/12	3/6	4/18	6/9	4/12	1/12	10/21	0/3	34/114
Team Gls F:	4	3	0	1	5	7	2	1	5	0	28
Team Gls A:	7	4	5	1	12	2	6	7	5	1	50
Total mins:	225	209	227	4	67	26	88	122	326	0	1,294
Starts (sub):	2 (2)	3	2 (2)	0 (1)	0 (1)	0 (2)	1 (1)	1 (2)	1 (6)	0	10 (17)
Goals:	0	0	0	0	0	1	0	1	1	0	3
Assists:	0	0	0	0	0	1	0	1	0	0	2
Clean sheets:	0	0	0	0	0	0	0	0	0	0	1
Cards (Y/R):	0	0	1	0	0	0	0	0	0	0	1

League Performance Totals

Goals

▶ Forssell:	3
▦ Team-mates:	23
Total:	**26**
▶ own goals:	2

Assists

▶ Forssell:	2
▦ Team-mates:	26
Total:	**28**

Cards

▶ Forssell:	1
▦ Team-mates:	56
Total:	**57**

Cup Games

	Apps	Goals	Cards
FA Cup	5	3	0
Carling Cup	3	2	0
Total	**8**	**5**	**0**

Career History

Career Milestones

Club Debut:
vs Fulham (H), D 2-2, Premiership
▶ **14.09.03**

Time Spent at the Club:
▶ **2.5 Seasons**

First Goal Scored for the Club:
vs Fulham (H), D 2-2, Premiership
▶ **14.09.03**

Full International:
▶ **Finland**

Premiership Totals

92-06

Appearances	96
Goals	25
Assists	12
Yellow Cards	3
Red Cards	0

Clubs

Year	Club	Apps	Gls
03-06	Birmingham	76	27
	B.M'gladbach		
00-01	Crystal Palace	62	18
98-05	Chelsea	53	12
	HJK Helsinki		

Off the Pitch

Age:

- ▶ Forssell: 25 years, 2 months
- ▦ Team: 27 years, 8 months
- | League: 26 years, 11 months

Height:

- ▶ Forssell: 5'10"
- ▦ Team: 5'11"
- | League: 5'11"

Weight:

- ▶ Forssell: 10st 10lb
- ▦ Team: 11st 12lb
- | League: 12st

19 Clinton Morrison
Forward

Player Details:

Date of Birth:	14.05.1979
Place of Birth:	Tooting
Nationality:	Irish
Height:	5'10"
Weight:	11st 2lb
Foot:	Right

Season Review 05/06

Clinton Morrison became the club's then-record signing when he arrived in the summer of 2002 from Crystal Palace in a deal that saw Andrew Johnson move in the opposite direction. A Republic of Ireland international, Morrison scored his first goals for the club as Blues came back from two goals down to earn a draw at Liverpool. And the Tooting born youngster went on to earn a permanent place in the annals of Blues' history by scoring the first goal in a 3-0 win over local rivals Aston Villa in the first top flight Second City derby in 16 years. Whilst the goals were not free-flowing for Morrison during his time at St. Andrew's - 16 goals in 97 games - he won many admirers for his work rate and unselfish play. He made just one appearance for Blues during the 2005/06 season before returning to Palace in a £2 million move.

Player Performance 05/06

League Performance

Percentage of total possible time player was on pitch   ⊖ position in league table at end of month

Month:	Aug	Sep	Oct	Nov	Dec	Jan	Feb	Mar	Apr	May	Total
	13	14	19	19	19	18	18	18	18	18	
	1%	0%	0%	0%	0%	0%	0%	0%	0%	0%	0%
Team Pts:	4/12	2/9	0/12	3/6	4/18	6/9	4/12	1/12	10/21	0/3	34/114
Team Gls F:	4	3	0	1	5	7	2	1	5	0	28
Team Gls A:	7	4	5	1	12	2	6	7	5	1	50
Total mins:	3	0	0	0	0	0	0	0	0	0	3
Starts (sub):	0 (1)	0	0	0	0	0	0	0	0	0	0 (1)
Goals:	0	0	0	0	0	0	0	0	0	0	0
Assists:	0	0	0	0	0	0	0	0	0	0	0
Clean sheets:	0	0	0	0	0	0	0	0	0	0	0
Cards (Y/R):	0	0	0	0	0	0	0	0	0	0	0

League Performance Totals

Goals
- ▶ Morrison: 0
- ▷ Team-mates: 26
- **Total: 26**
- ▶ own goals: 2

Assists
- ▶ Morrison: 0
- ▷ Team-mates: 28
- **Total: 28**

Cards
- ▶ Morrison: 0
- ▷ Team-mates: 57
- **Total: 57**

Cup Games

	Apps	Goals	Cards
FA Cup	0	0	0
Carling Cup	0	0	0
Total	**0**	**0**	**0**

Career History

Career Milestones

Club Debut:
vs Everton (A), D 1-1, Premiership
▶ **28.08.02**

Time Spent at the Club:
▶ **3 Seasons**

First Goal Scored for the Club:
vs Liverpool (A), D 2-2, Premiership
▶ **11.09.02**

Full International:
▶ **Rep. Ireland**

Premiership Totals

92-06	
Appearances	88
Goals	15
Assists	13
Yellow Cards	11
Red Cards	0

Clubs

Year	Club	Apps	Gls
05-06	Crystal Palace	44	13
02-05	Birmingham	97	16
97-02	Crystal Palace	181	71

Off the Pitch

Age:

- ▶ Morrison: 27 years
- ▷ Team: 27 years, 8 months
- | League: 26 years, 11 months

Height:

- ▶ Morrison: 5'10"
- ▷ Team: 5'11"
- | League: 5'11"

Weight:

- ▶ Morrison: 11st 2lb
- ▷ Team: 11st 12lb
- | League: 12st

8 Walter Pandiani
Forward

Season Review 05/06

Walter Pandiani's transfer to Blues came with literally seconds to spare before the midnight deadline of the January 2005 window. The Uruguayan international striker was signed from Spanish club Deportivo La Coruna on loan until the end of that season and the move was made permanent in early August 2005 for £3 million.

Pandiani had made an immediate impact at St. Andrew's by scoring after just 12 minutes of his debut against Southampton and he went on to notch three more goals in 14 appearances during the 2004/05 season.

Unfortunately his second campaign at Blues proved less fruitful with just two goals from 21 appearances and he returned to Spain to join Espanyol in January 2006.

Player Details:

Date of Birth:	27.04.1976
Place of Birth:	Montevideo
Nationality:	Uruguayan
Height:	6'
Weight:	11st 9lb
Foot:	Left/Right

Player Performance 05/06

League Performance

Percentage of total possible time player was on pitch   Ⓖ position in league table at end of month

Month:	Aug	Sep	Oct	Nov	Dec	Jan	Feb	Mar	Apr	May	Total
	71%	36%	33%	27%	34%	6%	0%	0%	0%	0%	21%
	13	14	19	19	19	18	18	18	18	18	
Team Pts:	4/12	2/9	0/12	3/6	4/18	6/9	4/12	1/12	10/21	0/3	34/114
Team Gls F:	4	3	0	1	5	7	2	1	5	0	28
Team Gls A:	7	4	5	1	12	2	6	7	5	1	50
Total mins:	256	97	118	48	185	16	0	0	0	0	720
Starts (sub):	3 (1)	0 (3)	2 (1)	0 (2)	2 (2)	0 (1)	0	0	0	0	7 (10)
Goals:	0	1	0	0	1	0	0	0	0	0	2
Assists:	1	0	0	1	0	0	0	0	0	0	2
Clean sheets:	0	0	0	0	0	0	0	0	0	0	0
Cards (Y/R):	1	0	0	0	0	0	0	0	0	0	1

League Performance Totals

Goals

- ▶ Pandiani: 2
- ▷ Team-mates: 24
- **Total: 26**
- ▶ own goals: 2

Assists

- ▶ Pandiani: 2
- ▷ Team-mates: 26
- **Total: 28**

Cards

- ▶ Pandiani: 1
- ▷ Team-mates: 56
- **Total: 57**

Cup Games

	Apps	Goals	Cards
FA Cup	1	0	0
Carling Cup	3	0	1
Total	**4**	**0**	**1**

Career History

Career Milestones

Club Debut:

vs Southampton (H), W 2-1, Prem.

▶ **02.02.05**

Time Spent at the Club:

▶ **1 Season**

First Goal Scored for the Club:

vs Southampton (H), W 2-1, Prem.

▶ **02.02.05**

Full International:

▶ **Uruguay**

Premiership Totals

92-06

Appearances	31
Goals	6
Assists	5
Yellow Cards	3
Red Cards	0

Clubs

Year	Club	Apps	Gls
05-06	Birmingham	35	6
	RCD Mallorca		
	Deportivo La Coruna		

Off the Pitch

Age:

- ▶ Pandiani: 30 years, 1 month
- ▷ Team: 27 years, 8 months
- | League: 26 years, 11 months

Height:

- ▶ Pandiani: 6'
- ▷ Team: 5'11"
- | League: 5'11"

Weight:

- ▶ Pandiani: 11st 9lb
- ▷ Team: 11st 12lb
- | League: 12st

The Academy

▶ Neil Kilkenny duels with Liverpool's Dietmar Harmann

The major plus point from a largely disappointing 2005/06 season for Blues has been the emergence of several young Academy players into the first team fold.

In recent years the occasional player has stepped up from the club's youth development programme.

But this term the trickle has become a torrent with SIX Academy graduates making their bow at first team level.

The transformation began in the unlikely surroundings of Scunthorpe United on 20 September 2005 as debutants Neil Kilkenny,

Marcos Painter and Peter Till came off the bench to help Blues win comfortably in the Coca Cola Cup.

Kilkenny, in particular, grabbed the opportunity with both hands and showed his pedigree with a mature performance that earned him his first start in the following weekend's Premiership game against Liverpool.

The midfielder, then just 19, made an impressive home debut to help Blues earn a creditable draw with the European champions in the late September sunshine at St. Andrew's.

He was unfortunate to get sent off for handball towards the end but that was a minor blip on a red-

► Marcos Painter in FA Cup action against Reading

letter day in the career of the Enfield-born teenager.

Kilkenny has gone on to clock up over 20 appearances in the Blues first team and he will hopefully play a big part in the club's future having signed a long term contract to keep him at St. Andrew's until 2009.

Blues acted quickly to snap up the England youth international after he was released by Arsenal at the age of 17.

Steve Hopcroft, Blues' Recruitment Officer, believes that Kilkenny has benefited from the club's policy of blooding youngsters in the reserves at the earliest available opportunity.

"Steve Bruce has revolutionised the pathway through from youth to first team football here by creating an under 21 team at reserve team level," explains Hopcroft.

"Our young players can now see a clear and structured route for their continued development that is geared towards them grasping the opportunities that lie before them.

"We now have 16 and 17-year-olds playing for the reserves every week.

"Neil Kilkenny could not see this pathway through as a 17-year-old at Arsenal which led to him becoming frustrated and unfulfilled.

▶ Mathew Birley gets away from Chelsea's Claude Makalele

"After securing his release one season early from his contract, we beat a host of other clubs to secure his signature and the main reason was that we could show Neil how we were going to get him from youth team to first team."

Whilst Kilkenny's recruitment came at a relatively late stage, the opposite can be said for Painter. The defender's debut in the Blues first team at Glanford Park was the culmination of almost a decade's hard work by the Academy coaches to mould him into a player good enough to perform at the top level.

Hopcroft continues: "Howard Wilkinson's Charter for Excellence forced clubs who were serious about developing young players to become part of the Premier League Academy Programme.

"This meant that from the age of nine boys would receive a high level of coaching from qualified staff in state-of-the-art facilities and would be subjected to a stimulating games programme against boys of the same age at other Academy clubs.

"This is the route that Painter took and one that has seen him develop from a schoolboy to a Republic of Ireland under 21 international and now a fully fledged member of the Blues first team squad.

"Marcos is adamant that he has become the player he is today because of the Academy

▶ Mathew Sadler battles with Bolton

system and the structure that is in place at Birmingham City."

After making his bow against Scunthorpe, Painter had to wait a little longer for his first chance to shine in the Premiership but when it duly arrived he too grasped it with relish.

Painter came into the back four for the Premiership clash with Fulham at St. Andrew's in December and produced an accomplished display to ensure a clean sheet and three crucial points in a 1-0 home win.

Till, meanwhile, has yet to add to that solitary Blues appearance but he has instead enjoyed two productive loan spells, the first ironically back at the ground where he made his debut, Scunthorpe, and then Boston United.

The winger-cum-striker scored one goal in nine appearances for the Iron before switching to Boston where he has clocked up over a dozen games for the League Two outfit.

Till was joined at York Street for three months by fellow Blues colleague Asa Hall who also gained valuable first team experience via a loan spell with Steve Evans' side this season.

A number of other Academy graduates have taken the same route by spending time on loan at lower

▶ Sam Oji pointing the way in the Reserves

league clubs and made a good impression, notably goalkeeper Colin Doyle at Millwall.

Meanwhile, back at St. Andrew's, Mat Birley and Sam Oji have to a lesser extent broken on to the first team scene.

Birley has made three first substitute appearances, including a run-out against reigning Premiership champions Chelsea at Stamford Bridge, whilst Oji made his bow in the FA Cup replay win over Reading.

Academy manager Richard Stevens has been delighted to see so many of his rising stars gain first team recognition this season.

Stevens believes that it is a sign that the work done behind the scenes by the Academy over the recent years is now finally beginning to bear fruit.

"It has been really good for us as an Academy," admits Stevens. "We've worked hard for five or six years and we've had to fight the fight.

"We have seen a few players begin to flourish this year and some of that is down to the work of my predecessors, Brian (Eastick) and Stuart (Hall).

"And with the next crop coming through, including the likes of Nick Wright and Sone Aluko, it is an exciting time for the club."

Finally, a review of the Academy season would not be complete without mention of the re-emergence of one of Stevens and co's most popular protégés. Mat Sadler has endured terrible bad luck with injury since breaking through into the first team back in 2002.

But the defender looks to have finally put his problems behind him and has put in some impressive performance at left back since being recalled to the side during the last month of the season.

Stevens has not been surprised by the impact Sadler has made after four years in the wilderness. "As a 16-year-old, Matt was regarded as one of the best left-backs in the country by England's coaches," said Stevens.

"That is why he was given a chance as a 17-year-old at Blues and he has grown up into a man now. "He had so much so young that he struggled to deal with being injured for two years.

"Matt has always set himself really high standards and injuries test you to the limit.

"He didn't have the answers to his questions but I know he is buzzing once again."

▶ Colin doyle tastes FA Cup passion on loan at Forest

Under 18's results

Date	Opponent	H/A	Result
Sat 20 Aug	Middlesbrough	A	Won 2-0
Wed 31 Aug	Arsenal	H	Won 3-0
Sat 3 Sep	West Ham United	H	Drew 1-1
Sat 10 Sep	Southampton	A	Lost 0-6
Sat 17 Sep	Norwich City	H	Lost 0-2
Sat 24 Sep	Bristol City	H	Drew 1-1
Sat 1 Oct	Tottenham Hotspur	A	Lost 0-2
Sat 8 Oct	Coventry City	H	Drew 0-0
Sat 15 Oct	MK Dons	A	Won 3-0
Sat 22 Oct	Leicester City	H	Won 3-1
Sat 5 Nov	Reading	A	Won 2-0
Sat 12 Nov	Watford	A	Drew 1-1
Sat 19 Nov	Cardiff City	H	Lost 1-2
Sat 3 Dec	Aston Villa	H	Lost 0-2
Sat 10 Dec	Bristol City	A	Lost 0-1
Thu 15 Dec	Man Utd (FAYC3)	H	Lost 0-2
Sat 7 Jan	Coventry City	A	Lost 2-3
Sat 14 Jan	MK Dons	H	Drew 0-0
Sat 21 Jan	Leicester City	A	Drew 0-0
Sat 4 Feb	Reading	H	Drew 1-1
Sat 18 Feb	Cardiff City	A	Lost 0-4
Sat 25 Feb	Aston Villa	A	Lost 0-4
Sat 11 Mar	Millwall	A	Lost 0-2
Sat 18 Mar	Crystal Palace	H	Lost 1-4
Sat 1 Apr	Chelsea	A	Won 1-0
Sat 8 Apr	Charlton Athletic	H	Won 2-0
Wed 19 Apr	Tottenham Hotspur	H	Won 2-0
Sat 22 Apr	Ipswich Town	A	Drew 5-5
Fri 5 May	Watford	H	Lost 2-3

2006/07: The Opposition

Barnsley

BARNSLEY FC

Nickname:	The Tykes	Telephone:	01226 211 211
Manager:	Andy Ritchie	Ticket Office:	01226 211 200
Chairman:	Gordon Shepherd	Club Shop:	01226 211 400
Website:	www.barnsleyfc.co.uk		

Season Review 05/06

Barnsley gained promotion via the Playoffs after seeing off Huddersfield and then Swansea. Despite having been a striker himself, boss Andy Ritchie put together a defence that kept 19 clean sheets over the course of the League One season.

The Tykes were far from being defensively-minded, however, winning many admirers with some of their inventive attacking displays.

Points / Position

won drawn lost H home A away

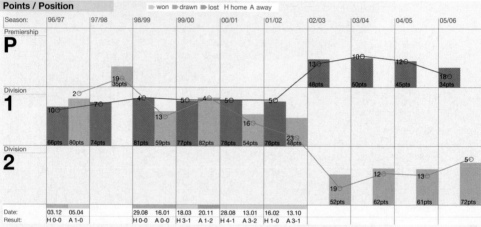

Season:	96/97	97/98	98/99	99/00	00/01	01/02	02/03	03/04	04/05	05/06

Premiership **P**

Division **1** — 10 (66pts), 2 (80pts), 7 (74pts), 4 (81pts), 13 (59pts), 5 (77pts), 4 (82pts), 5 (78pts), 16 (54pts), 5 (76pts), 19/35pts, 23/48pts, 13 (48pts), 10 (50pts), 12 (45pts), 18/34pts

Division **2** — 19 (52pts), 12 (62pts), 13 (61pts), 5 (72pts)

Date:	03.12	05.04		29.08	16.01	18.03	20.11	28.08	13.01	16.02	13.10
Result:	H 0-0	A 1-0		H 0-0	A 0-0	H 3-1	A 1-2	H 4-1	A 3-2	H 1-0	A 3-1

Goals 05/06

Goals by Time Period

11	7	12	9	10	13
0	15	30	45	60	75	90
4	8	4	10	8	10

scored
conceded

Goals by Area

Scored (Conceded)

15 (10)

42 (25)

5 (9)

Goals by Position

Scored | Conceded

- forward: 24
- midfield: 27
- defence: 7
- own goals: 4

- forward: 22
- midfield: 16
- defence: 6

Goal by Situation

Scored | Conceded

- set piece: 17
- open play: 41
- own goals: 4

- set piece: 16
- open play: 28

All-Time Records

Total Championship Record

Total Matches Played 0	Total Goals Scored ▶ 0
Total Matches Won ▶ 0	Total Goals Conceded ▶ 0
Total Matches Drawn ▶ 0	Total Points ▶ 0
Total Matches Lost ▶ 0	Total Players Used ▶ 0

All-Time Record vs Birmingham

Competition	Played	Won	Drawn	Lost	For	Against
League	60	16	14	30	79	103
FA Cup	5	2	2	1	8	6
League Cup	0	0	0	0	0	0
Other	2	1	0	1	5	2
Total	**67**	**19**	**16**	**32**	**92**	**111**

Barnsley

Oakwell Stadium

Stadium History

The Oakwell of today is unrecognisable from the place that Barnsley called home prior to the 1990's. Three of the four stands were knocked down and replaced, whilst the original West Stand was made all-seater. Furthermore, disabled facilities were significantly improved with the building of the Corner Stand in 1997.

Completion of the East Stand in 1993 enabled the Tykes to proudly boast that they were the first club in South Yorkshire to have executive boxes built in their stadium.

Stadium Statistics 05/06

Highest attendance
13,063 v Huddersfield Town 31.12.05

Lowest attendance
6,996 v Tranmere Rovers 06.12.05

Average attendance
9,045

How to Get There

Travel Information

Car parking
There is space for around 500 vehicles in a visitors car park at the ground.

Bus
Fans arriving at Barnsley Bus Station face a 10 minute walk to the ground.

Train
Barnsley Station is located in the town centre, just a five minute walk away from Oakwell.

Area Map

Local Map

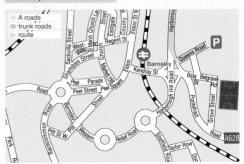

Burnley

Nickname:	The Clarets	Telephone:	0870 443 1882
Manager:	Steve Cotterill	Ticket Office:	0870 443 1914
Chairman:	Barry Kilby	Club Shop:	0870 443 1882
Website:	www.burnleyfootballclub.com		

Season Review 05/06

It was a season of little excitement at Turf Moor, with a mid-season push for the Playoffs proving to be the only real highlight. The goals of much-maligned striker Ade Akinbiyi were badly missed after he left for Sheffield United in January.

A worrying end to the campaign saw Steve Cotterill's team win just two of their final 14 Championship matches.

Points / Position

won drawn lost H home A away

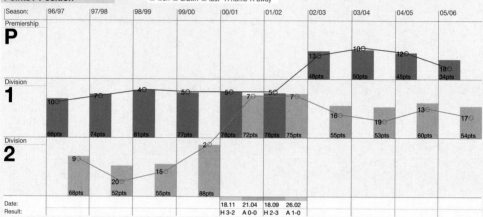

Season:	96/97	97/98	98/99	99/00	00/01	01/02	02/03	03/04	04/05	05/06
Premiership P							13○ 48pts	10○ 50pts	12○ 45pts	18○ 34pts
Division 1	10○ 66pts	7○ 74pts	4○ 81pts	5○ 77pts	5○ 78pts	7○ 72pts	5○ 76pts / 7○ 75pts / 16○ 55pts	19○ 53pts	13○ 60pts	17○ 54pts
Division 2		9○ 68pts	20○ 52pts	15○ 55pts	2○ 88pts					

Date:	18.11	21.04	18.09	26.02
Result:	H 3-2	A 0-0	H 2-3	A 1-0

Goals 05/06

Goals by Time Period

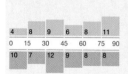

4	8	9	6	8	11
0	15	30	45	60	75	90
10	7	12	9	8	8

scored
conceded

Goals by Area

Scored (Conceded)

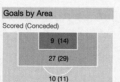

9 (14)

27 (29)

10 (11)

Goals by Position

Scored	Conceded

- forward: 20
- midfield: 22
- defence: 3
- own goals: 1

- forward: 28
- midfield: 14
- defence: 11
- own goals: 1

Goal by Situation

Scored	Conceded

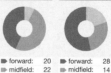

- set piece: 12
- open play: 33
- own goals: 1

- set piece: 23
- open play: 30
- own goals: 1

All-Time Records

Total Championship Record

Total Matches Played	Total Goals Scored
92	84

Total Matches Won	Total Goals Conceded
29	93

Total Matches Drawn	Total Points
27	114

Total Matches Lost	Total Players Used
36	42

All-Time Record vs Birmingham

Competition	Played	Won	Drawn	Lost	For	Against
League	78	36	16	26	123	99
FA Cup	4	3	0	1	7	3
League Cup	1	1	0	0	3	2
Other	0	0	0	0	0	0
Total	**83**	**40**	**16**	**27**	**133**	**104**

Burnley

Turf Moor

Stadium History

Having been in existence for just nine months, Burnley moved to Turf Moor in February 1883. It is believed that the ground was the first to play host to royalty, as Prince Albert, the son of Queen Victoria, attended a game in October 1886.

Much development has taken place since then, most recently the building of two new stands during the mid-1990's. The James Hargreaves Stand was swiftly followed by the Jimmy McIlroy Stand, giving the Clarets a modern venue to be proud of.

Seating Plan

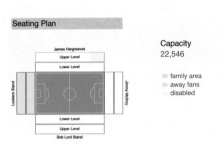

James Hargreaves
Upper Level
Lower Level

Lookers Stand

Jimmy McIlroy

Lower Level
Upper Level
Bob Lord Stand

Stadium Statistics 05/06

Capacity
22,546

family area
away fans
disabled

Highest attendance
17,912 v Stoke City 26.12.05

Lowest attendance
10,431 v Cardiff City 10.09.05

Average attendance
12,461

How to Get There

Travel Information

Car parking
Due to matchday parking restrictions, away fans are advised to use the cricket club on Belvedere Road

Bus
The main Bus Station is located just off Centenary Way, not far from Turf Moor.

Train
The nearest stations are Burnley Central (20 minute walk) and Burnley Manchester Road (15 minute walk).

Area Map

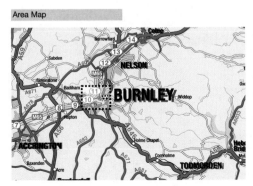

Local Map

A roads
trunk roads
route

Cardiff City ○

Nickname:	The Bluebirds	Telephone:	02920 221 001
Manager:	Dave Jones	Ticket Office:	0845 345 1400
Chairman:	Sam Hammam	Club Shop:	0845 345 1485
Website:	www.cardiffcityfc.co.uk		

Season Review 05/06

Cardiff spent the season on the fringes of a Playoff place, but ultimately fell away to finish 11th. On-loan midfielder Jason Koumas played a starring role, with Cameron Jerome demonstrating enough ability in attack to earn a summer move to Birmingham.

Producing consistent performances proved difficult for the Bluebirds, with back-to-back victories only achieved twice during the Championship campaign.

Points / Position

won drawn lost H home A away

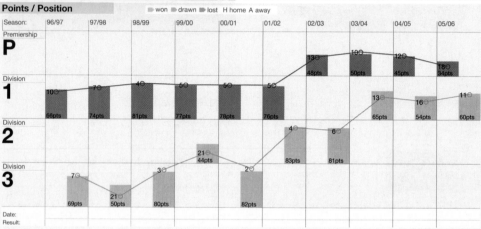

Goals 05/06

Goals by Time Period

11	10	6	10	12	9
0	15	30	45	60	75	90
6	9	6	10	14	14

- scored
- conceded

Goals by Area
Scored (Conceded)

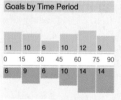

11 (22)
36 (31)
11 (6)

Goals by Position

Scored / Conceded

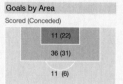

- forward: 29
- midfield: 19
- defence: 10

- forward: 28
- midfield: 21
- defence: 7
- own goals: 3

Goal by Situation

Scored / Conceded

- set piece: 19
- open play: 39

- set piece: 15
- open play: 41
- own goals: 3

All-Time Records

Total Championship Record

Total Matches Played
▶ 92

Total Matches Won
▶ 29

Total Matches Drawn
▶ 27

Total Matches Lost
▶ 36

Total Goals Scored
▶ 106

Total Goals Conceded
▶ 110

Total Points
▶ 114

Total Players Used
▶ 48

All-Time Record vs Birmingham

Competition	Played	Won	Drawn	Lost	For	Against
League	54	20	10	24	67	72
FA Cup	1	0	0	1	2	5
League Cup	0	0	0	0	0	0
Other	0	0	0	0	0	0
Total	**55**	**20**	**10**	**25**	**69**	**77**

Cardiff City

Ninian Park

Stadium History

Ninian Park, named after Lord Ninian Crichton-Stuart, became home to Cardiff in 1910. A 2-1 friendly defeat against Aston Villa on September 1 marked the first match played at the venue, and drew a crowd of over 7,000 spectators.

Much work had been required to turn land used primarily as a waste tip into a flat surface capable of staging football, with many volunteers playing a key role in the process. Nowadays, plans to build a new and improved stadium are in place.

Seating Plan

Popular Bank

Canton Stand

Grange Terrace

Grandstand

Capacity
20,000

🔻 family area
🔻 away fans
    disabled

Stadium Statistics 05/06

Highest attendance
16,403 v Plymouth Argyle 26.12.05

Lowest attendance
8,724 v Ipswich Town 28.11.05

Average attendance
11,720

How to Get There

Travel Information

Car parking
Spaces are available at a car park opposite the ground, and at the Leckwith Road Athletics Stadium.

Bus
There are regular services to Ninian Park from Cardiff Central Bus Station.

Train
Ninian Park Halt is served by trains from Cardiff Central Station, and is just a 2-3 minute walk from the ground.

Area Map

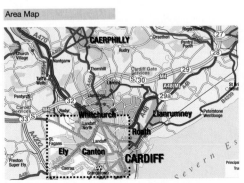

Local Map

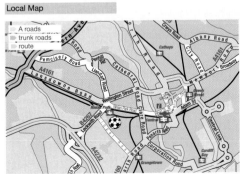

Colchester United °

Nickname:	The U's	Telephone:	0871 226 2161
Manager:	—	Ticket Office:	0871 226 2161
Chairman:	Peter Heard	Club Shop:	01206 715 309
Website:	www.cu-fc.com		

Season Review 05/06

Phil Parkinson was the toast of Colchester after leading his side to a surprise promotion, but he could not resist the overtures of Hull during the summer. The unfashionable Layer Road club overcame a shaky start and even managed a run of nine straight League One wins at home.

Amazingly, no team in the division performed in front of a lower average gate than the men from Essex.

Points / Position

won drawn lost H home A away

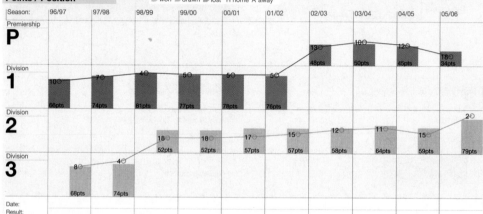

Season:	96/97	97/98	98/99	99/00	00/01	01/02	02/03	03/04	04/05	05/06

Premiership

P

Division **1** — 10 66pts / 7 74pts / 4 81pts / 5 77pts / 5 78pts / 5 76pts / 13 48pts / 10 50pts / 12 45pts / 18 34pts

Division **2** — 18 52pts / 18 52pts / 17 57pts / 15 57pts / 12 58pts / 11 64pts / 15 59pts / 2 79pts

Division **3** — 8 68pts / 4 74pts

Date:
Result:

Goals 05/06

Goals by Time Period

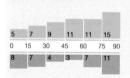

scored
conceded

Goals by Area

Scored (Conceded)

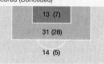

13 (7)
31 (28)
14 (5)

Goals by Position

Scored		Conceded	

Scored
forward: 23
midfield: 18
defence: 13
own goals: 4

Conceded
forward: 22
midfield: 17
defence: 1

Goal by Situation

Scored
set piece: 16
open play: 38
own goals: 4

Conceded
set piece: 10
open play: 30

All-Time Records

Total Championship Record

Total Matches Played	0	Total Goals Scored	0
Total Matches Won	0	Total Goals Conceded	0
Total Matches Drawn	0	Total Points	0
Total Matches Lost	0	Total Players Used	0

All-Time Record vs Birmingham

Competition	Played	Won	Drawn	Lost	For	Against
League	0	0	0	0	0	0
FA Cup	1	0	0	1	0	2
League Cup	2	0	1	1	2	3
Other	0	0	0	0	0	0
Total	**3**	**0**	**1**	**2**	**2**	**5**

Colchester United

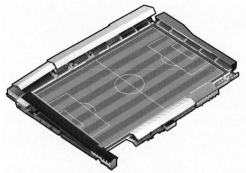

Stadium History

Layer Road opened its doors in August 1909, but it wasn't until 1937 that Colchester United were formed and took over the ground from previous occupants Colchester Town. In more recent times, ownership has changed hands between the local Borough council and the club on a couple of occasions.

It is hoped that a new 10,000-capacity community stadium at Cuckoo Farm will be constructed in time for the team to start playing there by the beginning of the 2007/08 season.

Seating Plan

Capacity
6,200

family area
away fans
disabled

Stadium Statistics 05/06

Highest attendance
5,920 v Southend United 04.03.06

Lowest attendance
2,721 v Barnsley 13.08.05

Average attendance
3,969

How to Get There

Travel Information

Car parking
Limited street parking is available in the area surrounding the ground.

Bus
The number 64 travels along Layer Road, and can be caught from the town centre.

Train
Away supporters are advised to use Colchester (North) Station.

Area Map

Local Map

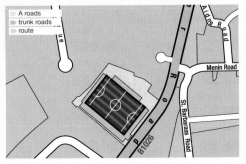

A roads
trunk roads
route

153

Coventry City

Nickname:	The Sky Blues	Telephone:	0870 421 1987
Manager:	Micky Adams	Ticket Office:	0870 421 1987
Chairman:	Geoffrey Robinson	Club Shop:	0870 421 1987
Website:	www.ccfc.co.uk		

Season Review 05/06

Coventry made real progress over the course of the campaign, brushing aside a slow start to finish in a creditable eighth place. The brand new Ricoh Arena proved to be a happy hunting ground for the Sky Blues, with just four visiting teams emerging victorious.

Gary McSheffrey always looked dangerous, whilst Dele Adebola and Stern John struck up a decent partnership in attack.

Points / Position

won • drawn • lost H home A away

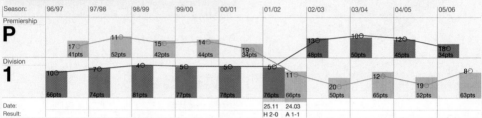

Season:	96/97	97/98	98/99	99/00	00/01	01/02	02/03	03/04	04/05	05/06
Premiership **P**	17 41pts	11 52pts	15 42pts	14 44pts	19 34pts		13 48pts	10 50pts	12 45pts	18 34pts
Division **1**	10 66pts	7 74pts	4 81pts	5 77pts	5 78pts	5 76pts / 11 66pts	20 50pts	12 65pts	19 52pts	8 63pts
Date:						25.11 24.03				
Result:						H 2-0 A 1-1				

Recent Meetings

25.11.01		
⚪⚪ **2-0**	Attendance: 18,279	
Referee: C.J.Foy		
O 17 Marcelo		
O 61 Marcelo		

24.03.02		
⚪⚪ **1-1**	Attendance: 17,945	
Referee: M.J.Brandwood		
O 60 Healy	O 80 Horsfield	

Goals 05/06

Goals by Time Period

11	9	13	12	7	10
0	15	30	45	60	75	90
9	13	14	9	5	15

• scored
• conceded

Goals by Area

Scored (Conceded)

22 (20)

35 (33)

5 (12)

Goals by Position

Scored | Conceded

• forward: 42
• midfield: 16
• defence: 2
• own goals: 2

• forward: 30
• midfield: 22
• defence: 12
• own goals: 1

Goal by Situation

Scored | Conceded

• set piece: 15
• open play: 45
• own goals: 2

• set piece: 21
• open play: 43
• own goals: 1

All-Time Records

Total Championship Record

Total Matches Played	▶ **92**
Total Matches Won	▶ **29**
Total Matches Drawn	▶ **28**
Total Matches Lost	▶ **35**

Total Goals Scored	▶ **123**
Total Goals Conceded	▶ **138**
Total Points	▶ **115**
Total Players Used	▶ **51**

All-Time Record vs Birmingham

Competition	Played	Won	Drawn	Lost	For	Against
League	42	12	13	17	51	64
FA Cup	2	1	0	1	3	8
League Cup	3	1	1	1	3	3
Other	0	0	0	0	0	0
Total	**47**	**14**	**14**	**19**	**57**	**75**

Coventry City

Ricoh Arena

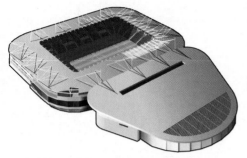

Stadium History

Coventry began the 2005-06 season in the impressive surroundings of the brand new Ricoh Arena. Having ended their 106-year stay at Highfield Road with a 6-2 demolition of Derby, the Sky Blues christened their new stadium with a 3-0 win against Q.P.R on August 20, 2005.

Built on a 70-acre site in the north of the city, the new ground is capable of housing 32,000 spectators. Football is not the only thing on offer at the venue, however, with the development also comprising a supermarket and casino.

Seating Plan

Marconi West Stand

Jewson South Stand

Coventry Evening Telegraph North Stand

NTL East Stand

Capacity
32,000

family area
away fans
disabled

Stadium Statistics 05/06

Highest attendance
26,851 v Wolverhampton Wanderers 02.01.06

Lowest attendance
16,156 v Millwall 10.12.05

Average attendance
21,301

How to Get There

Travel Information

Car parking
The Ricoh Arena offers around 2000 parking spaces on site.

Train
Coventry Station is a five minute taxi ride away from the new ground.

Bus
Six members-only bus routes to the stadium have been created.

Area Map

Local Map

Crystal Palace °

Nickname:	The Eagles	Telephone:	0208 768 6000
Manager:	Peter Taylor	Ticket Office:	0871 2000 071
Chairman:	Simon Jordan	Club Shop:	0208 768 6100
Website:	www.cpfc.co.uk		

Season Review 05/06

A campaign that began with high hopes of a return to the Premiership ended in bitter Playoff disappointment. Manager Iain Dowie then left for Charlton, with key men Andy Johnson and Fitz Hall also moving on to pastures new.

The Eagles struggled to fulfill their potential and will be hoping that new boss Peter Taylor can remedy that next season.

Points / Position

■ won ■ drawn ■ lost H home A away

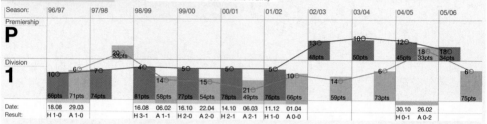

Season:	96/97	97/98	98/99	99/00	00/01	01/02	02/03	03/04	04/05	05/06
Premiership										
Division 1	10○ 66pts	6○ 71pts	7○ 74pts	4○ 81pts 14 58pts	5○ 77pts	5○ 54pts	5○ 78pts	21○ 49pts	13○ 48pts 10○ 76pts 66pts	18○ 50pts 14○ 59pts	12○ 45pts 6○ 73pts	18○ 33pts	18○ 34pts 6○ 75pts

| Date: | 18.08 | 29.03 | | 16.08 | 06.02 | 16.10 | 22.04 | 14.10 | 06.03 | 11.12 | 01.04 | | | | 30.10 | 26.02 | |
| Result: | H 1-0 | A 1-0 | | H 3-1 | A 1-1 | H 2-0 | A 2-0 | H 2-1 | A 2-1 | H 1-0 | A 0-0 | | | | H 0-1 | A 0-2 | |

Recent Meetings

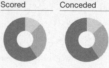

	11.12.01		01.04.02		30.10.04		26.02.05
○○ 1-0	Attendance: 20,119	○○○ 0-0	Attendance: 19,598	○○○ 0-1	Attendance: 28,916	○○ 2-0	Attendance: 23,376
Referee: A.R.Leake		Referee: S.J.Baines		Referee: D.J.Gallagher		Referee: P.Dowd	
○ 62 Mooney				○ 41 Johnson		○ 41 Johnson	
						○ 68 Johnson	

Goals 05/06

Goals by Time Period

8	11	13	12	8	15

0	15	30	45	60	75	90

7	10	7	7	4	13

■ scored
■ conceded

Goals by Area

Scored (Conceded)

18 (16)

42 (27)

7 (5)

Goals by Position

Scored	Conceded

- ■ forward: 37
- ■ midfield: 18
- ■ defence: 8
- ► own goals: 4

- ■ forward: 27
- ■ midfield: 13
- ■ defence: 6
- ► own goals: 2

Goal by Situation

Scored	Conceded

- ■ set piece: 17
- ■ open play: 46
- ► own goals: 4

- ■ set piece: 16
- ■ open play: 30
- ► own goals: 2

All-Time Records

Total Championship Record

Total Matches Played	► 46	Total Goals Scored	► 67
Total Matches Won	► 21	Total Goals Conceded	► 48
Total Matches Drawn	► 12	Total Points	► 75
Total Matches Lost	► 13	Total Players Used	► 23

All-Time Record vs Birmingham

Competition	Played	Won	Drawn	Lost	For	Against
League	36	15	6	15	50	42
FA Cup	3	1	1	1	3	5
League Cup	3	1	2	0	4	3
Other	0	0	0	0	0	0
Total	**42**	**17**	**9**	**16**	**57**	**50**

Crystal Palace

Selhurst Park

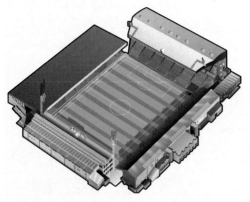

Stadium History

Having spent £2,570 on acquiring land and a further £30,000 on construction work, Crystal Palace moved into their new Selhurst Park home in 1924. Though the ground remained undeveloped until 1969, a friendly against Real Madrid in 1962 marked the installation of new floodlights mounted on pylons in each corner of the stadium.

In recent times, the venue has provided fellow London clubs Charlton Athletic and Wimbledon with temporary accommodation when they were without a home.

Seating Plan

Capacity
26,309

family area
away fans
disabled

Stadium Statistics 05/06

Highest attendance
23,843 v Leeds United 04.03.06

Lowest attendance
17,291 v Preston North End 24.09.05

Average attendance
19,457

How to Get There

Travel Information

Car parking
Plenty of street parking is available, while the local Sainsbury's car park can also be used.

Train
The nearest stations are Thornton Heath and Selhurst. Crystal Palace Station is nowhere near the stadium.

Bus
Buses from all the surrounding areas run past the ground.

Area Map

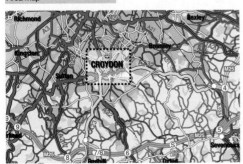

Local Map

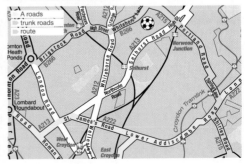

Derby County °

Nickname:	**The Rams**
Manager:	**Billy Davies**
Chairman:	**Peter Gadsby**
Website:	**www.dcfc.co.uk**

Telephone:	**0870 444 1884**
Ticket Office:	**0870 444 1884**
Club Shop:	**01332 209 000**

Season Review 05/06

Derby failed to build on what had been an impressive season in 2004/05, with Phil Brown only lasting a few months in the managerial hotseat. Caretaker replacement Terry Westley then did just enough to keep the Rams out of the relegation picture.

The summer appointment of former Preston boss Billy Davies has given many fans hope of better times to come at Pride Park.

Points / Position

● won ● drawn ● lost H home A away

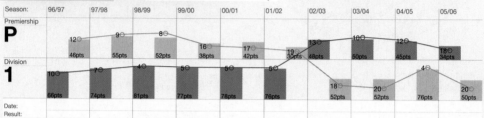

Season:	96/97	97/98	98/99	99/00	00/01	01/02	02/03	03/04	04/05	05/06
Premiership	12○ 46pts	9○ 55pts	8○ 52pts	16○ 38pts	17○ 42pts	19○ 30pts	13○ 48pts	10○ 50pts	12○ 45pts	18○ 34pts
Division 1	10○ 66pts	7○ 74pts	4○ 81pts	5○ 77pts	5○ 78pts	5○ 76pts		18○ 52pts	20○ 52pts 4○ 76pts	20○ 50pts
Date:										
Result:										

Recent Meetings

○○ 3-0 04.09.93 Attendance: 14,582

O Frain
O Saville
O Saville

○○ 1-1 26.02.94 Attendance: 19,598

O Johnson O Claridge

○○ 1-4 21.11.95 Attendance: 19,417
Referee: K.Breen

O Ward
O 5 Sturridge
O 40 Willems
O 47 Gabbiadini
O 73 Powell

○○ 1-1 20.04.96 Attendance: 16,757

O 56 Simpson O Breen

Goals 05/06

Goals by Time Period

6	10	10	9	8	10
0	15	30	45	60	75	90
9	6	10	12	11	19

● scored
● conceded

Goals by Area

Scored (Conceded)

10 (20)

35 (34)

8 (13)

Goals by Position

Scored		Conceded	
● forward:	16	● forward:	39
● midfield:	29	● midfield:	19
● defence:	6	● defence:	8
● own goals:	2	● own goals:	1

Goal by Situation

Scored		Conceded	
● set piece:	22	● set piece:	21
● open play:	29	● open play:	45
● own goals:	2	● own goals:	1

All-Time Records

Total Championship Record

Total Matches Played	▶ 92
Total Matches Won	▶ 32
Total Matches Drawn	▶ 30
Total Matches Lost	▶ 30
Total Goals Scored	▶ 124
Total Goals Conceded	▶ 127
Total Points	▶ 126
Total Players Used	▶ 47

All-Time Record vs Birmingham

Competition	Played	Won	Drawn	Lost	For	Against
League	88	34	26	28	147	128
FA Cup	6	3	1	2	12	10
League Cup	4	1	0	3	4	11
Other	0	0	0	0	0	0
Total	**98**	**38**	**27**	**33**	**163**	**149**

Derby County

Pride Park

Stadium History

Her Majesty the Queen and the Duke of Edinburgh officially opened Pride Park, with a friendly against Sampdoria getting things underway on the pitch. That was in the summer of 1997, and two years later the capacity was increased to in excess of 33,000.

Having previously hosted an Under-21 match, the ground staged a full international as England defeated Mexico 4-0 in a May 2001 friendly. Despite no longer playing in the Premiership, Derby regularly attract crowds of around 25,000.

Seating Plan

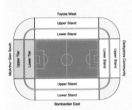

Capacity
33,597

family area
away fans
disabled

Stadium Statistics 05/06

Highest attendance
30,391 v Sheffield Wednesday 30.04.06

Lowest attendance
21,434 v Reading 31.12.05

Average attendance
24,166

How to Get There

Travel Information

Car parking
Away fans are advised to park at Wilmorton College.

Train
It is a 15 minute walk from Derby Railway Station to Pride Park.

Bus
Shuttle buses run to the ground from the bus station in the city centre.

Area Map

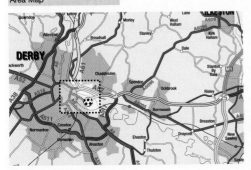

Local Map

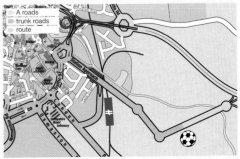

Hull City

Nickname:	**The Tigers**
Manager:	**Phil Parkinson**
Chairman:	**Adam Pearson**
Website:	www.hullcityafc.premiumtv.co.uk

Telephone:	**0870 837 0003**
Ticket Office:	**0870 837 0004**
Club Shop:	**0870 837 0005**

Season Review 05/06

Hull enjoyed a fairly comfortable season back at Championship level and were never unduly troubled by the threat of relegation. Victory over local rivals Leeds in April was the undoubted highlight of a solid campaign.

The summer departure of popular manager Peter Taylor came as a massive blow to the club, but his youthful replacement, Phil Parkinson, has shown plenty of promise.

Points / Position

won drawn lost H home A away

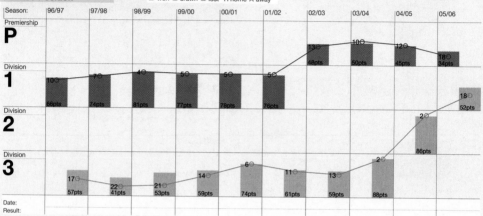

Goals 05/06

Goals by Time Period

6	6	10	10	6	11
0	15	30	45	60	75	90
7	10	10	7	11	10

 scored
 conceded

Goals by Area

Scored (Conceded)

15 (14)

25 (27)

9 (14)

Goals by Position

Scored		Conceded	
forward:	24	forward:	18
midfield:	18	midfield:	28
defence:	4	defence:	6
own goals:	3	own goals:	3

Goal by Situation

Scored		Conceded	
set piece:	11	set piece:	12
open play:	35	open play:	40
own goals:	3	own goals:	3

All-Time Records

Total Championship Record

Total Matches Played	**46**
Total Matches Won	**12**
Total Matches Drawn	**16**
Total Matches Lost	**18**

Total Goals Scored	**49**
Total Goals Conceded	**55**
Total Points	**52**
Total Players Used	**33**

All-Time Record vs Birmingham

Competition	Played	Won	Drawn	Lost	For	Against
League	50	14	15	21	69	76
FA Cup	1	0	0	1	0	2
League Cup	0	0	0	0	0	0
Other	0	0	0	0	0	0
Total	**51**	**14**	**15**	**22**	**69**	**78**

Hull City

KC Stadium

Stadium History

Constructed in 14 months, the KC Stadium opened for business with a friendly victory against Sunderland on December 18, 2002. Built at a cost of £43.5m, the stadium complex was the first in Britain to be located within a parkland setting.

Moving to this state-of-the-art venue has had a positive effect on the pitch, with Hull securing successive promotions and establishing themselves in the Championship. The ground is also home to the city's rugby league team, while other facilities such as a skate park can be found on the council-owned site.

Seating Plan

Ideal Standard Stand
Eastern

Smith & Nephew North Stand

MKM South Stand

Devries Honda Stand
Western

Capacity
25,504

family area
away fans
disabled

Stadium Statistics 05/06

Highest attendance
23,486 v Leeds United 01.04.06

Lowest attendance
17,698 v Reading 18.10.05

Average attendance
19,841

How to Get There

Travel Information

Car parking
There is a car park at the ground costing £2.50.

Train
Paragon Station is around 10 minutes walk from the stadium.

Bus
A park and ride service operates from the Priory Park site on the way into Hull.

Area Map

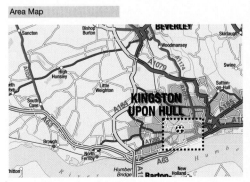

Local Map

A roads
trunk roads
route

Ipswich Town °

Nickname:	The Tractor Boys	Telephone:	01473 400 500
Manager:	Jim Magilton	Ticket Office:	0870 111 0555
Chairman:	David Sheepshanks	Club Shop:	01473 400 501
Website:	www.itfc.co.uk		

Season Review 05/06

Ipswich struggled to adapt to life without Darren Bent, Shefki Kuqi, Kelvin Davis and Tommy Miller. Manager Joe Royle had little choice but to put his faith in youth and saw the Tractor Boys slump to a disappointing 15th-place finish.

Legendary skipper Jim Magilton looked set for an emotional summer exit, but instead found himself succeeding Royle as boss.

Points / Position

won   drawn   lost   H home A away

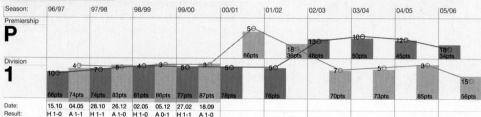

Season:	96/97	97/98	98/99	99/00	00/01	01/02	02/03	03/04	04/05	05/06

Premiership **P**

00/01 5 66pts
01/02 18 36pts
02/03 13 48pts
03/04 10 50pts
04/05 12 45pts
05/06 18 34pts

Division **1**

96/97 10 66pts
97/98 4 74pts
98/99 7 74pts / 5 83pts
99/00 4 81pts / 3 86pts
00/01 5 77pts / 3 87pts
01/02 5 78pts
02/03 5 76pts
03/04 7 70pts
04/05 5 73pts / 3 85pts
05/06 15 56pts

| Date: | 15.10 | 04.05 | 28.10 | 26.12 | 02.05 | 05.12 | 27.02 | 18.09 |
| Result: | H 1-0 | A 1-1 | H 1-0 | A 1-0 | H 1-0 | A 0-1 | H 1-1 | A 1-0 |

Recent Meetings

05.12.98	02.05.99	18.09.99	27.02.00
OO **1-0** Attendance: 15,901	OO **1-0** Attendance: 27,685	OOO **0-1** Attendance: 19,758	OO **1-1** Attendance: 20,493
Referee: M.J. Jones	Referee: R. Pearson	Referee: B.Knight	Referee: A.R.Leake
O 16 Petta	O 60 Furlong	O 10 Furlong	O 17 Mowbray (O.G) O 44 Johnson

Goals 05/06

Goals by Time Period

7	7	8	11	10	10
0	15	30	45	60	75	90
5	7	14	16	10	14

scored
conceded

Goals by Area
Scored (Conceded)

15 (18)

26 (39)

12 (9)

Goals by Position

Scored		Conceded	
forward:	19	forward:	40
midfield:	21	midfield:	21
defence:	12	defence:	3
own goals:	1	own goals:	2

Goal by Situation

Scored		Conceded	
set piece:	26	set piece:	19
open play:	26	open play:	45
own goals:	1	own goals:	2

All-Time Records

Total Championship Record

Total Matches Played
92

Total Matches Won
38

Total Matches Drawn
27

Total Matches Lost
27

Total Goals Scored
138

Total Goals Conceded
122

Total Points
141

Total Players Used
42

All-Time Record vs Birmingham

Competition	Played	Won	Drawn	Lost	For	Against
League	54	26	10	18	87	68
FA Cup	4	2	0	2	4	4
League Cup	5	1	0	4	5	11
Other	0	0	0	0	0	0
Total	**63**	**29**	**10**	**24**	**96**	**83**

Ipswich Town

Portman Road

Stadium History

Having shared what is now the training pitch behind the Britannia Stand with the local cricket club for a number of years, Ipswich moved to the site of today's Portman Road in the early 1900's.

The Supporters' Association funded several developments in the 1950's, most notably raising £30,500 towards the building of a new West Stand. Since the turn of the Millennium, further work has taken place. The impressive Greene King and North stands cost around £22m to build.

Seating Plan

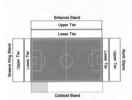

Capacity
30,300

- family area
- away fans
- disabled

Stadium Statistics 05/06

Highest attendance
29,184 v Norwich City 18.09.05

Lowest attendance
22,551 v Preston North End 29.08.05

Average attendance
24,252

How to Get There

Travel Information

Car parking
There are roughly 800 spaces available in car parks around the stadium.

Train
The ground is about 400 metres away from Ipswich Station.

Bus
Bus stops are located on nearby Princes Street, Civic Drive and Handford Road.

Area Map

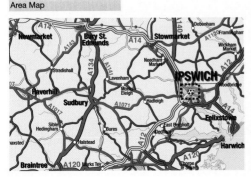

Local Map

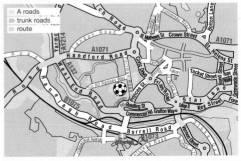

Leeds United °

Nickname:	United	Telephone:	0113 367 6000
Manager:	Kevin Blackwell	Ticket Office:	0845 121 1992
Chairman:	Ken Bates	Club Shop:	0870 125 3337
Website:	www.leedsunited.com		

Season Review 05/06

A promising campaign ended in bitter disappointment for Leeds as they missed out on promotion against Watford in the Playoff Final. Kevin Blackwell's team were a permanent fixture in the top six, but rarely threatened to go up automatically.

Rob Hulse, David Healy and Robbie Blake all contributed a decent amount of goals, with Eddie Lewis providing a number of vital assists.

Points / Position

won drawn lost H home A away

Season:	96/97	97/98	98/99	99/00	00/01	01/02	02/03	03/04	04/05	05/06
Premiership P	11	5	4	3	4	5	13 / 15	18 / 19	12 / 18	
	46pts	59pts	67pts	69pts	68pts	66pts	48pts / 47pts	50pts / 33pts	45pts / 34pts	
Division 1	10	7	4	5	5	5			14	5
	66pts	74pts	81pts	77pts	78pts	78pts			60pts	78pts

Date:							31.08	01.01	27.03	20.09
Result:							H 2-1	A 0-2	H 4-1	A 2-0

Recent Meetings

OOO 2-1 31.08.02 Attendance: 27,164
Referee: P.A.Durkin
O 32 Devlin   O 50 Bowyer
O 58 Johnson

OOO 2-0 01.01.03 Attendance: 40,034
Referee: P.Dowd
O 6 Bakke
O 67 Viduka

OOO 0-2 20.09.03 Attendance: 34,305
Referee: D.J.Gallagher
O 79 Savage
O 84 Forssell

OOO 4-1 27.03.04 Attendance: 29,069
Referee: M.R.Halsey
O 12 Hughes   O 3 Viduka
O 67 Hughes
O 69 Forssell
O 82 Forssell

Goals 05/06

Goals by Time Period

3	4	11	11	14	14
0	15	30	45	60	75	90
5	5	7	6	8	7

 scored
 conceded

Goals by Area
Scored (Conceded)

13 (11)
38 (20)
6 (7)

Goals by Position

Scored
- forward: 40
- midfield: 12
- defence: 4
- own goals: 1

Conceded
- forward: 11
- midfield: 20
- defence: 3
- own goals: 4

Goal by Situation

Scored
- set piece: 27
- open play: 29
- own goals: 1

Conceded
- set piece: 11
- open play: 23
- own goals: 4

All-Time Records

Total Championship Record

Total Matches Played **92**
Total Matches Won **35**
Total Matches Drawn **33**
Total Matches Lost **24**

Total Goals Scored **106**
Total Goals Conceded **90**
Total Points **138**
Total Players Used **46**

All-Time Record vs Birmingham

Competition	Played	Won	Drawn	Lost	For	Against
League	80	27	23	30	95	102
FA Cup	4	3	0	1	8	6
League Cup	2	2	0	0	5	1
Other	0	0	0	0	0	0
Total	**86**	**32**	**23**	**31**	**108**	**109**

Leeds United

Elland Road

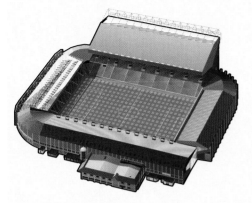

Stadium History

Having previously housed rugby and then Leeds City Football Club, Elland Road became home to the newly-formed Leeds United in 1919. A fire devastated the West Stand in September 1956, with damage estimated at £100,000. The stadium has recovered from that dark day, and can now boast a 17,000-capacity East Stand.

Unfortunately, recent financial problems forced the club to sell the ground on a 25-year sale and lease-back deal, though they do have the right to repurchase it at any time.

Seating Plan

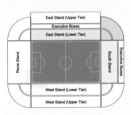

Stadium Statistics 05/06

Capacity
40,204

family area
away fans
disabled

Highest attendance
27,843 v Sheffield Wednesday 21.01.06

Lowest attendance
18,353 v Derby County 28.09.05

Average attendance
22,354

How to Get There

Travel Information

Car parking
Visiting supporters are directed into Car Park A, at a cost of £3 per car.

Bus
Shuttle buses start running from the railway station to the ground two hours before kick-off.

Train
Elland Road is around a 35 minute walk from Leeds Station.

Area Map

Local Map

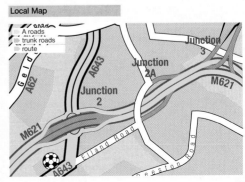

Leicester City

Nickname:	The Foxes
Manager:	Rob Kelly
Chairman:	Andrew Taylor
Website:	www.lcfc.co.uk

Telephone:	0870 040 6000
Ticket Office:	0870 499 1884
Club Shop:	0870 040 6000

Season Review 05/06

The Foxes endured a disappointing campaign, only moving away from the relegation places following the departure of manager Craig Levein. A run of 28 points from the final 16 games then helped caretaker boss Rob Kelly secure the role on a permanent basis.

Midfielder Joey Gudjonsson was very much the star performer, even managing to score from the halfway line against Hull.

Points / Position

won drawn lost   H home A away

Season:	96/97	97/98	98/99	99/00	00/01	01/02	02/03	03/04	04/05	05/06
Premiership **P**	9 / 47pts	10 / 53pts	10 / 49pts	8 / 55pts	13 / 48pts	20 / 28pts / 48pts	13 / 48pts	10 / 50pts	18 / 33pts / 12 / 45pts	18 / 34pts
Division **1**	10 / 66pts	7 / 74pts	4 / 81pts	5 / 77pts	5 / 78pts	5 / 76pts	2 / 92pts		15 / 57pts	16 / 54pts
Date:								13.03 H 0-1	13.12 A 2-0	
Result:										

Recent Meetings

13.12.03

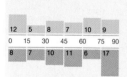 **0-2**   Attendance: 30,639

Referee: M.A.Riley

O 42 Morrison
O 66 Forssell

13.03.04

 **0-1**   Attendance: 29,491

Referee: M.D.Messias

O 53 Ferdinand

Goals 05/06

Goals by Time Period

12	5	8	7	10	9
0	15	30	45	60	75	90
8	7	10	11	6	17

 scored
 conceded

Goals by Area

Scored (Conceded)

13 (18)
32 (32)
6 (9)

Goals by Position

Scored	Conceded

 forward: 29   forward: 29
 midfield: 16   midfield: 20
 defence: 6   defence: 8
 own goals: 2

Goal by Situation

Scored	Conceded

 set piece: 14   set piece: 25
 open play: 37   open play: 32
 own goals: 2

All-Time Records

Total Championship Record

Total Matches Played	Total Goals Scored
92	100
Total Matches Won	**Total Goals Conceded**
25	105
Total Matches Drawn	**Total Points**
36	111
Total Matches Lost	**Total Players Used**
31	50

All-Time Record vs Birmingham

Competition	Played	Won	Drawn	Lost	For	Against
League	116	48	20	48	197	196
FA Cup	9	6	3	0	19	10
League Cup	0	0	0	0	0	0
Other	0	0	0	0	0	0
Total	**125**	**54**	**23**	**48**	**216**	**206**

Walkers Stadium

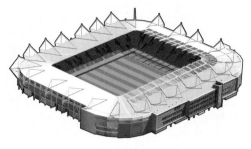

Stadium History

Having beaten Tottenham 2-1 in a memorable final match at their legendary Filbert Street home, Leicester made the short journey to the Walkers Stadium. Former fox Gary Lineker was handed the honour of officially opening the state-of-the-art facility.

Promotion to the Premiership was achieved during the inaugural season at the new venue, but relegation swiftly followed. In June 2003, England defeated Serbia & Montenegro in the first full international to be staged in the city.

Seating Plan

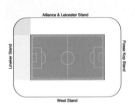

Capacity
32,500

- family area
- away fans
- disabled

Stadium Statistics 05/06

Highest attendance
25,578 v Reading 25.03.06

Lowest attendance
18,856 v Watford 22.11.05

Average attendance
22,233

How to Get There

Travel Information

Car parking
There is plenty of street parking available, particularly in the Upperton Road area.

Train
Leicester Station is located in the city centre, some 20-25 minutes walk from the ground.

Bus
Numbers 36, 52, 52a, 52b, 52c and 53 regularly go to and from the city centre.

Area Map

Local Map

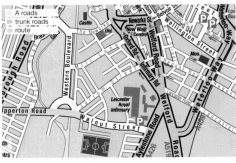

Luton Town ○

Nickname: **The Hatters**
Manager: **Mike Newell**
Chairman: **Bill Tomlins**
Website: **www.lutontown.co.uk**

Telephone: **01582 411 622**
Ticket Office: **01582 416 976**
Club Shop: **01582 488 864**

Season Review 05/06

Luton burst onto the Championship scene in spectacular fashion, rarely dropping out of the top-six until mid-December. Though the Hatters eventually finished in tenth, they won many admirers for approaching the game in such a positive fashion.

The achievements of manager Mike Newell also attracted attention, with both Leicester and Crystal Palace expressing an interest in securing his services.

Points / Position

won ▶ drawn ▶ lost H home A away

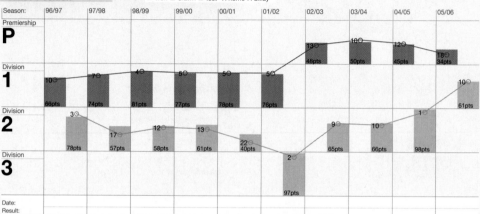

Season:	96/97	97/98	98/99	99/00	00/01	01/02	02/03	03/04	04/05	05/06
Premiership **P**										
Division **1**	10 / 66pts	7 / 74pts	4 / 81pts	5 / 77pts	5 / 78pts	5 / 76pts	13 / 48pts	10 / 50pts	12 / 45pts	18 / 34pts, 10 / 61pts
Division **2**		3 / 78pts	17 / 57pts	12 / 58pts	13 / 61pts	22 / 40pts		9 / 65pts	10 / 66pts	1 / 98pts
Division **3**							2 / 97pts			
Date: Result:										

Goals 05/06

Goals by Time Period

8	11	9	10	9	19
0	15	30	45	60	75	90
7	10	10	12	7	21

▬ scored
▬ conceded

Goals by Area

Scored (Conceded)

27 (13)

31 (43)

8 (11)

Goals by Position

Scored	Conceded
▶ forward: 32	▶ forward: 34
▶ midfield: 25	▶ midfield: 24
▶ defence: 5	▶ defence: 7
▶ own goals: 4	▶ own goals: 2

Goal by Situation

Scored	Conceded
▶ set piece: 19	▶ set piece: 15
▶ open play: 43	▶ open play: 50
▶ own goals: 4	▶ own goals: 2

All-Time Records

Total Championship Record

Total Matches Played
▶ **46**

Total Matches Won
▶ **17**

Total Matches Drawn
▶ **10**

Total Matches Lost
▶ **19**

Total Goals Scored
▶ **66**

Total Goals Conceded
▶ **67**

Total Points
▶ **61**

Total Players Used
▶ **24**

All-Time Record vs Birmingham

Competition	Played	Won	Drawn	Lost	For	Against
League	50	10	15	25	53	90
FA Cup	2	1	0	1	2	2
League Cup	5	0	3	2	6	8
Other	0	0	0	0	0	0
Total	**57**	**11**	**18**	**28**	**61**	**100**

Luton Town

Stadium History

Following spells playing at Dunstable Road and Dallow Lane, Luton moved to Kenilworth Road in 1905. One of the stands burnt down during a fire in 1920, and was replaced by the Main Stand of today. Having set a record attendance for the ground of 30,069 in the late 1950's, the capacity has since fallen to just over 10,000.

The club experimented with a plastic playing surface in more recent times, though this was removed and replaced with conventional grass in the early 1990's.

Seating Plan

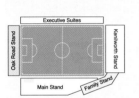

Capacity
10,300

▶ family area
▶ away fans
  disabled

Stadium Statistics 05/06

Highest attendance
10,248 v Wolverhampton Wanderers 10.09.05

Lowest attendance
7,474 v Crewe Alexandra 22.11.05

Average attendance
9,139

How to Get There

Travel Information

Car parking
There is limited street parking near the ground, with a multi-storey car park in the town centre.

Train
Luton Station is a 10 minute walk from Kenilworth Road.

Bus
Take the number 31 from opposite the railway station, and ask for the Oak Road stop.

Area Map

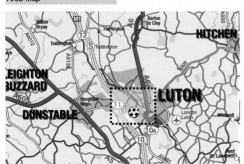

Local Map

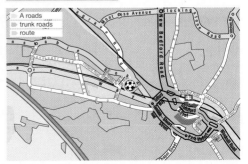

A roads
trunk roads
route

Norwich City

Nickname:	The Canaries	Telephone:	01603 760 760
Manager:	Nigel Worthington	Ticket Office:	0870 444 1902
Chairman:	Roger Munby	Club Shop:	0870 444 1902
Website:	www.canaries.co.uk		

Season Review 05/06

The Canaries struggled to adjust to life back in the Championship, failing to recover from a sluggish start to the campaign. Manager Nigel Worthington came in for much criticism, particularly in light of some woeful displays away from Carrow Road.

Though the team could only manage a ninth-place finish, the club came top of the division in average attendance terms.

Points / Position

won drawn lost H home A away

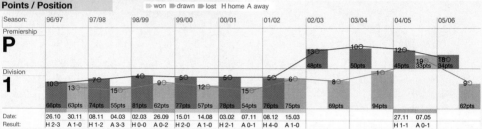

Season:	96/97	97/98	98/99	99/00	00/01	01/02	02/03	03/04	04/05	05/06

Premiership P — 13 48pts, 10 50pts, 12 45pts, 19 33pts, 18 34pts

Division 1 — 10 66pts, 13 63pts, 7 74pts, 15 55pts, 4 81pts, 9 62pts, 5 77pts, 12 57pts, 5 78pts, 15 54pts, 5 76pts, 6 75pts, 8 69pts, 1 94pts, 9 62pts

| Date: | 26.10 | 30.11 | 08.11 | 04.03 | 02.03 | 26.09 | 15.01 | 14.08 | 03.02 | 07.11 | 08.12 | 15.03 | | | 27.11 | 07.05 | |
| Result: | H 2-3 | A 1-0 | H 1-2 | A 3-3 | H 0-0 | A 0-2 | H 2-0 | A 1-0 | H 2-1 | A 0-1 | H 4-0 | A 1-0 | | | H 1-1 | A 0-1 | |

Recent Meetings

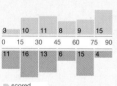

O O 4-0 — 08.12.01 — Attendance: 17,310
Referee: G.Laws
O 30 Mooney
O 44 Mooney
O 46 Marcelo
O 57 Mooney

O O O-1 — 15.03.02 — Attendance: 18,258
Referee: M.D.Messias
O 22 John

O O 1-1 — 27.11.04 — Attendance: 29,120
Referee: G.Poll
O 9 Morrison O 64 Huckerby

O O 1-0 — 07.05.05 — Attendance: 25,477
Referee: S.G.Bennett
O 45 Ashton

Goals 05/06

Goals by Time Period

3	10	11	8	9	15
0	15	30	45	60	75	90

11	16	13	6	15	4

scored
conceded

Goals by Area
Scored (Conceded)

15 (17)
36 (36)
5 (12)

Goals by Position

Scored		Conceded	
forward:	37	forward:	23
midfield:	10	midfield:	27
defence:	4	defence:	10
own goals:	5	own goals:	5

Goal by Situation

Scored		Conceded	
set piece:	16	set piece:	21
open play:	35	open play:	39
own goals:	5	own goals:	5

All-Time Records

Total Championship Record

Total Matches Played	46
Total Matches Won	18
Total Matches Drawn	8
Total Matches Lost	20

Total Goals Scored	56
Total Goals Conceded	65
Total Points	62
Total Players Used	31

All-Time Record vs Birmingham

Competition	Played	Won	Drawn	Lost	For	Against
League	48	16	14	18	71	71
FA Cup	4	1	3	0	3	2
League Cup	4	1	1	2	5	5
Other	1	0	1	0	1	1
Total	**57**	**18**	**19**	**20**	**80**	**79**

Norwich City

Carrow Road

Stadium History

Norwich moved to Carrow Road in 1935, and the stadium has come a long way since then. Despite hosting the likes of European giants Bayern Munich and Inter Milan, the record attendance at the ground of 43,984 was set in a 1963 FA Cup tie with Leicester City.

The recently-constructed 8,000 capacity Jarrold Stand is a sign that the club is moving in the right direction, while Delia Smith's personal touch ensures that business is brisk on the catering front.

Seating Plan

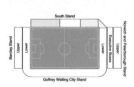

Stadium Statistics 05/06

Capacity
27,470

■ family area
■ away fans
□ disabled

Highest attendance
27,470 v Hull City 27.09.05

Lowest attendance
23,838 v Cardiff City 01.11.05

Average attendance
24,952

How to Get There

Travel Information

Car parking
Norfolk County Hall offers around 2000 spaces, while there are plenty of car parks in the city centre.

Bus
No services run to, or near, the ground.

Train
Carrow Road is a five minute walk from Norwich Station.

Area Map

Local Map

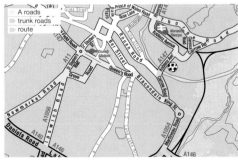

Plymouth Argyle ○

Nickname:	The Pilgrims
Manager:	Ian Holloway
Chairman:	Paul Stapleton
Website:	www.pafc.co.uk

Telephone:	01752 562 561
Ticket Office:	0871 222 1288
Club Shop:	01752 558 292

Season Review 05/06

Despite winning at eventual champions Reading on the opening day of the season, manager Bobby Williamson did not last much longer in the role. Tony Pulis was appointed as his successor and guided the Pilgrims to 14th place, before departing for Stoke in the summer.

Plymouth fans will be hoping that new boss Ian Holloway can bring a little more attacking flair to the team.

Points / Position

○ won ○ drawn ○ lost H home A away

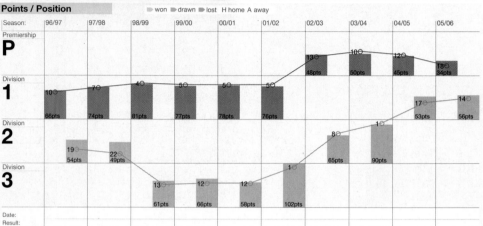

Goals 05/06

Goals by Time Period

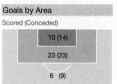

9	5	7	7	3	8
0	15	30	45	60	75	90

| 5 | 6 | 10 | 13 | 7 | 5 |

○ scored
○ conceded

Goals by Area

Scored (Conceded)

10 (14)

23 (23)

6 (9)

Goals by Position

Scored		Conceded	
○ forward:	14	○ forward:	27
○ midfield:	19	○ midfield:	14
○ defence:	3	○ defence:	3
○ own goals:	3	○ own goals:	2

Goal by Situation

Scored		Conceded	
○ set piece:	19	○ set piece:	14
○ open play:	17	○ open play:	30
○ own goals:	3	○ own goals:	3

All-Time Records

Total Championship Record

Total Matches Played	► 92
Total Matches Won	► 27
Total Matches Drawn	► 28
Total Matches Lost	► 37
Total Goals Scored	► 91
Total Goals Conceded	► 110
Total Points	► 109
Total Players Used	► 44

All-Time Record vs Birmingham

Competition	Played	Won	Drawn	Lost	For	Against
League	24	5	7	12	26	51
FA Cup	0	0	0	0	0	0
League Cup	10	3	1	6	9	13
Other	0	0	0	0	0	0
Total	**34**	**8**	**8**	**18**	**35**	**64**

Plymouth Argyle

Home Park

Stadium History

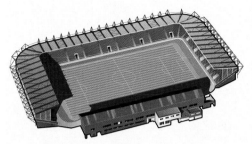

Originally home to Devonport Albion Rugby Club, the Home Park Recreation Ground was unused for three years prior to 1901. Football then began to take place at the venue, leading to Plymouth Argyle turning professional in 1903.

The stadium was badly damaged during a World War II air raid, but went on to play host to Pele and his Santos team in March 1973. Recent rebuilding work has seen development on three sides of the ground, raising the capacity to in excess of 20,000.

Seating Plan

Capacity
20,922

family area
away fans
disabled

Stadium Statistics 05/06

Highest attendance
17,726 v Leeds United 02.01.06

Lowest attendance
10,460 v Crewe Alexandra 13.09.05

Average attendance
13,776

How to Get There

Travel Information

Car parking
A large free car park is situated next to the ground.

Train
Plymouth North Road Station is a fair way from Home Park, but has direct links from all over the country.

Bus
Regular services run from the city centre to the required Milehouse area of Plymouth.

Area Map

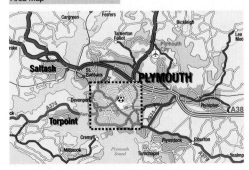

Local Map

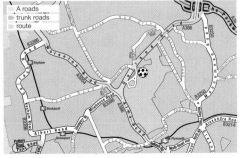

Preston North End

Nickname:	The Lilywhites		Telephone:	0870 442 1964
Manager:	Paul Simpson		Ticket Office:	0870 442 1966
Chairman:	Derek Shaw		Club Shop:	0870 442 1965
Website:	www.pnefc.co.uk			

Season Review 05/06

A 22-match unbeaten run midway through the season helped Preston reach the Playoffs, where they were beaten at the semi-final stage by Leeds. Manager Billy Davies then left for Derby, with Carlisle boss Paul Simpson replacing him at Deepdale.

The lilywhites kept 24 Championship clean sheets in 2005/06, but will be weakened by the departure of defender Claude Davis.

Points / Position

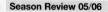

won | drawn | lost | H home A away

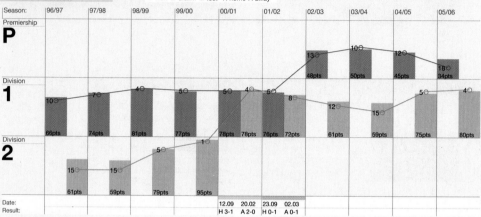

Season:	96/97	97/98	98/99	99/00	00/01	01/02	02/03	03/04	04/05	05/06

Premiership **P**

Division **1**

Division **2**

| Date: | | | | 12.09 | 20.02 | 23.09 | 02.03 |
| Result: | | | | H 3-1 | A 2-0 | H 0-1 | A 0-1 |

Goals 05/06

Goals by Time Period

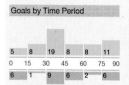

5	8	19	8	8	11
0	15	30	45	60	75	90
6	1	9	6	2	6

 scored
conceded

Goals by Area

Scored (Conceded)

8 (11)

35 (14)

16 (5)

Goals by Position

Scored		Conceded	
forward:	21	forward:	14
midfield:	22	midfield:	10
defence:	14	defence:	3
own goals:	2	own goals:	3

Goal by Situation

Scored		Conceded	
set piece:	17	set piece:	13
open play:	40	open play:	14
own goals:	2	own goals:	3

All-Time Records

Total Championship Record

Total Matches Played	92	Total Goals Scored	126
Total Matches Won	41	Total Goals Conceded	88
Total Matches Drawn	32	Total Points	155
Total Matches Lost	19	Total Players Used	50

All-Time Record vs Birmingham

Competition	Played	Won	Drawn	Lost	For	Against
League	76	29	19	28	115	107
FA Cup	2	0	0	2	1	3
League Cup	3	1	0	2	3	3
Other	2	1	0	1	2	2
Total	**83**	**31**	**19**	**33**	**121**	**115**

Preston North End

Deepdale

Stadium History

Housing the National Football Museum, located in the Sir Tom Finney and Bill Shankly Kop stands, Deepdale is a ground steeped in history. The stadium is currently three-quarters of the way through a total redevelopment program that began in 1996, as the club look to turn their home into a 30,000-capacity arena.

During the summer of 2005 the venue played host to several matches in the Women's European Championships, further highlighting its modern capabilities.

Seating Plan

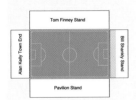

Capacity
22,225

- family area
- away fans
- disabled

Stadium Statistics 05/06

Highest attendance
19,350 v Leeds United 30.04.06

Lowest attendance
12,453 v Stoke City 16.09.05

Average attendance
14,619

How to Get There

Travel Information

Car parking
Moor Park High School and Deepdale Primary School charge £5 for parking.

Train
Preston Station is around 1.5 miles away from Deepdale.

Bus
Numbers 5, 6 and 19 stop at the bus station, and travel along Deepdale Road.

Area Map

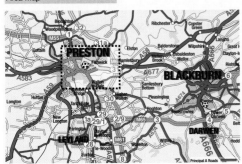

Local Map

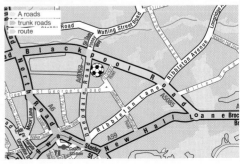

QPR

Nickname:	The Superhoops	Telephone:	020 8743 0262
Manager:	Gary Waddock	Ticket Office:	0870 112 1967
Chairman:	Gianni Paladini	Club Shop:	020 8749 6862
Website:	www.qpr.co.uk		

Season Review 05/06

Boardroom friction did little to help matters on the pitch at Loftus Road, with Rangers finishing the season just above the relegation places. Manager Ian Holloway had been sent on "gardening leave" in February and was replaced by coach Gary Waddock.

A return of just five points from the final 11 games of the campaign highlighted the sense of uncertainty at the club.

Points / Position

won ■ drawn ■ lost H home A away

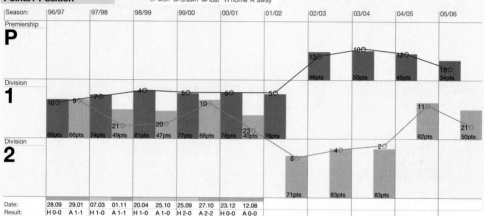

Season:	96/97	97/98	98/99	99/00	00/01	01/02	02/03	03/04	04/05	05/06
Premiership P							13○ 48pts	10○ 50pts	12○ 45pts	18○ 34pts
Division 1	10○ 66pts	9○ 66pts	7○ 74pts / 21 49pts	4○ 81pts / 20 47pts	5○ 77pts / 10 66pts	5○ 78pts / 23 40pts	5○ 76pts		11○ 62pts	21○ 50pts
Division 2							8 71pts	4○ 83pts	2○ 83pts	

| Date: | 28.09 | 29.01 | 07.03 | 01.11 | 20.04 | 25.10 | 25.09 | 27.10 | 23.12 | 12.08 |
| Result: | H 0-0 | A 1-1 | H 1-0 | A 1-1 | H 1-0 | A 1-0 | H 2-0 | A 2-2 | H 0-0 | A 0-0 |

Goals 05/06

Goals by Time Period

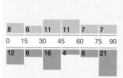

8	6	11	11	7	7
0	15	30	45	60	75	90
12	6	16	4	6	21

■ scored
■ conceded

Goals by Area

Scored (Conceded)

14 (11)

29 (47)

7 (7)

Goals by Position

Scored	Conceded

■ forward: 24   ■ forward: 29
■ midfield: 20   ■ midfield: 21
■ defence: 5   ■ defence: 12
■ own goals: 1   ■ own goals: 3

Goal by Situation

Scored	Conceded

■ set piece: 19   ■ set piece: 18
■ open play: 30   ■ open play: 44
■ own goals: 1   ■ own goals: 3

All-Time Records

Total Championship Record

Total Matches Played	92	Total Goals Scored	104
Total Matches Won	29	Total Goals Conceded	123
Total Matches Drawn	25	Total Points	112
Total Matches Lost	38	Total Players Used	56

All-Time Record vs Birmingham

Competition	Played	Won	Drawn	Lost	For	Against
League	40	9	13	18	39	57
FA Cup	2	2	0	0	4	1
League Cup	3	3	0	0	9	2
Other	0	0	0	0	0	0
Total	45	14	13	18	52	60

Loftus Road

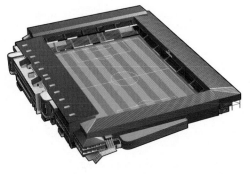

The club led a somewhat nomadic existence for many years, occupying several grounds prior to arriving at Loftus Road and only settling there at the third time of asking in the early 1960's. Development was soon underway, with the South Africa Road Stand the first to be completed.

A plastic pitch was installed during the 1980's, and lasted seven seasons before being replaced with natural grass. More recently, the stadium offered a temporary two-year home to West London neighbours Fulham.

Seating Plan

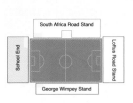

Stadium Statistics 05/06

Capacity
18,500

Highest attendance
16,152 v Watford 22.04.06

family area
away fans
disabled

Lowest attendance
10,901 v Preston North End 22.11.05

Average attendance
13,440

How to Get There

Travel Information

Car parking
Street parking is available near the ground.

Train
Acton Central Station is a bus ride away from Loftus Road.

Tube
The nearest stations are White City on the Central line and Shepherds Bush on the Hammersmith & City line.

Bus
Number 283 goes to nearby Bloemfontein Road.

Area Map

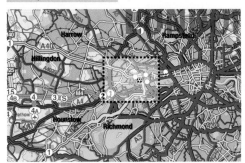

Local Map

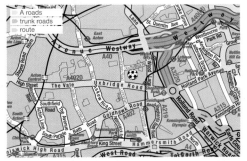

Sheff Wed

Nickname:	The Owls	Telephone:	0870 999 1867
Manager:	Paul Sturrock	Ticket Office:	0870 999 1867
Chairman:	Dave Allen	Club Shop:	0870 999 1867
Website:	www.swfc.co.uk		

Season Review 05/06

Paul Sturrock's team achieved their goal of Championship survival, helped in no small part by a terrific level of support. Things looked bleak during the early months of the campaign, but the Owls eventually found their feet.

Northern Ireland international Chris Brunt was particularly outstanding, weighing in with seven goals and six assists in the league.

Points / Position

won drawn lost H home A away

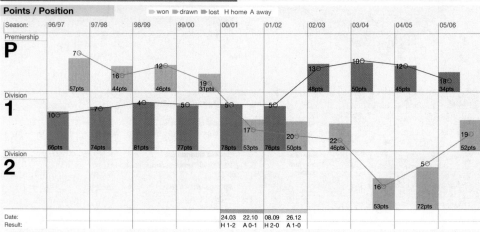

Season:	96/97	97/98	98/99	99/00	00/01	01/02	02/03	03/04	04/05	05/06

Premiership
P
7 57pts | 16 44pts | 12 46pts | 19 31pts | | | 13 48pts | 10 50pts | 12 45pts | 18 34pts

Division 1
10 66pts | 7 74pts | 4 81pts | 5 77pts | 5 78pts | 17 53pts | 5 76pts | 20 50pts | 22 46pts | 19 52pts

Division 2
16 53pts | 5 72pts

| Date: | | | | | 24.03 | 22.10 | 08.09 | 26.12 | | |
| Result: | | | | | H 1-2 | A 0-1 | H 2-0 | A 1-0 | | |

Goals 05/06

Goals by Time Period

8	2	6	4	10	9
0	15	30	45	60	75	90
6	9	13	7	7	10

scored
conceded

Goals by Area

Scored (Conceded)

11 (16)

21 (33)

7 (3)

Goals by Position

Scored		Conceded	
forward:	15	forward:	34
midfield:	13	midfield:	11
defence:	7	defence:	6
own goals:	4	own goals:	1

Goal by Situation

Scored		Conceded	
set piece:	15	set piece:	22
open play:	20	open play:	29
own goals:	4	own goals:	1

All-Time Records

Total Championship Record

Total Matches Played	Total Goals Scored
46	39
Total Matches Won	**Total Goals Conceded**
13	52
Total Matches Drawn	**Total Points**
13	52
Total Matches Lost	**Total Players Used**
20	37

All-Time Record vs Birmingham

Competition	Played	Won	Drawn	Lost	For	Against
League	74	27	20	27	122	126
FA Cup	3	1	1	1	5	4
League Cup	1	0	0	1	0	2
Other	0	0	0	0	0	0
Total	**78**	**28**	**21**	**29**	**127**	**132**

Sheff Wed

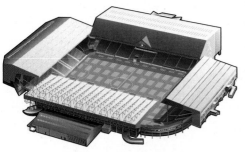

Stadium History

Sheffield Wednesday moved to Hillsborough in 1899, though it wasn't until 1914 that their new home changed its name from the Owlerton Stadium. Chesterfield were beaten 5-1 in the club's opening game at the ground, the first of 19 consecutive victories at the venue.

April 15, 1989 was the darkest day in the stadium's history, as 96 Liverpool fans lost their lives during an FA Cup semifinal. The disaster led to nationwide safety improvements, and Hillsborough went on to host several matches during Euro 96.

Seating Plan

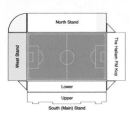

Capacity
39,859

◈ family area
▨ away fans
◌ disabled

Stadium Statistics 05/06

Highest attendance
33,439 v Sheffield United 18.02.06

Lowest attendance
20,244 v Plymouth Argyle 22.11.05

Average attendance
24,853

How to Get There

Travel Information

Car parking
Parking is available at the nearby Owlerton Greyhound Stadium.

Bus
Numbers 53, 77 and 80 run to Hillsborough from the Flat Street Bus Terminus.

Train
Sheffield Railway Station is in the city centre, some 3 miles from the ground.

Area Map

Local Map

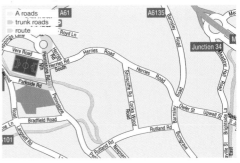

Southampton

Nickname:	The Saints	Telephone:	0870 220 0000
Manager:	George Burley	Ticket Office:	0870 220 0150
Chairman:	Michael Wilde	Club Shop:	0870 220 0130
Website:	www.saintsfc.co.uk		

Season Review 05/06

Southampton failed to make an immediate return to the Premiership, paying the price for drawing 19 of their 46 games. Many fans were delighted to see Harry Redknapp desert his managerial post in December, particularly as George Burley took over.

Five wins from the final six games of the season represented a strong finish and further boosted morale in the camp.

Points / Position

▶ won ▶ drawn ▶ lost H home A away

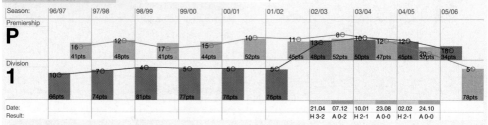

Season:	96/97	97/98	98/99	99/00	00/01	01/02	02/03	03/04	04/05	05/06
Premiership P							10○	8○	10○	18○
	16○	12○	17○	15○		11○	13○		12○ 12○	
	41pts	48pts	41pts	44pts	52pts	45pts	48pts 52pts	50pts 47pts	45pts 32pts	34pts
Division 1	10○	7○	4○	5○	5○	5○			20○	5○
	66pts	74pts	81pts	77pts	78pts	76pts				78pts
Date:							21.04	07.12	10.01	23.08 02.02 24.10
Result:							H 3-2	A 0-2	H 2-1	A 0-0 H 2-1 A 0-0

Recent Meetings

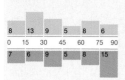

○○ 0-0	Attendance: 31,656	
Referee: G.P.Barber		

○○ 2-1	Attendance: 29,071	10.01.04
Referee: S.G.Bennett		
○ 16 Clemence	○ 6 Ormerod	
○ 67 Kenna		

○○ 0-0	Attendance: 27,568	24.10.04
Referee: M.L.Dean		

○○ 2-1	Attendance: 28,797	02.02.05
Referee: P.Walton		
○ 12 Pandiani	○ 52 Camara	
○ 41 Blake		

Goals 05/06

Goals by Time Period

8	13	9	5	8	6
0	15	30	45	60	75	90
7	6	9	5	8	15

▶ scored
▶ conceded

Goals by Area

Scored (Conceded)

10 (15)
34 (31)
5 (4)

Goals by Position

Scored	Conceded

▶ forward: 24 ▶ forward: 28
▶ midfield: 18 ▶ midfield: 14
▶ defence: 5 ▶ defence: 7
▶ own goals: 2 ▶ own goals: 1

Goal by Situation

Scored	Conceded

▶ set piece: 18 ▶ set piece: 23
▶ open play: 29 ▶ open play: 26
▶ own goals: 2 ▶ own goals: 1

All-Time Records

Total Championship Record

Total Matches Played	▶ 46
Total Matches Won	▶ 13
Total Matches Drawn	▶ 19
Total Matches Lost	▶ 14
Total Goals Scored	▶ 49
Total Goals Conceded	▶ 50
Total Points	▶ 58
Total Players Used	▶ 40

All-Time Record vs Birmingham

Competition	Played	Won	Drawn	Lost	For	Against
League	34	14	9	11	39	33
FA Cup	3	1	0	2	5	6
League Cup	3	2	1	0	9	3
Other	0	0	0	0	0	0
Total	40	17	10	13	53	42

Southampton

St Mary's Stadium

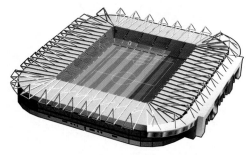

Stadium History

Following a 103-year stay at The Dell, Southampton moved to their brand new £32m stadium in time for the start of the 2001–02 season.

It took three months for a victory to arrive, leading many to believe that the venue was somehow jinxed. In truth, the poor early results were probably a consequence of visiting players feeling less intimidated than on previous visits to the South Coast. In October 2002, the stadium played host to England vs FYR Macedonia in a Euro 2004 Qualifier.

Seating Plan

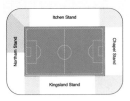

Capacity
32,251

family area
away fans
disabled

Stadium Statistics 05/06

Highest attendance
30,173 v Leeds United 19.11.05

Lowest attendance
19,086 v Luton Town 11.12.05

Average attendance
23,613

How to Get There

Travel Information

Car parking
City centre parking is an option, due to restrictions nearer the ground.

Train
It is a 30 minute walk from Southampton Station to the stadium.

Bus
A free park and ride scheme for away supporters is in operation just off Junction 8 of the M27.

Area Map

Local Map

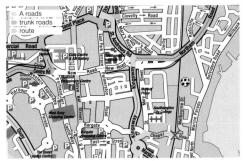

Southend United ○

Nickname:	The Shrimpers	Telephone:	01702 304 050
Manager:	Steve Tilson	Ticket Office:	08444 770 077
Chairman:	Ron Martin	Club Shop:	01702 351 117
Website:	www.southendunited.co.uk		

Season Review 05/06

Southend took to League One like ducks to water, brushing off the tag of relegation favourites to win the division. Manager Steve Tilson continued the good work of the previous campaign, leading the team to eight straight league wins in the early part of the season.

Though the team ethic was vital to the Shrimpers' success, Freddy Eastwood's goals proved crucial.

Points / Position

won ▶ drawn ▶ lost H home A away

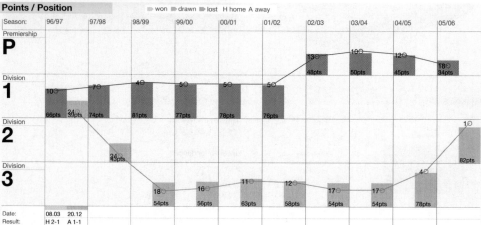

Season:	96/97	97/98	98/99	99/00	00/01	01/02	02/03	03/04	04/05	05/06
Premiership P										
							13○ 48pts	10○ 50pts	12○ 45pts	18○ 34pts
Division 1	10○ 66pts	7○ 24pts 39pts 74pts	4○ 81pts	5○ 77pts	5○ 78pts	5○ 76pts				
Division 2		24○ 45pts								1○ 82pts
Division 3			18○ 54pts	16○ 56pts	11○ 63pts	12○ 58pts	17○ 54pts	17○ 54pts	4○ 78pts	
Date:	08.03	20.12								
Result:	H 2-1	A 1-1								

Goals 05/06

Goals by Time Period

10	10	11	11	11	19
0	15	30	45	60	75	90
1	9	11	6	10	6

 scored
 conceded

Goals by Area

Scored (Conceded)

19 (17)

42 (17)

11 (9)

Goals by Position

	Scored		Conceded
▶ forward:	46	▶ forward:	23
▶ midfield:	19	▶ midfield:	13
defence:	6	defence:	3
▶ own goals:	1	▶ own goals:	4

Goal by Situation

	Scored		Conceded
▶ set piece:	25	▶ set piece:	12
open play:	46	open play:	27
▶ own goals:	1	▶ own goals:	4

All-Time Records

Total Championship Record

Total Matches Played		Total Goals Scored	
▶	0	▶	0

Total Matches Won		Total Goals Conceded	
▶	0	▶	0

Total Matches Drawn		Total Points	
▶	0	▶	0

Total Matches Lost		Total Players Used	
▶	0	▶	0

All-Time Record vs Birmingham

Competition	Played	Won	Drawn	Lost	For	Against
League	10	4	2	4	16	14
FA Cup	2	0	0	2	2	8
League Cup	3	0	1	2	0	8
Other	0	0	0	0	0	0
Total	**15**	**4**	**3**	**8**	**18**	**30**

Southend United

Roots Hall

Stadium History

Until 1988, Roots Hall was the newest ground in the Football League. Southend purchased the site in 1952 and beat Norwich 3-1 in the first game to be played there on August 20, 1955. Constructing the stands was a long process, however, and it wasn't until 1966 that building work was finally completed.

Significant further development did not take place until the 1990's, with a second tier added to the South Stand and the West Stand roof extended.

Seating Plan

Capacity	Stadium Statistics 05/06

Capacity
12,392

family area
away fans
disabled

Highest attendance
11,387 v Bristol City 06.05.06

Lowest attendance
5,261 v Oldham Athletic 04.09.05

Average attendance
8,053

How to Get There

Travel Information

Car parking
The ground has a £3 car park behind the Main Stand.

Train
The nearest stations are Prittlewell (5 minute walk) and Southend Central (15 minute walk).

Bus
The main bus station is located close to Southend Central Railway Station.

Area Map

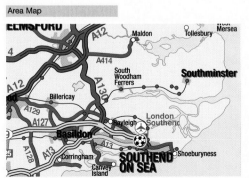

Local Map

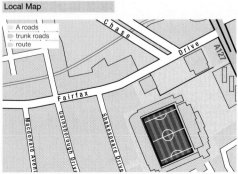

Stoke City

Nickname:	The Potters	Telephone:	01782 592 222
Manager:	Tony Pulis	Ticket Office:	01782 592 204
Chairman:	Peter Coates	Club Shop:	01782 592 244
Website:	www.stokecityfc.com		

Season Review 05/06

It was a season of managerial uncertainty at Stoke, with Johan Boskamp threatening to leave on several occasions prior to his summer exit. In his short time at the club, the Dutchman introduced an attacking brand of football that pleased both players and supporters alike.

Tony Pulis has since returned as boss and will be looking to turn a mid-table side into genuine Playoff contenders.

Points / Position

won drawn lost H home A away

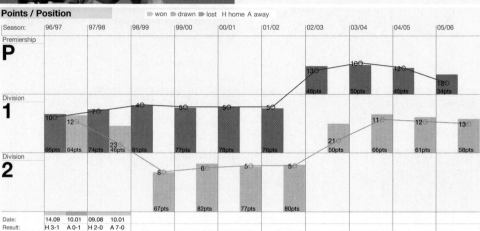

Goals 05/06

Goals by Time Period

scored
conceded

Goals by Area

Scored (Conceded)

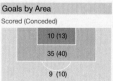

10 (13)

35 (40)

9 (10)

Goals by Position

Scored		Conceded	
forward:	30	forward:	30
midfield:	12	midfield:	21
defence:	10	defence:	9
own goals:	2	own goals:	3

Goal by Situation

Scored		Conceded	
set piece:	13	set piece:	21
open play:	39	open play:	39
own goals:	2	own goals:	3

All-Time Records

Total Championship Record

Total Matches Played	92
Total Matches Won	34
Total Matches Drawn	17
Total Matches Lost	41
Total Goals Scored	90
Total Goals Conceded	101
Total Points	119
Total Players Used	48

All-Time Record vs Birmingham

Competition	Played	Won	Drawn	Lost	For	Against
League	80	37	17	26	113	101
FA Cup	8	2	3	3	10	9
League Cup	0	0	0	0	0	0
Other	0	0	0	0	0	0
Total	**88**	**39**	**20**	**29**	**123**	**110**

Stoke City

Stadium Name

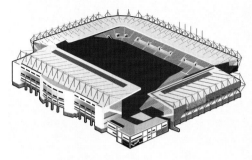

Stadium History

The Britannia Stadium took less than a year to build, and was constructed at a cost of £14.7m. The first competitive match to be played at the new ground came in the League Cup, as Stoke drew 1-1 with Rochdale on August 27, 1997.

Following their inception in the 2002-03 season, the first three Football Conference Playoff finals were all staged at the home of the Potters. In addition to housing football, the state-of-the-art facility has also played host to concerts by the likes of rock band Bon Jovi.

Seating Plan

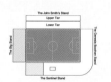

Stadium Statistics 05/06

Capacity
28,218

▨ family area
▨ away fans
☐ disabled

Highest attendance
20,408 v Leeds United 28.12.05

Lowest attendance
10,121 v Crystal Palace 13.03.06

Average attendance
14,432

How to Get There

Travel Information

Car parking
Away supporters can use the South Car Park, but must secure a space in advance from the club ticket office.

Bus
Buses run to the stadium at regular intervals from Glebe Street.

Train
The nearest railway station is Stoke-on-Trent.

Area Map

Local Map

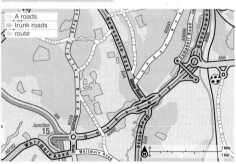

Sunderland ○

Nickname:	The Black Cats	Telephone:	0191 551 5000
Manager:	—	Ticket Office:	0845 671 1973
Chairman:	—	Club Shop:	0191 551 5050
Website:	www.safc.com		

Season Review 05/06

The Black Cats plumbed new depths as they collected just 15 Premiership points, breaking their own unwanted record in the process. Manager Mick McCarthy paid the price for the abject failure, but caretaker replacement Kevin Ball fared no better.

Victory against Fulham in the final home game of the season at least ensured that the fans at the Stadium of Light witnessed a league win.

Points / Position

▨ won ▧ drawn ▨ lost H home A away

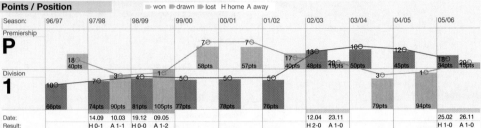

Season:	96/97	97/98	98/99	99/00	00/01	01/02	02/03	03/04	04/05	05/06
Premiership **P**					7○	7○	17○ 40pts	13○ 48pts	18○ 50pts	12○ 45pts	18○ 34pts	20○ 15pts
		18○ 40pts			58pts	57pts		19pts			
Division **1**	10○	7○	3○ 4○	1○	5○	5○	5○		3○	1○	
	66pts	74pts	90pts 81pts	105pts	77pts	78pts	76pts		79pts	94pts	
Date:		14.09	10.03	19.12	09.05			12.04	23.11		25.02	26.11
Result:		H 0-1	A 1-1	H 0-0	A 1-2			H 2-0	A 1-0		H 1-0	A 1-0

Recent Meetings

23.11.02	**12.04.03**	**26.11.05**	**25.02.06**
○○ **0-1** Attendance: 38,803	○○ **2-0** Attendance: 29,132	○○ **0-1** Attendance: 32,442	○○ **1-0** Attendance: 29,257
Referee: R.Styles	Referee: P.Dowd	Referee: U.D.Rennie	Referee: S.G.Bennett
○ 89 Morrison	○ 43 Hughes ○ 60 Dugarry	○ 68 Gray	○ 39 Heskey

Goals 05/06

Goals by Time Period

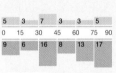

5	3	7	3	3	5
0	15	30	45	60	75	90
9	6	16	8	13	17

▨ scored
▨ conceded

Goals by Area

Scored (Conceded)

9 (18)

11 (39)

6 (12)

Goals by Position

Scored	Conceded
▶ forward: 10	▶ forward: 39
▶ midfield: 11	▶ midfield: 25
▨ defence: 4	▨ defence: 4
▶ own goals: 1	▶ own goals: 1

Goal by Situation

Scored	Conceded
▨ set piece: 10	▨ set piece: 18
▨ open play: 15	▨ open play: 50
▶ own goals: 1	▶ own goals: 1

All-Time Records

Total Championship Record

Total Matches Played	Total Goals Scored
▶ **46**	▶ **76**
Total Matches Won	Total Goals Conceded
▶ **29**	▶ **41**
Total Matches Drawn	Total Points
▶ **7**	▶ **94**
Total Matches Lost	Total Players Used
▶ **10**	▶ **30**

All-Time Record vs Birmingham

Competition	Played	Won	Drawn	Lost	For	Against
League	98	47	18	33	160	127
FA Cup	9	2	2	5	8	14
League Cup	0	0	0	0	0	0
Other	0	0	0	0	0	0
Total	**107**	**49**	**20**	**38**	**168**	**141**

Sunderland

Stadium of Light

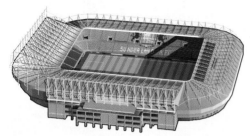

Stadium History

Opened in July 1997, and standing on the banks of the River Wear, the Stadium of Light is an impressive structure. Initially housing 42,000 spectators, the capacity was increased to nearer 50,000 by the extension to the North Stand and other improvements.

The ground has played host to two England internationals, a friendly against Belgium in 1999 and a Euro 2004 qualifier against Turkey in 2003. Unfortunately for the Black Cats, filling such a large arena has proved difficult.

Seating Plan

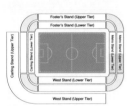

Capacity
48,300

family area
away fans
disabled

Stadium Statistics 05/06

Highest attendance
44,003 v Arsenal 01.05.06

Lowest attendance
28,226 v Fulham 04.05.06

Average attendance
33,904

How to Get There

Travel Information

Car parking
The Stadium of Light provides 1,146 parking spaces for supporters as well as space for up to 24 coaches on match days.

Metro
Between Stadium of Light and St Peter's stations.

Area Map

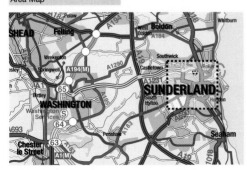

Local Map

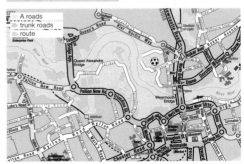

West Brom °

Nickname:	The Baggies
Manager:	Bryan Robson
Chairman:	Jeremy Peace
Website:	www.wba.co.uk

Telephone:	08700 668 888
Ticket Office:	08700 662 800
Club Shop:	08700 662 810

Season Review 05/06

Bryan Robson's men were unable to repeat the "Great Escape" of twelve months earlier, suffering relegation after a two-season Premiership stay. The Baggies were unable to recover from a crushing 6-1 loss at Fulham in February, failing to win another game from then on.

On the plus side, Albion won a new fan in the shape of 2001 Wimbledon champion Goran Ivanisevic.

Points / Position

● won ● drawn ● lost H home A away

Season:	96/97	97/98	98/99	99/00	00/01	01/02	02/03	03/04	04/05	05/06

Premiership

P

| | | | | | | | 13○ 48pts | 19○ 26pts | 10○ 50pts | | 12○ 45pts | 17○ 34pts | 18○ 34pts | 19○ 30pts |

Division

1

| 10○ 66pts | 16○ 57pts | 7○ 74pts | 10○ 61pts | 4○ 81pts | 12○ 59pts | 5○ 77pts | 21○ 49pts | 5○ 78pts | 6○ 74pts | 5○ 76pts | 2○ 89pts | 2○ 86pts | | | |

Date:	04.02	16.03	28.03	23.11	13.03	07.11	11.09	04.03	17.02	17.09	07.11	29.01	22.03	19.10		18.12	06.03	11.03	27.08
Result:	H 2-3	A 0-2	H 1-0	A 0-1	H 4-0	A 3-1	H 1-1	A 3-0	H 2-1	A 1-1	H 0-1	A 0-1	H 1-0	A 1-1		H 4-0	A 0-2	H 1-1	A 3-2

Recent Meetings

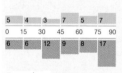

18.12.04		06.03.05		27.08.05		11.03.06	
○○ **4-0**	Attendance: 28,880	○○ **2-0**	Attendance: 25,749	○○ **2-3**	Attendance: 23,993	○○ **1-1**	Attendance: 28,041
Referee: M.A.Riley		Referee: S.W.Dunn		Referee: G.Poll		Referee: P.Dowd	
○ 4 Savage		○ 53 Clement		○ 12 Horsfield	○ 10 Heskey	○ 49 Forssell	○ 70 Ellington
○ 23 Morrison		○ 64 Campbell		○ 64 Horsfield	○ 26 Jarosik		
○ 30 Heskey					○ 33 Heskey		
○ 80 Anderton							

Goals 05/06

Goals by Time Period

5	4	3	7	5	7
0	15	30	45	60	75	90

6	6	12	9	8	17

● scored
● conceded

Goals by Area

Scored (Conceded)

6 (11)

18 (40)

7 (7)

Goals by Position

Scored	Conceded

● forward: 19
● midfield: 6
● defence: 6

● forward: 35
● midfield: 17
● defence: 3
● own goals: 3

Goal by Situation

Scored	Conceded

● set piece: 9
● open play: 22

● set piece: 18
● open play: 37
● own goals: 3

All-Time Records

Total Championship Record

Total Matches Played	Total Goals Scored
▶ 0	▶ 0

Total Matches Won	Total Goals Conceded
▶ 0	▶ 0

Total Matches Drawn	Total Points
▶ 0	▶ 0

Total Matches Lost	Total Players Used
▶ 0	▶ 0

All-Time Record vs Birmingham

Competition	Played	Won	Drawn	Lost	For	Against
League	112	47	32	33	152	128
FA Cup	8	6	1	1	16	7
League Cup	2	1	1	0	3	1
Other	0	0	0	0	0	0
Total	**122**	**54**	**34**	**34**	**171**	**136**

West Brom

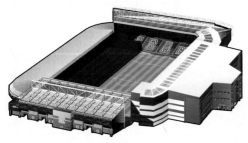

Stadium History

The home of West Bromwich Albion was the first Football League ground to be built in the 20th Century, and was opened on September 3rd 1900. Nearly 50 years later, in 1949, The Hawthorns recorded another first with the introduction of an electronic turnstile aggregator.

More recently, completion of the £7.5m East Stand in time for the start of the 2001-02 season meant that the stadium was fully enclosed. Both the ticket office and club shop are now located within this modern part of the arena.

Seating Plan

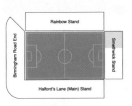

Rainbow Stand

Birmingham Road End

Smethwick Stand

Halford's Lane (Main) Stand

Stadium Statistics 05/06

Capacity
28,003

▨ family area
▨ away fans
  disabled

Highest attendance
27,623 v Manchester United 18.03.06

Lowest attendance
23,144 v Fulham 03.12.05

Average attendance
25,403

How to Get There

Travel Information

Car parking
The club has its own car park alongside the Tom Silk Building in Halfords Lane. The car park is stewarded, and costs £4 for the duration of the game. There are other car parks, such as along Halfords Lane, but street parking there is limited.

Train
The Hawthorns railway station is situated on Halfords Lane, 250 metres south of the stadium itself. There is also a Metro tram link which services the main route from Birmingham to Wolverhampton.

Area Map

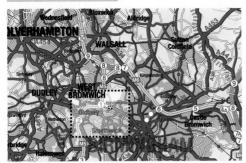

Local Map

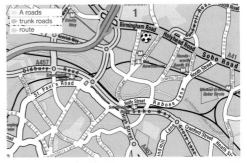

Wolves

Nickname:	Wolves	Telephone:	0870 442 0123
Manager:	–	Ticket Office:	0870 442 0123
Chairman:	Rick Hayward	Club Shop:	0870 442 0123
Website:	www.wolves.co.uk		

Season Review 05/06

Wolves were perhaps the biggest disappointment of the 2005/06 Championship season, failing even to make the Playoffs. Manager Glenn Hoddle was unable to get the most out of a talented group of players and decided to leave his post during the summer.

Expensive striker Tomasz Frankowski failed to find the net, whilst fans' favourite George Ndah was forced to hang up his boots.

Points / Position

won drawn lost H home A away

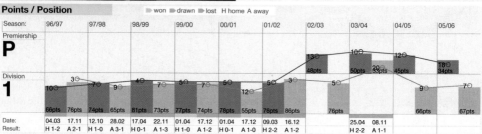

Season:	96/97	97/98	98/99	99/00	00/01	01/02	02/03	03/04	04/05	05/06
Date:	04.03	17.11	12.10	28.02	17.04	22.11	01.04	17.12	01.04	17.12	09.03	16.12		25.04	08.11
Result:	H 1-2	A 2-1	H 1-0	A 3-1	H 0-1	A 1-3	H 1-0	A 1-2	H 0-1	A 1-0	H 2-2	A 1-2		H 2-2	A 1-1

Recent Meetings

	16.12.01		09.03.02		08.11.03		25.04.04
OO **2-1** Attendance: 21,482		OO **2-2** Attendance: 22,104		OO **1-1** Attendance: 28,831		OO **2-2** Attendance: 29,494	
Referee: R.D.Furnandiz		Referee: S.W.Mathieson		Referee: G.P.Barber		Referee: M.L.Dean	
O 38 Blake	O 40 Marcelo	O 36 John	O 20 Butler	O 66 Iversen	O 49 Forssell	O 34 Forssell	O 6 Cameron
O 66 Rae A		O 45 Devlin	O 29 Lescott			O 41 Morrison	O 75 Cort

Goals 05/06

Goals by Time Period

8	9	10	7	7	9
0	15	30	45	60	75	90
6	7	7	6	7	9

 scored
 conceded

Goals by Area

Scored (Conceded)

18 (14)

24 (20)

8 (8)

Goals by Position

Scored		Conceded	

	forward:	33		forward:	21
	midfield:	14		midfield:	12
	defence:	2		defence:	6
	own goals:	1		own goals:	3

Goal by Situation

Scored	Conceded

	set piece:	9		set piece:	16
	open play:	40		open play:	23
	own goals:	1		own goals:	3

All-Time Records

Total Championship Record

Total Matches Played	Total Goals Scored
92	122
Total Matches Won	**Total Goals Conceded**
31	101
Total Matches Drawn	**Total Points**
40	133
Total Matches Lost	**Total Players Used**
21	39

All-Time Record vs Birmingham

Competition	Played	Won	Drawn	Lost	For	Against
League	112	55	25	32	185	136
FA Cup	4	2	1	1	6	5
League Cup	3	2	0	1	5	3
Other	0	0	0	0	0	0
Total	**119**	**59**	**26**	**34**	**196**	**144**

Molineux

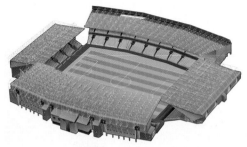

Stadium History

Wolverhampton Wanderers have called Molineux home since 1889. From humble beginnings, where spectators sat on dirt banks, the stadium has evolved into a modern football arena.

Sir Jack Hayward's money saw the transformation of an ageing venue during the 1990's, with all four sides of the ground being redeveloped. During the summer of 2003 it was decided to change the name of the John Ireland Stand to the Steve Bull Stand, thus honouring a modern Wolves hero.

Seating Plan

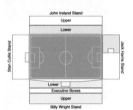

Capacity
29,400

- family area
- away fans
- disabled

Stadium Statistics 05/06

Highest attendance
27,980 v Reading 26.12.05

Lowest attendance
21,683 v Crewe Alexandra 11.02.06

Average attendance
23,624

How to Get There

Travel Information

Car parking
Parking is available in Wolverhampton city centre (5-minute walk).

Train
Wolverhampton Station is a 15 minute walk away from Molineux.

Bus
Numbers 503 and 504 run from the bus station and stop at the ground.

Area Map

Local Map

Championship Fixture List 2006/07

Home matches in bold.

Date	Opponent
August	
05.08.06	**Colchester**
8.8.06	Sunderland
12.8.06	Stoke
19.8.06	**C Palace**
26.8.06	Cardiff
September	
9.9.06	**Hull City**
12.9.06	QPR
16.9.06	**Ipswich**
23.9.06	Leeds
30.9.06	**Leicester**
October	
14.10.06	Luton
17.10.06	**Norwich**
21.10.06	Derby
28.10.06	**West Brom**
31.10.06	Coventry
November	
4.11.06	Plymouth
11.11.06	**Barnsley**
18.11.06	**Wolves**
25.11.06	Burnley
29.11.06	Southampton
December	
2.12.06	**Plymouth**
9.12.06	**Preston**
16.12.06	Sheff Wed
23.12.06	Southend
26.12.06	**QPR**
30.12.06	**Luton**

Date	Opponent
January	
1.1.07	Ipswich
13.1.07	**Leeds**
20.1.07	Leicester
30.1.07	**Southend**
February	
3.2.07	Colchester
10.2.07	**Stoke**
17.2.07	C Palace
20.2.07	**Sunderland**
24.2.07	Hull City
March	
3.3.07	**Cardiff**
10.3.07	**Derby**
13.3.07	Norwich
17.3.07	West Brom
31.3.07	**Coventry**
April	
7.4.07	**Burnley**
9.4.07	Barnsley
14.4.07	**Southampton**
21.4.07	Wolves
28.4.07	**Sheff Wed**
May	
6.5.07	Preston